Feminist Media Studies

Feminist Media Studies

ALISON HARVEY

polity

Copyright © Alison Harvey 2020

The right of Alison Harvey to be identified as Author of this Work has been asserted in accordance with the UK Copyright, Designs and Patents Act 1988.

First published in 2020 by Polity Press

Polity Press
65 Bridge Street
Cambridge CB2 1UR, UK

Polity Press
101 Station Landing
Suite 300
Medford, MA 02155, USA

All rights reserved. Except for the quotation of short passages for the purpose of criticism and review, no part of this publication may be reproduced, stored in a retrieval system or transmitted, in any form or by any means, electronic, mechanical, photocopying, recording or otherwise, without the prior permission of the publisher.

ISBN-13: 978-1-5095-2446-4
ISBN-13: 978-1-5095-2447-1(pb)

A catalogue record for this book is available from the British Library.

Library of Congress Cataloging-in-Publication Data
Names: Harvey, Alison, author.
Title: Feminist media studies / Alison Harvey.
Description: Medford, MA : Polity Press, 2019. | Includes bibliographical references and index.
Identifiers: LCCN 2019005172 (print) | LCCN 2019009884 (ebook) | ISBN 9781509524501 (Epub) | ISBN 9781509524464 (hardback) | ISBN 9781509524471 (pbk.)
Subjects: LCSH: Feminism and mass media.
Classification: LCC P96.F46 (ebook) | LCC P96.F46 H38 2019 (print) | DDC 305.42--dc23
LC record available at https://lccn.loc.gov/2019005172

Typeset in 11 on 13pt Adobe Garamond Pro
by Fakenham Prepress Solutions, Fakenham, Norfolk NR21 8NL
Printed and bound in Great Britain by CPI Group (UK) Ltd, Croydon

The publisher has used its best endeavours to ensure that the URLs for external websites referred to in this book are correct and active at the time of going to press. However, the publisher has no responsibility for the websites and can make no guarantee that a site will remain live or that the content is or will remain appropriate.

Every effort has been made to trace all copyright holders, but if any have been overlooked the publisher will be pleased to include any necessary credits in any subsequent reprint or edition.

For further information on Polity, visit our website:
politybooks.com

Contents

Acknowledgements	*page* vi
1 Introduction to Intersectional Feminist Media Studies	1
2 Feminist Media Critique	32
3 Representing Gender	58
4 Transnational Feminist Media Studies	84
5 Feminist Digital Media Studies	112
6 Gendered Media Work	142
7 The Future of Feminist Media Studies and Action	168
References	180
Index	205

Acknowledgements

Gratitude and recognition are important feminist gestures, and a brief acknowledgements section cannot do justice to the countless feminists who have shaped this book. Thank you to all the killjoys, fighters, and quiet resisters making this a world where feminist media studies can flourish. Because of your work, researchers and activists around the world are able to track enduring and emerging inequalities as well as forms of solidarity.

Thanks to my writing day compatriots Vanessa Ciccone, Bridget Conor, Amanda Earley, Galina Miazhevich, and Jess Perriam for the quiet and vocal inspiration (and a great many afternoon coffees and teas). Huge thanks to Leah Bassel for her fabulous company and incredible feedback throughout the writing process.

To the University of Leicester library and the British Library for providing the space and research materials needed to complete this book; to my British Library membership patrons Luke Robson and Ray Murphy; and to critical reader Marcos Moldes.

To those who provided generous feedback on chapters as well as reading suggestions and copious intellectual support – Rena Bivens, Koen Leurs, Kaitlynn Mendes, Katie Moylan, Bibi Reisdorf, Tamara Shepherd, and Natasha Whiteman. An extra big thank you to Jessalynn Keller for reading and commenting on multiple drafts, and being a vocal champion of the book. A shout out to Mark Banks for being the most inspiring and supportive mentor anyone could ask for. I feel extremely lucky to count amongst my colleagues and friends such brilliant, kind, and supportive people.

To the Fourchettes, an amazing feminist research network that inspires everything I do. In addition to those already mentioned, shout outs to Mél Hogan, ME Luka, Mélanie Millette, and Andrea Zeffiro.

To the vibrant, brilliant, life-giving community of feminist scholars, the Media & Gender research group hosted by the University of Leicester. The conversations, debates, and presentations I've been lucky enough to participate in have been a fabulous source of inspiration and encouragement. The group is too dynamic to list each member, but I must thank its longstanding organizers and contributors Jess Bain, Jilly Boyce Kay, Melanie Kennedy, and Helen Wood for being excellent colleagues.

Acknowledgements

To the University of Leicester for the time to read, think, and write in the form of a study leave, and all the wonderful colleagues at Queensland University of Technology; the Institute for Culture and Society at Western Sydney University; RMIT; Monash University; and Griffith University, for hosting me and organizing stimulating exchanges during my sabbatical in Australia.

To Mary Celeste Kearney and Jonathan Gray for graciously allowing me to include Kearney's "Manifesta for Feminist Media Criticism" in the final chapter of this book. A shout out also to the venue where this piece was originally published, *Antenna*, and its contributors, for six years of terrific, accessible media and cultural critique.

To my family, especially my feminist cheerleaders – Mom, Jess, and Aleigha. Thank you for the emotional support Dad, Kyle, Louise, Nathan, and the Chan clan. And endless gratitude to Hilary, without whose support, encouragement, feedback, and belief in me this book would not have been possible.

And last but not least, to Liesbet van Zoonen for writing the first *Feminist Media Studies* book. This foundational text has done so much for feminist media scholars, shaping our thought, grounding our research, and bolstering our teaching. Staking out a field is hard work, and I am forever grateful for the ongoing generative power of van Zoonen's text.

1 Introduction to Intersectional Feminist Media Studies

To say we live in a media-saturated world is a truism. Take a walk in most populated areas, and you will have all the evidence needed to support the claim. In fact, we need only survey our everyday routines to observe the pervasiveness of media content and technologies. For example, today on my way to work I passed through a busy central London train station and encountered as usual a diverse range of mediated practices. A free daily newspaper was thrust into my hands, where I spotted an image of the reality television host turned American president. Travellers clustered around the station entrance, phones in their hands, loading up maps, texts with directions, and travel guides. My phone buzzed with notifications as friends from Canada, the United States, and the United Kingdom commented on a leaked internal memo written by a Google employee on women's biological inferiority in technological aptitude. A shopfront I walked by announced a clothing store opening with a huge advertisement featuring a pouting woman slouching in underwear, and a muscular, topless man giving the camera a smouldering glare. A large group of teens sat on their suitcases awaiting check-in for trains to Paris, playing mobile games, taking selfies, and recording video of a young man playing one of the pianos dotted throughout the station. Next to the train information board, a large television screen featured the nation's second female Prime Minister in a discussion about the UK's future upon leaving the European Union. I observed all of this within 60 seconds, in addition to countless other people scrolling and tapping on their phones and laptops, checking their email and social media.

This example shows how pervasive media are in a major metropolis like London, though media studies from a range of global contexts indicate that this is the case around the world, with important differences according to place, community, and individual identity. From my anecdote, it may seem reasonable to conclude that experiences of mediation are universal rather than marked by gender. For instance, both men and women are leaders of countries, male and female models are equally sexualized in advertising, and mobile content creation and consumption are activities observed across genders. This might suggest that long-standing criticisms made about the media – that it sexualizes women, frames them as passive rather than active, and excludes them from production – are outdated. However, as this book will demonstrate, despite the ubiquity of these mediated activities, media forms and practices continue to be deeply gendered, with our access, activities, representation, and participation in media production and engagement shaped not only by our gender but also by our race, class, sexuality, ethnicity, ability, religion, and location in the world. Mediated content – in advertising, digital gaming, social media, selfies, news reporting, and more – is stratified by relations of gender and global systems of power that differently enable the participation of people and groups based on who they are. So too is the production of media, from the big-budget films of Hollywood and Bollywood to the user-generated content of Facebook and Sina Weibo. This text will explore how this gendering in contemporary media culture occurs on a global level. In doing so, it will introduce the reader to intersectional feminist media studies as an approach to understanding enduring and emerging trends in media and communication and to conceiving of action for change.

Building on the foundational text authored by Liesbet van Zoonen (1994), this book takes stock of the field that has blossomed since she set out the key debates, terms, and stakes of feminist media studies. In addition to tracing the issues that remain and the challenges that arise with changes in the media landscape – including but not limited to new media technologies, increasingly globalized media systems, and emergent political discourses and practices – this book is unique in how it draws on concepts and insights from a range of complementary fields. By engaging with classical and contemporary work from a diverse body of scholarship – from feminist theory to game studies, postcolonial theory to science and technology studies, queer and critical race theory to platform studies – the book situates feminist media studies as vital to researching and analysing a range of timely and significant issues across subject areas. By taking an interdisciplinary and multi-method approach to synthesizing key concepts and debates in feminist media studies, it provides a sense of the value of this approach for readers interested in media, communication, and cultural studies as well as those who increasingly need to engage with media in a range of social and humanities-focused fields, including but not limited to anthropology, education, sociology, politics, criminology, and law.

This chapter provides an overview of the central ideas relevant to undertaking feminist media studies today and highlights the significance and exigency of an intersectional approach to feminist media research and action. This primary emphasis on **intersectionality** is central to the book, and while the concept will be explored in more detail at the end of this chapter, it is important to define it at the outset. An intersectional feminist media studies approach is one that accounts for the complexity of lived experience and addresses the interconnected and inseparable character of oppression based on gender, race, class, sexuality, age, ability, religion, nationality, and other social stratifications. In what follows, we review the contributions of a feminist approach to media studies through an introduction to its core concepts and key questions, the 'waves' of feminist histories, and theoretical debates about gender as an individual or structural concern as articulated through postfeminism and intersectionality.

Putting the feminism in media studies

Not all research exploring gender and the media necessarily originates from a feminist media studies tradition, because this is dependent on how the researcher understands **gender** and its relationship to the media. In many quarters of society, it is commonplace to conceive of gender as a natural attribute based on embodied physical traits, which then predispose a person to particular tastes, behaviours, and ways of knowing and feeling. The framing of gender as immutable, fixed, and universal is a form of **essentialism**. This understanding of women and men as inherently different has been deployed in a range of contexts to explain discrepancies in treatment and status as well as to justify diverse inequalities in access to education and employment, experiences of violence and incarceration, and beyond. Feminist approaches, on the other hand, are informed by the critical theories of **poststructuralism**, which challenge gender essentialism by understanding reality as given meaning through social forces, including language and institutions such as the family, school, and the media. It is therefore tied to critical theories of sexuality detailing how normalized heterosexuality contributes to oppressive gender relations as well as the invisibility of other identities, lives, and communities in public life (Berlant and Warner 1998). A feminist perspective, then, refutes ideas of 'natural' gender norms and sexual relations, understanding expectations about masculinity and femininity to be **social constructs** that maintain male dominance as well as **heteronormative** understandings of the social world. The media here is a significant actor in shaping how we understand gender and sexuality as it conveys messages about the expected social and cultural roles taken up by people based on their identification as men or women.

Gender is therefore understood as an **identity**, comprised of the attributes and traits we express and are ascribed by our social and cultural affiliations. Depending on one's standpoint, it might be considered an identity we choose (such as the identity of a striker on a football team), become (such as the identity of a high school graduate), or are born into (such as the identity of a Black British person). In critical media studies, including feminist media studies, gender along with other markers of identity is understood to be a **subjectivity**, which refers to how our sense of self is situated within relations of power that normalize some behaviours while framing other ways of being as 'unnatural'. Subjectivities, including what we understand to be appropriate performances of gender, are produced by systems of power that authorize them and exclude others (Butler 1990).

From a poststructuralist perspective, the media plays a key role in this process of **subjectification** as well as in **signification**, which refers to the social meanings we construct from images, symbols, and words, including what are circumscribed as normalized and expected gender performances. In how it does this, the media is central to the circulation of ideologies, which refers to a set of ideas and values. A feminist ideology would include, for example, the idea that our society is shaped by relations of unequal power based on gender. A capitalist ideology would involve the idea that we exist on an equal playing field and therefore success is achievable by anyone with hard work. Ideologies are not neutral; they construct visions of how the world is organized and what actions are valuable as well as what is unnecessary, unimportant, or irrelevant. The power of the media in supporting the dominance of a set of ideas, or what is called **hegemonic ideology**, is vitally important, as it serves to represent and reproduce ideological norms within particular types of stories, or **discourses**, that may be more or less acceptable in society. While discourses, including those about gender, are powerful, they do not determine our actions and are open to contestation and resistance (Foucault 1990).

While these ideas are central to feminist media studies as an approach to research, criticism, analysis, and action, it would be a mistake to believe they are irrefutable or agreed upon in the scholarship or beyond it in popular culture and discourse. Feminism is as diverse as women and men are, and the way we understand gender, sexuality, identity, and bodies is multifaceted and in flux. Just as there is no unified or singular feminine identity or experience, there are multiple understandings of feminism as a politics, an approach, and a way of thinking, shaped by historical as well as geographical location. This is important because defining feminism is not simply a matter of words but also of practices; feminism is not only a set of diverse ideas but also entails a commitment to action, transformation, and change. This is what distinguishes feminist media studies from the study of media and gender, which would include research essentializing gendered preferences and practices rather than challenging the notion of natural or innate behaviours and interests.

As we will see throughout this book, feminist action related to media studies encompasses a broad agenda aimed at understanding how gendered relations are mediated, how gender plays a role in the consumption and creation of media, and how the tools of media can be used to achieve greater inclusion and equity across the world. This book is unique in its emphasis on delineating how feminist media studies is as much about ways of understanding how media are used, consumed, and produced in a manner marked by gendered subjectivities as it is about imagining the potential for media to contribute to a more just and equal world for those excluded within hegemonic systems of power.

A historical perspective on the development, origins, debates, and contributions of feminism can give us a sense of the multifaceted nature of its aims and objectives. Histories of feminist thought commonly identify three waves of distinct feminist objectives, actions, and debates, with a fourth wave potentially arising now. It is important to remember that this way of thinking about history risks introducing breaks that are excessively rigid and thus inaccurate. Furthermore, there is a great deal of disagreement between feminist scholars about what is to be included within each of these waves, and about their points of origin (Rivers 2017). Therefore, when thinking about the history of feminism it is preferable to see its phases or moments as indicative or suggestive of important sets of questions, commitments, and conflicts, rather than as firm historical periods. The notion of waves is, however, useful for indicating the importance of the historically shaped social, political, economic, and cultural contexts affecting questions of gender-based activism, and the central role of media for feminist work in these moments.

Each wave of feminist theory and action also consists of a series of concurrent social movements, sharing and diverging in their perspectives and approaches towards the aim of women's equal rights in society. Furthermore, many of the discussion topics within specific waves tend to arise across them, indicating that we have not found a simple set of answers in this approach – and indeed that the considerations of feminist media studies, and feminist thought more broadly, are complex and ongoing. One major criticism of the 'waves' model is that it tends to frame the thinkers and questions associated with each wave as being in conflict with each other, with new generations rejecting the work of their feminist predecessors. Such a simplistic understanding needs to be resisted when engaging with feminist media analysis, in order to focus instead on the lessons to be learned and the continuities of challenges despite shifts in our mediated society. It is also necessary to reflect on who benefits from a focus on disagreement rather than on the potential power offered by forming intergenerational collectives across waves. Therefore, in introducing these waves, I will stray from the more commonplace stories told about them in order to emphasize the ongoing challenges and questions associated with each period, pointing especially to the multiplicity of women's experiences and the part played by media in each wave.

The first wave

As with all waves, no agreed date has been attributed to the first wave of feminism. In fact, the time period associated with this moment in feminist history is very wide, ranging from the mid-1880s to the early 1900s. Many locate the 'beginning' of a formal project of feminism even earlier, at a convention held in Seneca Falls, New York in 1848 – a first example of how frequently feminist histories are centred around US-based actors. At this convention, 300 men and women came together to rally for women's equality. The meeting resulted in the drafting by Elizabeth Cady Stanton of the Seneca Falls Declaration, a document outlining a new movement for equality, its aims, and its political tactics.

The primary rallying issue behind this gathering was women's suffrage, the fight to gain the vote for women. Historically, the right to vote in democratic countries across the world has been limited in various ways. In Britain, for instance, voting was restricted to property owners (who could legally only be men) for hundreds of years. The suffrage movement in the UK was organized to reform these laws to allow non-propertied people the right to vote and therefore to participate in the political process, a shift that was particularly important given the decisions being made about sexual and reproductive regulation that were directly impacting on the lives and rights of women.

One critique of historical accounts centred on the Seneca Falls meeting and declaration is that they emphasize the organizing of White women at the expense of the role played by the abolitionist movement to end slavery, which was led by African American and First Nation women throughout the 1880s (Kinser 2004). Organizing to gain equal rights for people of colour was tied to the recognition of women as people, and yet many histories of feminism in the US do not include these activities. The White-washing of history and politics is something to keep in mind throughout this book and while engaging in intersectional feminist media studies. For some, 'feminism' is not a term they identify with because they disagree in some way with the fight for gender equality. However, because feminism has been dominated by privileged groups of straight White, highly educated, middle-class women and their issues, it may also not be a movement with which women of colour, poor women, LGBTQ+ people, and other marginalized communities can comfortably identify (hooks 1981). From the earliest days of feminist thought and organizing to the present, **White feminism** – treating the experiences, struggles, and desires of White women as if they were universal to all women – has been a danger to be recognized and avoided by adopting an intersectional approach.

One example of this was the 2016 celebration in Canada of the 100th anniversary of women being granted the right to vote. The selection of this date overlooked the fact that Indigenous people in Canada were denied the right to vote until the 1960s. Similarly, in apartheid-era South Africa, Black voters were systematically disenfranchised, with equal voting being introduced only in 1994. Centennial celebrations of 'universal suffrage' thus refer largely to White women gaining the right to vote and ignore the continued oppression of women of colour and Indigenous women by the state. The media contribute to this erasure of women of colour in the suffrage movement, for example in the 2015 film *Suffragette*, which focuses exclusively on White women's organizing in the UK. This framing of women as having a single common experience is a troubling tendency that must be resisted when engaging in feminist analysis of the media. As this example from the history of first wave feminism shows, we need to consider how race, indigeneity, and class also shape gendered experiences, access, rights, and representation, and how this is reflected in media content, production, and consumption. Mukherjee's (2018) research, for instance, examines the role played by Indian women in the suffrage movement, revealing the transnational and global history of first wave feminism often neglected in US- and UK-centric accounts.

Race is a key consideration because, as already mentioned, feminism in its first wave was entangled with the abolitionist movement, which sought to end the transatlantic slave trade and give rights to enslaved peoples. Many historical accounts of abolitionism emphasize the role of male figures, but women in the movement were active in organizing, and challenged the denial of their rights based on their status as women *and* as slaves. Activists challenged the default position of the propertied White man in legal systems. A famous example comes from a speech by emancipated slave Sojourner Truth at an Ohio-based Women's Rights Convention, titled 'Ain't I a woman?' Feminist scholar bell hooks, who we will return to throughout this book, titles one of her explorations of Black women and feminism after this speech, noting that a failure on the part of feminists to recognize the role of their race and class position alienates poor women and Black women from the movement (hooks 1981). This is not simply implicit in the emphasis on White women's experiences, as we see with celebrations of universal suffrage, but is explicit too in how, for example, Elizabeth Cady Stanton put women's rights activism in opposition to Black male suffrage, thereby placing Black women in a situation where they had to choose between fighting oppression based on race or gender. Such a failure to acknowledge the relationship between forms of subjugation and discrimination as they intersect with gender has been an enduring challenge for feminist approaches, and has inspired many core concepts and key questions still relevant to feminist media studies today.

The second wave

Historicization of the second wave of feminism has faced similar criticism for its emphasis on the struggles of White, middle-class women in the US. In particular, *The Feminine Mystique*, the famous 1963 book by journalist Betty Friedan, has been subject to critique. In this book, Friedan reflects on her interviews with her former classmates about their suburban lives fifteen years after they completed their education. She argues that in the US after the Second World War, the only socially acceptable identity a woman could take on was that of the 'housewife-mother'. This limited positioning of women in the media, advertising, and psychology texts, she contends, resulted in widespread unhappiness. Despite the insistence across media and social institutions that a woman's place was in the home, with fulfilment to be found in domestic work and child-raising, Friedan's respondents and her own experiences revealed a desire for more. She concludes her book by demanding greater opportunities for women to pursue further education and a career, challenging the status quo of gender relations and calling for reforms to family structures, reproduction, sexuality, and work.

The Feminine Mystique was very influential in raising awareness about women's lives, partly because of its huge readership – it was the best-selling non-fiction book of 1964. As a result of its popular success, US politicians took notice of the book and the status of women, leading to the Equal Pay Act of 1963, legislating that men and women should be paid the same amount for the same work. Friedan received hundreds of letters from readers and went on to co-found the National Organization for Women in 1966, which had as its mission 'true equality for all women', recognizing their humanity, fighting for economic advances, and advancing women's autonomy beyond the domestic sphere.

One critique of *The Feminine Mystique* and the discussion that ensued about women's lives was that it focused entirely on a fairly narrow, privileged group of women. Other women living in America in this period did not have stable economic situations allowing them to be housewives, working instead in low-paid, physically and emotionally demanding jobs to sustain themselves and their families. Some could not identify with the role of the wife because they were not heterosexual, and there was no provision for gay marriage. For these women, a framing of the experience of the feminine subject as wedded to a man and a strictly domestic working life did not reflect their own lives, and their absence from this vision is striking given that the book was written at a time when the civil rights movement was challenging the segregation of and legal discrimination against Black people in the US. Furthermore, the desire to dissolve the family did not reflect the perspectives and experiences of women of colour, as the familial unit is a significant part of their communities, and social networks were targeted as a source of strength to be dismantled in slavery and genocide throughout US history (Davis 1983). But these alternative viewpoints did not appear to be as media-friendly at the time, leading to their lack of visibility. This raises important questions in feminist media studies: *What stories about women do we see and hear being told in the media, and which bodies, identities, and lives are not present? What is the vision of feminism we see portrayed and how? Who gets to speak and whose voices are silenced?*

However, as with the first wave, reformers of women's rights during this period were embedded in a range of organized movements in the US, including the anti-Vietnam War movement and the civil rights movement for Black, Chicano and Chicana, Asian-American, and gay and lesbian people, who also had as their mission equal rights and the recognition of marginalized people as fully human members of society. When women's voices were not being featured or heard in these groups, this raised questions of gender equality. As this reminds us, features of oppression do not operate separately and we cannot conceptually or practically address 'race', 'gender', 'sexuality', or other embodied subjectivities that shape our experiences as unique considerations. In tandem, we need to recognize the implications of relative **privilege** and how this means that gendered experiences of the world are not universal. When we refer to 'women's experience' but only mean White women or middle-class women or straight women, we are saying that women without the latter's sexual, class, and racial privilege are not themselves women. We will return to the idea of privilege and alternatives to universality in the discussion of intersectionality.

Taking a transnational view on the second wave's organizing for women's liberation around the world highlights the intersectional nature of the movement. In some places, 'liberation' entailed a focus on unique experiences of oppression, such as poverty and gender in India (Patel 1985), sexual liberation in Japan (Shigematsu 2012), and the valuation of women's domestic labour in Italy (Federici 1975). A key critique arising in this moment of women's liberation on the global level is how sexual, reproductive, and domestic norms contribute to the differential treatment and oppression of women. Rights were sought across the world for women's greater autonomy over their bodies, including access to contraception and abortion. In the US, this also prominently featured critiques of beauty regimes and cultural objects such as make-up, bras, and high heels, which activists framed as oppressive tools of **patriarchy**, the dominant gender power system wherein men are commonly found in leading positions and women are subordinated. For example, the 1969 Miss America beauty pageant was the site of feminist protest by the Redstockings group, who agitated against the sexual **objectification** of women by throwing feminine items into a trashcan. This is the origin of the common trope of 'bra-burning' feminists, and indicates how the media can focus on iconic images, symbols, and metaphors to the detriment of a fuller discussion of the issues at hand (Ashley and Olsen 1998).

As these examples show, the media played a key role in second wave actions, particularly in **consciousness-raising**, or ensuring the wider visibility of issues related to women's rights. A major target of the movement in the 1960s was getting an Equal Rights Amendment to the Constitution passed through Congress, enshrining the right to social, political, and economic equality for men and women. Print publications and the use of highly visible forms of action such as rallies were essential to this, and allowed women interested in these issues to discuss and debate topics including the differences and connections between biological sex and gender performance (de Beauvoir 1949), compulsory heterosexuality (Rich 1980), and the relationship between capitalism and the subjugation of women (Firestone 1970). Through these discussions, gender equality became linked to class, sexuality, and race as well as the environment, imperialism and colonialism, and sexism within many quarters of society, from major institutions such as law and medicine to everyday matters including clothing, television, and family dynamics. It was in this period that the now-familiar expression '**the personal is political**' was popularized, highlighting the need to consider what had been historically dismissed as 'women's problems' within business, law, the media, and politics. This politicization of the personal not only shifted conceptual framings but also led to new institutional practices, from the opening of women's shelters for domestic assault survivors, to organizing against rape, to launching court battles to criminalize sexual harassment in the workplace.

Second wave feminism can be seen as focused on supporting women's autonomy over their bodies through access to contraception and abortion, and on increasing the number of women in domains previously dominated by men, such as education, politics, and the corporate world. Public awareness and discussion of women's rights, issues, and criticisms of patriarchy were amplified. As we will see, these were shifts that prepared the ground for topical action as well as debate in later waves, demonstrating the continuities across feminism's history.

The third wave

With the more recent feminist waves, the diversity of perspectives, actions, and missions becomes even more difficult to summarize, but they can be productively understood through the lens of individual agency versus structural critique. Accounts of the emergence of the third wave in the 1980s frequently define it in opposition to the concerns and actions of the second wave, framing its predecessor's activists as militant and anti-sex. The mission of the third wave is thus often characterized as the pursuit of a more playful, fun, sexy feminism. Lacy bras, along with high heels, make-up, and other beauty and fashion regimens once framed as tools of patriarchy, are embraced rather than scorned as discussions turn to the plurality of women's desires and pleasures.

Media is a central element of the third wave, as an object of scrutiny as well as a tool for action. Take for instance the so-called 'sex wars', where prominent feminist activists and scholars debated the harms of pornography versus the liberating potential of sex and its representation. Sexual freedoms and the loosening of restrictive social norms related to women's sexuality became important features of feminist action throughout the 1960s and 1970s on a global level, but in the 1980s and 1990s debates emerged around how much **agency** we could ascribe to women's participation in porn, and the impact of this content on individuals and society. We can see similar concerns at play in the activism against the infamous Page Three girl in the British tabloid *The Sun*, a daily feature of a topless young woman that ran from 1970 until 2015, despite calls to end pornography in the press having started in the 1980s.

In debates about the mediatized sexualization of female bodies, questions arise about the potential effects of such images, particularly given their pervasiveness, and the relationship between these framings and social problems ranging from sexual assault and workplace harassment to anorexia, low self-esteem, and body problems in girls and women. But there are other considerations, including complicated questions about pleasure and desire, the complexities of power in sexual performances, and participation in and through the media. It is easy to frame this as a question of playfulness and sexual liberation versus a puritanical prudishness spouted by the feminist **killjoy** – a figure explored by Ahmed (2010) that arises regularly in relation to feminist analysis. The feminist of the second wave is often constructed as joyless, angry, radical, and man-hating – an image fostered by conservative voices in the media in a backlash against the gains of feminism. As we will see, the killjoy figure appears throughout feminist history in attempts to denigrate expressions of feminist critique and reify limited ideas of what constitutes an acceptable feminism. While many of the arguments about the negative repercussions of feminism in society emerged in the 1980s (Faludi 1991), similar narratives about the harm it allegedly causes to family life and to men's economic and psychological well-being continue to circulate in the media today.

The questions raised by the sex wars related to individual choice, resistance, and freedom on the one hand, and to structural power and systemic gendered and sexualized violence on the other. These perspectives underpin many debates and lingering questions in feminist media studies, again demonstrating how challenges are not necessarily resolved despite their association with one or other of the feminist waves. Such debates continue to arise today with discussions of, for instance, **rape culture** and the concept of **the male gaze**, as will be examined in Chapter 3. It was in the context of this plurality of perspectives that the field of feminist media studies originated, informed by the insights of critical communication and cultural studies as well as queer theory (Probyn 2001). It is therefore a field of study that, rather than offering simplistic conclusions, is by necessity attuned to the tensions and contradictions in feminist thought in relation to the media and its important role in shaping, representing, reproducing, and challenging gender dynamics.

One critical trend in third wave feminism is the dismissal of a universal experience of womanhood rooted in the body, challenging taken-for-granted ideas about nature, gender, identity, sexuality, and heteronormativity. As noted above, this is linked to the rise of poststructuralist as well as postmodern and postcolonial thought in academic quarters in the 1990s. Feminist thought in this wave challenged familiar binaries and constructs naturalizing differences between men and women. Biological explanations for inequalities between people premised on genetics, hormones, and bodily difference, such as the ability to bear children, are here rejected in favour of approaches exploring how gender and sexuality are socialized through educational, political, and economic institutions, and not least through the media with its production and circulation of images, narratives, and symbols associated with normative expressions of masculinity and femininity. Through the telling and re-telling of these stories about men and women, we come to know what is acceptable in gender performance, and also what is unintelligible. In her analysis of how delimited gender identities and heterosexuality become normative, Judith Butler (1990) demonstrates that it is through the repetition of performances, rather than essential truths about the body, that ideas of what is correct feminine and masculine behaviour are constructed. This understanding of gender and sexuality as a dynamic process presents an opportunity for interventions, through what she calls '**gender trouble**', though it is important to note that this is not an easy proposition within unequal relations of power. Real dangers threaten those who resist the gender binary and presumed heterosexuality. One need only consider the tremendous structural, institutionalized, and everyday violence faced by **transgender** people to understand the stakes of making this kind of trouble. A report by Stonewall (Bachmann and Gooch 2017) indicated that 41 per cent of transgender people had experienced a hate crime in the previous 12 months, with 25 per cent facing discrimination in housing and/or the provision of public services based on their identities.

Despite these and other statistics indicating persistent structural inequalities based on gender and its intersections with sexuality, race, and class, individual power is a key concept of the third wave. **Empowerment** emerged as a major buzzword in this period, linked to two different sets of discourses and actions associated with the figure of the girl/grrl. The Spice Girls, a British pop group that rose to fame in the mid-1990s, proclaimed 'girl power' as their slogan, popularizing the topic of women's power outside of the more academic discussions outlined above. With their bold assertive style, emphasis on female friendships before romantic relationships, and repeated calls for girls to recognize and seize their power, the Spice Girls ushered in a moment of mainstream feminism unlike anything seen before, appealing in particular to youth cultures with their celebration of girls. Many, however, characterize this as an apolitical moment in the third wave, in which feminism was made safe and nonthreatening through its co-optation by popular culture and association with hyperfeminized imagery (Taft 2004). Girl power, as articulated not only by the Spice Girls but within a range of media texts from *Buffy the Vampire Slayer* to *Time Magazine*, heavily emphasized a break with traditional feminism in favour of a fresh, feisty, fun approach focused on the strength and power of the individual rather than on a critique of structures such as law, the economy, and educational institutions in their perpetuation of gender inequalities. Furthermore, 'girl power' was strongly linked to the creation of a new market, that of the tween girl, a consumer group positioned somewhere between childhood and adolescence. Tweendom as a category links the empowerment of this feminine consumer subject to their purchasing power (Coulter 2014), a move that indicates how feminism can be co-opted and commercialized in commodity capitalism if framed in a sufficiently unthreatening manner.

The alternate figure to the subject constructed within 'girl power' discourse is that of the Riot Grrl, based in an underground punk movement focused on challenging the stories and images circulated about young women in the media. Participants in this movement reject discourses of victimization as well as the traditional beauty standards commonly portrayed in teen magazines and other media, instead embracing a do-it-yourself aesthetic and reclaiming terms such as 'slut' and 'bitch' in a show of strength. Self-made media are at the core of the Riot Grrl movement, including music and zines (independent, self-published magazines), and the content of these texts focuses heavily on resistance to hegemonic discourses about gender but also age, race, class, and sexuality through discussions of taboo topics including masturbation, sexual violence, and queer desire (Kearney 1998). As a space enabling the creation and circulation of alternative images of femininity, the Riot Grrl movement is seen as a politicized site of media critique and action in the third wave, though as Kearney notes those who were able to participate were typically more privileged young women in terms of their race and class backgrounds.

The increasing adoption of the internet in North America in the mid to late 1990s allowed feminist action to circulate in new ways, including the exploration of and experimentation with gender performance in online communities as well as the sharing of feminist ideas across wider geographical areas. Networked communication facilitates the circulation of DIY media artefacts such as online zines by Riot Grrls, as well as other forms of creative expression via blogs and social media sites. In her research on girls' blogging activities, Keller (2015) notes that digital media creates new opportunities for girls to experiment with feminist identities and link into broader peer networks to talk about the issues they face in society. In Chapter 5, we consider the challenges and opportunities presented by the critical activist and creative work of girls and women becoming visible in digital culture in some parts of the world.

As with the previous two waves, third wave topics and the growth of mainstream discourses about female empowerment arose in a historical context worthy of consideration. Gonick (2006) traces the rise of the girl as a subject and argues that the idea of empowered young femininity is tied to **neoliberalism**, defined as a political-economic phenomenon emphasizing the responsibility of the individual in tandem with the dismantling of social welfare and community services funded by the state. In this context the discussion shifts away from structural inequalities such as pay gaps based on gender to focus on individuals' personalities, efforts, and circumstances. This focus on individual action and personal responsibility rather than systems of power and collective action means that neoliberal policies, practices, and discourses are at odds with the politics of feminism but in alignment with the consumer-based empowerment observed in the girl power movement. While the rise of neoliberalism is linked to the third wave, it remains the context for undertaking feminist media studies today, as an emphasis on the individual, her power, and her responsibility for addressing gender-based exclusion remains dominant.

Defining a core set of thoughts and actions related to the third wave is complex because it is a moment in feminist critique where a range of ideas about gender in society coexist, at times in tension. The idea that feminist action is important in continuing to fight for equal rights circulates alongside the notion that feminism has ushered in societal ills such as the destruction of the family, and the sentiment that feminism's mission has been completely successful so we can now move past it as an ideology (McRobbie 2004). Despite these challenges, the third wave is a moment when feminist discourse becomes more prominent and even mainstream, though this visibility does not translate to a universal acceptance of its politics. Rather than arguing for a single perfect definition of feminism, the third wave's rich and complex discussions indicate the value of embracing the plurality of perspectives and multiple voices active in feminist thought, particularly those that remain focused on challenging structural power rather than supporting neoliberalism and consumerism.

As we will explore in Chapter 7, the commodification of feminist thought, from the sale of branded T-shirts proclaiming feminist slogans to the use of feminist discourse to sell lifestyle products, clashes with feminism's transformational politics, underpinned as it is by the desire to subvert oppressive social structures. Capitalism as an economic system that prioritizes profit over values such as equality and justice is not compatible with the aims and objectives of feminist action, and therefore sentiments that link feminist action to spending power or the marketplace fail to account for how economic power is stratified not only across gender but also between women. As such, while the third wave's plurality of perspectives and voices necessitates being willing to listen to others, it does not entail accepting that all standpoints are equally valid. A feminism that means everything means nothing (Kinser 2004). While feminist media studies as a critical project is broad and diverse in its positions, approaches, and questions, it is united by a commitment to understanding how the media contributes to gendered inequalities and in turn how it may be deployed to intervene for greater social justice.

The fourth wave

Unsurprisingly, given the model of a progression of waves, some argue that we have now entered a fourth wave of feminism. Rivers (2017) links this fourth wave to a range of trends in the contemporary media environment, including the spread of social and digital media, networked activism, celebrity feminism, transnational interactions between women living in different parts of the world, and postfeminism. Alternately, Banet-Weiser (2018) notes the prevalence within contemporary media cultures of **popular feminism**, where there is a recognition of structural inequalities and enduring sexism but a continuing focus on the individual's negotiations of the barriers these present. Many of these ideas will be reviewed in greater depth throughout the book, but here we note the significance of the debate about where we put the emphasis in talking about power and oppression. In the previous waves, feminist activists struggled with institutionalized forms of power such as the legal system (in the case of abolitionism and suffrage) and differential treatment based on gender within social, economic, and political structures. In recent mainstream articulations of feminism, however, prominence is given primarily to individual feelings of agency and empowerment.

The media contributes to the pervasive tension between the individual and the structural, particularly in relation to the idea of 'choice'. The danger here is that highlighting individualized experiences of power can obscure social, economic, and political inequalities. One example of this would be the call to 'love your body', circulating widely across popular feminist texts, women's magazines, advertisements, blogs, and vlogs. While this might seem like a positive, inclusive message, it overlooks the broad range of industries and structures perpetuating a narrow vision of feminine beauty and demanding the consumption of a multitude of diet, fitness, and cosmetic goods and services to reach an impossible ideal. This emphasis on loving one's body despite its imperfections results in the depoliticization of the experience of living in a gendered body, turning away from collective organizing to meet the demands of existing oppressive systems of capitalism and patriarchy.

The fourth wave of feminism also resurrects some of the most pressing debates of feminist history, but often without reference to their historical antecedents. For instance, celebrity feminism is often linked to recent well-publicized proclamations by actors, singers, and models of being a feminist (or not), as in the case of Beyoncé standing in front of a giant illuminated sign reading FEMINIST at the 2014 MTV Video Music Awards, or Taylor Swift rejecting and then claiming the identity of feminist. However, celebrity feminism is neither new nor unique to the fourth wave. The second wave was publicized through the mediation of celebrity figures such as Betty Friedan and Gloria Steinem, and the Spice Girls were central to the popularization of the third wave. Indeed, across all the waves, the understanding of what gender-based thought and action means is heavily mediated, circulating a limited range of stereotypes, icons, and myths, and contributing to the repetition of narrow stories about gender, sexuality, and feminism. Mediation of this kind tends to limit our focus to North American and European figures and contexts, hindering a transnational view of feminist action on a global level. All this raises several questions: *What is the result of framing familiar feminist questions as new? What benefits would arise from connecting feminist struggles across history and around the world? Why is girl power so much easier for celebrities to identify with than feminism?*

Ahistorical perspectives on feminism also emphasize intergenerational conflict, with several significant consequences, including a failure to recognize the contributions and insights of feminist antecedents or, even worse, dismissing and mocking their work as outdated, with older generations of feminists unable to comment meaningfully on the current context. Rivers uses the example of *Harry Potter* star Emma Watson acting as a champion of the United Nations-initiated #HeForShe campaign, and her use of a familiar stereotype of the 'nagging, aggressive, man-hating feminist' (2017: 68), otherwise known as the killjoy, to vouch for the palatability of this male-led, digitally mediated approach to gender justice. Within media coverage, feminism is frequently interrogated for its relevance, dismissed for its unwelcome opposition to normalized ways of doing things, or framed as a completed project that has met its goals and need not be revisited. The influence of celebrities on these positionings is variable, but they are certainly key figures through which stories about feminism are told in the public eye, and their contributions to the feminist conversation should not simply be dismissed or celebrated but explored and examined for how they coexist with and contribute to other feminist discourses (Hobson 2016).

In many ways, the definition of fourth wave feminism is rooted not in the political development of feminism but in practices associated with digital media and emerging technologies, in particular social media such as Twitter and blogging. We saw in the discussion of the third wave of feminism that the growth of the internet in the US was important to the circulation of ideas in that context, highlighting the fallacy of treating such digital practices as wholly new to the fourth wave. But it is unsurprising that the fourth wave has so little awareness of its antecedents, as a key argument in the backlash against the third wave was that feminism's aims had been met. For many in this contemporary moment of feminism, then, it may seem as though feminist ideas are new, unlikely, or surprising.

With feminist discourse returning to the public sphere, conversations about sexualized violence, threats to reproductive rights, the gender pay gap, sexist language and behaviour, and the under-representation of women in many fields have again become mainstream. While some of these conversations are familiar, particularly from the second wave of feminism, there are important differences. Discussions about transphobia and homophobia, racism and xenophobia, and reversals of hard-fought gains are more prominent, as is a recognition of the gender binary and its restrictive function in feminist action. These issues coalesce around the inclusion of transgender and non-binary people in a range of spaces and discussions. Despite insights from the third wave of feminism and poststructuralist theory about gender as a social and cultural rather than biological category, with trans-exclusionary radical feminism there has been a return to essentialism linking gender (and feminism) to a delimited idea of women's bodies. Intersectional, social justice-oriented feminist media studies, as we will discuss below, rejects the idea of the universal woman and focuses instead on the intersection of gender equity with other forms of oppression, including that experienced by transgender and genderqueer people, in all its complexity (see for example Ahmed 2016; Phipps 2016).

Whether or not we are in a fourth wave, and what it may enable and entail, are yet to be determined. But what this overview should indicate for feminist media studies is that even a simple definition of feminism as being 'about equal rights' is complicated by the social, cultural, economic, and political context in which these rights arise. The resurrection of issues and questions across waves demonstrates that feminism is not a completed project, as gains can be lost and rights rolled back. Furthermore, we have seen challenges across the history of feminism in recognizing and accounting for differences between women, and in understanding inequalities and organizing action to address them, with a key distinction between discourses emphasizing the individual and those focusing on the structures perpetuating oppression. Two core concepts in media culture – intersectionality and postfeminism – relate to these different perspectives, and we investigate these further now.

Intersectionality

Intersectionality is a concept widely attributed to critical race and legal scholar Kimberlé Crenshaw (1989), who argues that the tendency to consider race and gender as separate, mutually exclusive categories fails to account for how they are experienced as axes of double oppression for women of colour. Crenshaw's insights and the concept of intersectionality are typically associated with the third wave of feminism, but the history of this perspective demonstrates again how firm divisions between these waves are inaccurate. While not given the name intersectionality, the argument that experiences and identities are impacted by race, class, gender, religion, age, sexuality, and ability was articulated by the Combahee River Collective (1977) during the second wave. Black women, the collective argued, are obliged to struggle against sexist and racist societal norms in a manner that does not reflect the battles against oppression articulated by White feminists on the one hand or Black male liberation activists on the other. The collective posits that separatism – the political gesture of focusing on single issues rather than alliances across experiences of oppression – cannot work for Black women, who need to speak to their lived experiences as both gendered and racialized. Collins (2008) refers to this overarching system of oppression as a 'matrix of domination', a perspective that enables us to conceptualize experiences of privilege and subordination as lived in tandem. Such an approach counters the ways in which laws, policies, and the media continue to define forms of discrimination as distinct.

Intersectionality recognizes systems of oppression such as patriarchy, White supremacy, heteronormativity, and capitalism as interlocking and as disadvantaging and privileging individuals at multiple axes of identity. Intersectional approaches also recognize that oppressed people can themselves perpetuate the oppression of others, even as they attempt to challenge structural inequalities. Recognition of these differences and the relative power, privilege, and marginalization that different bodies and communities experience is central to a critical feminist media studies, as freedom from oppression is not possible only for some. Since our examination of the media needs to consider oppression in all its complexity, this necessarily extends to feminist methods of research and action in the media. Building a movement for a more just world entails an intersectional approach premised not on a single issue but on a broad vision, large-scale collaboration, and democratic inclusion (Weiner Mahfuz and Farrow 2012).

Intersectionality is not a grand feminist theory, and in feminist media studies it is important not to approach forms of oppression as an additive equation whereby we measure some forms of oppression as quantitatively more severe because they include several forms of subject positioning (such as thinking of the experiences of Black lesbian women in terms of gender + race + sexuality). Adding oppressions in this way, rather than considering the layered complexities of multiple forms of subjugation, can lead to what Martínez refers to as a 'hierarchy of competing oppressions' (1993: 23), whereby rather than seeking opportunities for collaboration or solidarity, experiences of inequality become a basis for competition. Sometimes referred to as the '**Oppression Olympics**', such competition can impede the efforts of intersectional feminist critique to acknowledge how women's issues have been consistently framed across history in relation to White, middle-class, Western, English-speaking, able-bodied, and cisgender straight women.

Intersectionality as theory and method enables consideration of the ways groups and individuals can experience some kinds of privilege and not others, thereby shaping their everyday lives. Under patriarchy, as a system of masculine power, men and boys will have gender privilege. This translates into benefits that women and girls will not be able to access equally simply because of their gender. Privilege refers to advantages that are not earned but that are contingent on the body and identity one was born with, and which may grant access to opportunities others will not be able to obtain. Consider, for instance, which gendered bodies are constantly and publicly instructed about the ways they must dress, navigate the city, and respond to harassment to avoid sexual assault. Not having to consider these dangers is a privilege.

When analysing the media from an intersectional feminist perspective, there are several axes of oppression and privilege to consider as they intersect with gender:

Race – White privilege, a system of power that prioritizes, naturalizes, and celebrates Whiteness as the norm or default, is apparent in the positioning of White women's experiences and struggles as universal. As we will see throughout this book, women of colour are represented in distinctly different ways from White women, who are afforded more visibility in the media as well as more diverse and positive roles. Racialized men too face limiting representations of themselves, which indicates how intersectionality as an approach encompasses masculinity as well. To capture the specific form of gender-based hatred (misogyny) Black women face in the media, Bailey (2010) coined the term **misogynoir**.

While initially focused on hip hop music, this term has been applied to a range of media and popular culture objects to examine the intersection of gendered and racialized discrimination faced by women, in particular the erasure of Black women and their experiences in the media, such as the key role played by women activists in the Black Lives Matter movement. It also addresses how Black women are objectified, sexualized, framed as disposable, and otherwise debased in media content produced by Black men (though misogynoir can be and is perpetuated by others as well). We will consider further examples from critical race theory in Chapter 3.

Class – In the rise of consumer or commodity feminism associated with purchasing power and choice in the market, we can see how class privilege is linked to expressions of contemporary womanhood. Being born with economic resources affords people opportunities and access to health, education, well-being, personal development, and career progression. *How are those without class privilege, such as working-class and poor women, represented in the media, and how does this support capitalist structures?* As we will see in our discussion of gendered media work and feminist political economy in Chapter 6, media representations contribute to how the bodies and lives of women with less economic capital are subject to intensive scrutiny and typically found lacking and otherwise objectionable.

Language – A great deal of feminist theory and feminist media studies (including this book) exclusively references texts in or translated into English. Not only do we hear relatively little about the thoughts and actions of women who communicate in other languages, but in the media these women tend to be framed in a manner similar to racialized women – as passive or untrustworthy. Communication in English grants many a form of privilege in a globalized world where the expectation is that everyone should speak this language, as we will discuss in Chapter 4. In considering the intersections of gender with race, language, migration, citizenship status, and religion, **postcolonial theory** provides insights into how a history of colonialism and imperialism contributes to a worldview that shapes representations of non-White, non-Western nations, peoples, and practices as Other (Said 1978).

Sexuality – Heteronormativity, 'the institutions, structures of understanding, and practical orientations that make heterosexuality seem not only coherent – that is, organized as a sexuality – but also privileged' (Berlant and Warner 1998), is produced in a range of institutions, including the media. In a system of compulsory heterosexuality, lesbian, gay, bisexual, and queer individuals face overt and implicit discrimination and exclusion, requiring them to engage in social and legal battles for the same rights as those with straight privilege. While we see gay and lesbian people represented more than ever before in media texts, from television shows to films to advertising, scholars question how the political power of queerness, challenging ideas about the nuclear family, essentialized gender, and capitalist structures, is evacuated from stereotypical media representations. Pathologizing representations and the erasure of queer people persist as well, with bisexuality represented, if at all, largely within a negative framing of bi people as disingenuous, greedy, or indecisive. In the field of **queer theory**, it is common to engage in media analysis that complicates the 'totalizing tendency' of heteronormativity (Warner 1991: 8). Queer approaches do not relate to the gender binary or other fixed categories of hetero- or homosexuality, but instead concern themselves with the intersections and combinations of non-straight sexualities (Doty 1993) in order to challenge the privileging of heterosexuality in public culture. We will examine further the contributions of this approach in Chapter 2.

Age – Media cultures tend to emphasize and value young femininity, framing the aging female body as sexless, failing, and shameful. In staging intergenerational conflict between feminists, the media also construct firm differences between women of varying ages rather than highlighting their shared interests and challenges. With the aging of the population in the Western world, an increasing number of texts have focused on the experiences of older women in a more positive way, but as we will see in Chapter 3, these representations tend to be quite limited as well.

Migration and citizenship status – Women who are refugees, immigrants, citizens, or Indigenous peoples of a nation-state experience different degrees of privilege. As with language, this is shaped by colonial histories and relationships between Indigenous people and settler populations as well as immigration policies and discourses. The stories circulating in the media about migrating women, whether forced or not, and Indigenous women tend to be again frequently delimited, showcasing how few women are afforded the opportunity to be represented in the media in a rich and robust manner. This will be discussed further in Chapter 4.

Gender identity – **Cisgender** people, designated a sex at birth that aligns to their internal sense of identity, experience the privilege of being recognized by others and within institutions, whereas genderqueer, non-binary, transgender, and otherwise non-gender-conforming people face pervasive and persistent discrimination, harassment, and violence in their everyday lives. In the US in particular there has been a noticeable increase in the number of media texts centred on the stories of transgender people. However, transgender people lack the privilege of having diverse stories told about their lives, and in many cases are denied the opportunity to work in the media (e.g. when cisgender actors are cast in the roles of transgender people, such as Jeffrey Tambour in the lead role in the television series *Transparent*). Furthermore, 'when trans people are granted mainstream visibility, it is often as spectacularized objects of suffering, not as political, speaking subjects' (Horak 2018: 2013), or as hypersexual and scheming individuals deserving of their victimization (Jackson et al. 2018). Relatedly, the language used in the media to refer to transgender people and the issues they face is often dehumanizing and inaccurate. A useful resource for feminist media scholars is the Media Reference Guide provided by GLAAD (n.d.), which includes a glossary of key terms as well as explanations of why some terms and framings contribute to the marginalization of transgender people.

Disability – The privilege of able-bodied people is easily spotted when we consider how many physical locations in our cities are difficult or impossible to access for those who use a wheelchair, and how language referring to physical and cognitive disabilities is used in everyday slurs (such as dumb, lame, and crazy). People with disabilities are largely represented in the media as victims, objects of pity, and as lacking or damaged. Their disability becomes the sum of their experience, dehumanizing a whole group of people, though challenges to this framing can be found in the media participation of young women with disabilities on social media such as YouTube (Reinke and Todd 2016). *How often are women with disabilities represented in the media, and how frequently in a way that is not about their lives beyond their disability? How is their disability used as a narrative device? How often are people with disabilities included in the production of media texts, including those that portray their experiences?*

Religion – Discriminatory media representations of religious groups are common, including in particular the portrayal of Muslim women. As we will see in Chapter 4, Islamophobia is used as a mechanism by which to not only delimit the narratives and images of the men and women who practise Islam, but also to assert the dominance of particular models of femininity. *How are other religious groups represented (or not) in the media? What do these framings tell us about which religions are privileged?*

Body shape and size – A common form of discrimination perpetuated by the media is fatphobia. The bodies granted visibility in our media cultures are almost always thin, fit, and toned, and the expectation that women should achieve such a body fuels the beauty, fitness, and health industries. While fat positivity is a growing activist campaign with strong parallels to queer organizing (Lebesco 2003), fat women are often defined first and foremost by their weight and body shape rather than other attributes, and fatness is commonly mocked as unattractive and the result of a loss of control or a failure of self-discipline.

Discussing privilege often appears to elicit guilt or denial from those who are part of privileged groups, partly because the lived experience of privilege is the opposite of oppression. Whereas someone who is structurally disadvantaged due to their disability will experience difficulty when trying to gain access to a space without a lift, the able-bodied will feel nothing when moving in the same space – because of their privilege. As McIntosh notes, 'White privilege is like an invisible weightless knapsack of special provisions, maps, passports, codebooks, visas, clothes, tools, and blank checks' (1988: n.p.). But recognizing privilege is not intended to close off conversations in feminist thought and analysis. The purpose of taking an intersectional perspective on privilege and power is to understand that our bodily lived experiences cannot be isolated from each other, and that some people are required to work harder to experience things others may take for granted.

In a feminist media analysis this entails understanding how the mediation of gender contributes to these forms of privilege and to the narrow stories told about women. *Who gets to be the strong female protagonist? Who is relegated to the sidekick? How are villains constructed as evil through traits associated with sexuality, gender identity, race, ability, or body size?* Molina-Guzmán and Cacho point out that intersectional research 'foregrounds women of color as interpreters and audiences; emphasizes how gender(s) intersect sexuality, class, race, nationality, or citizenship; and/or illustrates how gendered representations in the media are significant in the production of social, political, or cultural inequalities' (2013: 75). In doing so, it encourages us to consider who gets to research, critique, and produce the media. Such an approach necessitates questioning Whiteness as the unspoken default for women, and challenging this norm in our methods, sites of research, and analysis.

Postfeminism

Alongside growing awareness of the importance of intersectional approaches, another trend of interest within contemporary media cultures is the rise of postfeminist discourse, emphasizing personal empowerment, generational divides in feminism, and the sentiment that feminism's goals have been attained. Postfeminism is not equivalent to feminism and it is not a wave or form of feminism. One is not a postfeminist, nor is postfeminism a politics. Postfeminism cannot be intersectional, though we can and should take an intersectional approach to examining it. Instead, as Gill (2007) highlights in her exploration of the idea, postfeminism is a sensibility with several interrelated themes in media and culture. I review these now in some depth in recognition of the significance of its analysis in feminist media studies. Postfeminism's logic is premised on:

1) The idea that femininity is located in the body, and that women's power is derived from the cultivation and maintenance of a sexy body. Rather than returning to the essentialization of women as mothers and caretakers, postfeminist discourse emphasizes that women's power is linked to the self-disciplining of their bodies against criticisms related to weight gain, aging, and other failures linked to physical attractiveness.

2) The sexualization of culture, whereby sex and sexuality become pervasive across the media, from normalized reporting of rape in the news media to magazine articles celebrating pole-dancing as a form of fitness. This sexualization is uneven between men and women, as women are responsible for maintaining their sexual desirability as well as the emotional and physical health of their sexual relations, whereas men are addressed in the media as a uniformly sex-hungry and uncaring group. Young girls too become the targets for this sexualization, as girlishness is codified as sexy and pornographically themed objects are marketed to them.

3) The notion that women are active agents in the process of their own sexualization, participating in their framing as desirable figures rather than being passive victims of objectification. This sexual subjecthood is only available to some women – young, slim, and typically White – placing other women outside the acceptable frame of postfeminist femininity. As Gill says, this 'represents a shift in the

way that power operates: a shift from an external, male judging gaze to a self-policing narcissistic gaze. It can be argued that this represents a higher or deeper form of exploitation than objectification – one in which the objectifying male gaze is internalized to form a new disciplinary regime' (2007: 151). What would have once been criticized as straightforwardly sexist media representation is now self-aware and laughs at the idea of taking criticism seriously.

4) The seductive story of individual power, choice, and agency, which we have seen characterizes many of the debates in the third and fourth waves due to the rise of neoliberalism. Politics, structural inequalities, and cultural and social power do not feature in the discussion here. Instead, women are empowered in the choices and directions they take in their careers, relationships, and personal appearance. Rather than engaging in self-discipline of the body for male appreciation, women are framed as engaging in beauty and fitness regimes for their own self-satisfaction. As Gill points out, given how much choice women apparently have, it is perplexing that the look that is most valued across autonomous agents is so similar.

5) The normalization of an intensive degree of surveillance and discipline despite apparent freedoms, instructing women in a range of areas, from physical fitness and beauty practices to emotional well-being, caring for themselves and their male partners, managing their workplace communication and image, organizing their domestic spheres, and myriad other duties, all supposed to be performed to very high standards but without any sign of effort. The way this is gendered towards women is apparent in how the subject of self-help texts is largely female.

6) The idea that women are flawed and need to undertake a campaign of self-improvement. This is what Gill refers to as the makeover paradigm, which fuels the growth of reality shows focused on physical and self-transformation, from fashion choices to parenting to weight loss to cosmetic surgery. These bodies and subjects are often subject to class and body-size shame in the process of self-improvement, disciplining them in the acceptable femininity of postfeminist media culture.

7) The concept of essential sexual difference, which has been challenged by feminists and queer theorists for some time, becomes re-entrenched

as a dominant idea. Experts refer to evolutionary psychology and the 'natural' needs and desires of men and women, and decry the harms caused by political correctness and feminism in inhibiting men from enacting their true selves. In this way, gender essentialism and heteronormativity are reaffirmed, while critical social justice work on the oppressions faced by women and other marginalized people becomes easy to dismiss.

Postfeminist discourse is illuminated in research analysing media from the late 1990s and early 2000s, including the television series *Ally McBeal* and *Sex in the City* as well as *Bridget Jones's Diary* and other books in the genre known as 'chick lit'. These early, oft-cited exemplars have in common feminine subjects that are White, professional, and located in urban centres in the UK and the US. Indeed, Gill's definition of a postfeminist sensibility concludes by asking whether it re-centres the White woman as its subject. However, Gill's conceptualization of postfeminism has been productively extended more recently by Jess Butler (2013), in her analysis of the American singer Nicki Minaj. How race plays a key role in postfeminist media culture becomes apparent in Butler's reading of Minaj's play of hyperfemininity and masculine symbolism as well as her embrace of 'girl power'. Clearly, an analysis of postfeminist media cultures focused solely on White female subjects is insufficient. Dosekun (2015) demonstrates how postfeminist discourse circulates beyond the West, finding that the women in her study in Lagos, Nigeria are also hailed by this discourse, indicating the importance of taking a global, transnational approach to feminist media studies.

Analysis of postfeminist discourse in the media has become a central pivot in feminist media studies, and this cultural logic continues to have a strong resonance when considering contemporary media trends. It is a logic in which feminist and antifeminist ideas coexist despite their contradictions. **Antifeminism** has existed since women began to agitate for rights, with opponents disagreeing on a range of elements within feminism. Putative evidence against women's equality is frequently derived from sources in evolutionary psychology, pointing to historical trends across human life to justify sexist behaviour. Stereotypes about differences between men and women continue to be invoked in order to justify, for instance, women's domestic roles and men's positions of power. Some antifeminists say that they agree with equal rights, but claim that feminism is actually seeking to privilege or empower women over men. Despite the argument that feminism has succeeded in reaching its goals, to this day there are those who will fight against anyone expressing feminist ideas, at times violently.

Feminist Media Studies

While it might seem contradictory for these ideas to operate together, their coexistence is enabled by the depoliticization and commodification of feminism, linking women's power to spending, consumption, and the individual's ability to meet life's demands, rather than to collective action against structural inequalities. The emergence of **neoliberal feminism**, where women proclaim to be feminist but locate the solution to exclusion in individualized activities such as self care, further obscures the origins and aims of a feminist politics (Rottenberg 2013). The focus on individual practices has a disciplinary result, wherein women are obligated to self-regulate, and where any barriers to success they face must be attributed to personal failure rather than to social and cultural norms that privilege other subjects over them.

Undertaking feminist media studies

As this chapter has demonstrated, feminism is a complex political concept with diverse meanings, divergent perspectives, and a long and varied history. This does not make a feminist media studies impossible. Instead, we can understand this complexity as a productive power, fuelling an approach to media studies that is fundamentally comfortable with conflict, complications, difference, and debate, even among those who are engaged in this work. Rather than pursuing simple, binary understandings of what is right and what is wrong in media representations and practices, feminist media analysts need to be accepting of the challenges that emerge from the fact that each of us has only a partial perspective on the world (Haraway 1988). Such acceptance lies at the heart of an intersectional approach recognizing the pitfalls of taking a universalized perspective on women. This book therefore aims to provide the insights and directions needed to engage in intersectional feminist media studies, and in the process move the field forward in critical, fruitful, and ethical ways.

This chapter has outlined the historical and conceptual context for feminist media studies while also detailing the necessity of embracing intersectionality. Throughout, I have bolded key concepts and included difficult questions intended to generate further, more specific analysis and discussion. While no simple answers can be given, each chapter in this book provides a sense of the concepts, key debates, and possible directions for action that may form the basis of an investigation into these provocations. The structure of the chapters in this book largely follows this approach, beginning with core issues and theoretical context and then moving on to generative thematics and questions, concluding with examples of action, transformation, and strategies for countering the issues identified.

Rather than providing a literature review of feminist media studies so far, this book looks to the future of the field. To do so, it provides an original synthesis of interdisciplinary perspectives, concepts, and methods from media and communications and beyond. It thus lays the ground for wide-ranging interdisciplinary and intersectional feminist research into the media across the social sciences and humanities, as well as for action outside academia. These elements of the book – its interdisciplinarity, focus on intersectional approaches, and emphasis on critical analysis as well as action – constitute the book's major contribution to furthering the field of feminist media studies in ethical and just ways.

The act of knowledge production in research and critique is an important place to start with this project. In Chapter 2, I outline methods and approaches to feminist media studies, demonstrating both the practicalities and politics of this field through a discussion of a feminist ethics of care and practices of iteration, reflexivity, and situatedness in research design and analysis. I detail foundational and contemporary examples of feminist media critique to illustrate best practices for rigorous and ethical research, and demonstrate the intersectionality and international scope of this field across work analysing media texts, practices and cultures, and action.

Chapter 3 further explores the political question of what is made visible raised in Chapter 2 by considering representation in the media. Here we examine quantitative and qualitative research on the presence and visibility of women in fiction and non-fiction texts, considering in particular intersectional subject positions. This chapter explores key concepts for understanding why representation matters, its role in social life, and common representational regimes marked by unequal relations of power. It also examines how, with the growth of accessible media production opportunities and the harassment of women and girls online, visibility is a fraught goal.

Chapter 4 further complicates the issue of visibility by introducing transnational feminist media studies, drawing on scholarship from postcolonial and critical race theory to propose a decolonizing approach to the field attuned to global relations and flows. We examine in more detail the notions of agency, choice, freedom, and empowerment in light of transnational dynamics, and consider how such norms are shaped by global power relations premised on gendered colonial and imperialist histories. Here we also return to the politics of knowledge production in thinking about approaches to decolonizing feminist media research and critique.

Freedom is a key concept in Chapter 5, where we focus on the questions, challenges, and possibilities arising for feminist media studies and action as a result of the growth of digital media. I introduce a critical, historically informed approach to examining the relationship between digital media and social norms to better understand the opportunities and constraints inherent in the field. The gendering of technology, a key feature of feminist digital media studies, is considered through a discussion of the early myths of the internet in relation to freedom and equality. Looking at hashtag activism and selfie production in particular, we consider how challenges related to visibility and voice endure but also shift with new platforms and their politics.

While Chapter 5 explores gendered participation in digital media from the standpoint of communities of users, Chapter 6 explores women's work in media production on a global level. While it is commonplace to assume that inequalities in media representation can be attributed to a lack of women in the workplace and therefore addressed with strategies to get more girls into the industry, this chapter explores how an 'add more women and stir' approach overlooks the cultural and structural basis for women's exclusion. It also fails to account for the myriad ways in which women do make the media, historically and transnationally, but in a culture where their labour is consistently undervalued and unrecognized.

In Chapter 7, we conclude by considering how to move forward with intersectional feminist media studies given the theoretical, methodological, and practical challenges and opportunities explored throughout this book. While the plethora of feminisms that appear to circulate indicate intriguing directions for research, in this chapter I demonstrate how an attunement to our past and to the work of feminist predecessors is vital both for addressing pressing contemporary concerns and ultimately for ensuring the future of the field.

To conclude the present chapter, I want to account for the necessity of taking an intersectional approach to the field. Feminist scholars bell hooks and Donna Haraway both remind us that women's experiences are not monolithic or universally shared, but are subject to contextual and situated forces shaping how gendered lives will be lived. Consider, for instance, how the life of a Chinese worker constructing iPhones in Zhengzhou differs from that of a British vlogger making beauty tutorials in her bedroom. Gender always intersects with age, nationality, class, race and ethnicity as well as sexuality, ability, and religion. At the same time as we recognize difference, however, we need to be sure not to end our analysis there. The conclusion that all experiences are relative can lead to a sense of powerlessness in effecting change. Instead, feminist media scholars need to remain sensitive to and careful with differences while also recognizing the global systems of power and domination serving to marginalize people and groups based on gender and its intersections with other identities. Marginalization occurs in contextually specific ways, and our work must consider the nuances of each context we study. This is particularly important when considering global media, and how our locations impact on production, marketing, consumption, representation, and audience practices.

This mindset runs in direct opposition to a postfeminist logic in which feminism is discarded in a turn towards the power of the individual. Engaging in an intersectional feminist media critique therefore runs the risk of being framed as angry, humourless, and strident. The only route left, then, as Sara Ahmed urges, is to embrace the feminist killjoy, for this is where our collective intellectual power and resistance to oppression is to be found. As hooks asserts, 'when we dare to speak in a liberatory voice, we threaten even those who may initially claim to want our words. In the act of overcoming our fear of speech, of being seen as threatening, in the process of learning to speak as subjects, we participate in the global struggle to end domination' (1989: 18). Our critical approach to understanding the role of the media in supporting or challenging unequal global systems of power relies on finding this voice. In the next chapter, we look at approaches to research and critique that support this goal.

2 Feminist Media Critique

Chapter 1 foregrounded feminist media studies' rich history, characterized by complex and constructive debates about how to approach a feminist analysis of media across contexts, communities, and experiences. As a branch of critical media studies, this field's wide-ranging set of interests – in texts, institutions, identities, cultures, communities, and practices – necessitates an attendant multiplicity of methods and approaches to research. While feminist methodologies and social science research methods have been well-detailed in a range of books and articles, this chapter fills a gap by providing a cohesive overview of how feminist media studies have been conducted in all their diversity, in order to support those new to the field as well as experienced scholars seeking new methods in their work.

We consider here several classic and contemporary examples of feminist media critique as well as key theories and concepts for engaging with the media – whether the so-called old media industries of television, magazines, and newspapers, or new media including online platforms, digital games, and mobile communication. A number of the research methods for generating and analysing data outlined in this chapter are associated with studies of media, communication, and culture generally. Feminist media studies also draws on insights from, to name a few influences, queer theory, critical race theory, postcolonial critique, and poststructuralist theories of identity, wherein gender and other subject positions are understood to be contingent on social norms and cultural institutions in specific contexts. This fundamentally shapes how we engage in research and critique. Therefore, this chapter focuses on the distinctive elements and motivations underlying an intersectional feminist approach to critique, including how gendered subjects and relations are represented and performed in the media, how feminist methods can address issues of visibility and erasure arising for marginalized groups in media research, and the relationship between critique and feminist action for change in the media. While the methods reviewed here are not exclusive to feminist media studies, the politics and ethics underpinning them in their attunement to intersectional gender relations is what enables them to be deployed to meet the objectives of a feminist media critique. By providing insight into the politics of knowledge production, this chapter contributes to a deeper understanding of how the processes of research and critique are entwined with feminist aims for a more just and equal world.

While analysis of the media is at the heart of feminist media critique, there are many ways researchers might approach their object of empirical interest in this field. These approaches are organized around three broad categories: 1) the media as text; 2) people and cultures participating in media practices; and 3) action and intervention in and through the media. These are not mutually exclusive, and many feminist media scholars design multi-method studies putting these areas of focus in conversation with each other. This is fitting as the media are discursive, constituted of text, symbols, and images, as well as social, taking an important role in a variety of interpersonal, community, and institutional contexts. The media are also both a target and a resource for feminist activism. Consequently, the organization of this chapter around these three categories should be understood – as with the marking out of feminist waves in Chapter 1 – as a way of getting at similarities and distinctive features rather than as imposing firm divisions between modes of feminist media critique. Note as well that this is not a full account of all potential approaches, partly because this is a diverse area of thought and research and also because techniques for considering inequalities in the media are ever-changing, evolving, and emerging. Rather, this chapter should be read as a jumping off point for further investigation into forms of feminist media critique.

Feminist media critique is premised on the idea that our social realities are shaped by our experiences and contexts within an unequal system of power based on gender and other axes of oppression. As such, the types of research reviewed in this chapter share a common feature, which is that they are forms of **interpretivist** research methods. Interpretive approaches enable a consideration of the media, and of those who engage with it in their social, cultural, and historical contexts, which is well-suited to a critical feminist politics. Such research methods diverge in their starting points, but what underlies their design, questions, execution, and analysis is the understanding that there is no objective, neutral, outside perspective that researchers can take, and that therefore interpretation of social realities always occurs in the contexts they are embedded in. Researchers are, after all, themselves subjected to the power relations of the gender order they critique, and therefore cannot abstract their realities or those they research from the context in which they exist and make meaning. However, this does not mean that the conclusions derived from interpretivist approaches are biased or open to endless varied explanations. As with **positivist** research, which is based on testing predetermined hypotheses, those undertaking interpretivist projects also uphold standards of **rigour** and **ethics** in their research practices.

Generally speaking, rigorous research will ensure that techniques of producing and analysing research materials are appropriate for addressing the set research questions, and that the research methods are transparent. Ethical research conforms to the standard of **informed consent**, where participants in the research are made fully aware of the project's aims, methods, modes of analysis, and possible outcomes, as well as of their own rights and responsibilities, in advance. Feminist thought recognizes that power relations inherently inform knowledge production, including in research and critique. The power dynamics in our interactions and encounters as researchers create the potential for harms that may not be recognized as such in more legalist, institutionalized approaches to ethics. To address this, and to cultivate more rigorous and ethical research and critique, we turn now to the notion of a **feminist ethics of care** and how it can be fostered in the practices of **iteration**, **reflexivity**, and **situatedness**.

Principles of rigour and ethics in feminist media critique

The interpretations we make in feminist media studies are grounded in the contexts in which they occur and are examined. Therefore, it is not possible, necessary, or even desirable to generalize findings from one study to another. However, rather than generalizability, the criteria of iteration, reflexivity, and situatedness can be used to support a rigorous and ethical interpretivist approach. These standards of rigour are derived from the principles of qualitative research methods but are also inflected with the politics of a feminist analysis oriented towards care. For Leurs, who writes about feminist approaches to data-driven research, a feminist ethics of care is 'value-based and recognises the dependencies, partiality, political commitments and personal involvements of researchers' (2017: 138). According to Gillies and Alldred (2012), engaging in ethical feminist research entails a critical questioning of several elements of our critique. First, how should we represent women across differing locations, histories, and experiences, including the perspectives of Indigenous people, colonial subjects, and those from the Global South, who have been largely excluded from processes of knowledge-building (as we will see in Chapter 4)? Second, how might we reshape existing practices of knowledge production, such as the assumption of researcher objectivity and the idea that we can discover 'truths' or 'give voice' to those we conduct research with? Third, how might we use research methods to engage in social change and transformation, as in the forms of action research to be discussed later in this chapter? In their discussion of these concerns, Gillies and Alldred highlight how research is not innocent of power structures. Indeed, histories of research demonstrate that it can do harm. A feminist ethics of care entails acknowledging and mitigating against these potentially negative impacts, as well as seeking mutually beneficial encounters in our research. There is no step-by-step process to follow that will guarantee ethical and rigorous feminist research, but the criteria detailed below may be useful in guiding research design, execution, and critique.

Iteration – This is a research practice entailing a systematic and repetitive process of moving back and forth between what is being analysed, its social reality, and the researcher's interpretations and theoretical approach, to ensure that the meaning made in critique accords with the diverse viewpoints being considered. Iteration in qualitative research ensures that the researcher creates a dialogue between the empirical context under examination and their theoretical interests in analysis. The result is that the emerging interpretations the researcher makes, based on their research questions, existing literature, and theoretical framework, are set in dialogue with the material under review, what is often called research data. The researcher asks what the relation between these areas are, what they say together, and what insights can be inductively derived from them (Srivastava and Hopwood 2009). **Inductive** approaches focus on what theories, new understandings, and conclusions can be drawn from exploring the relationships, patterns, and similarities observed in the research, in contrast to **deductive** approaches which assume patterns and relations in hypotheses established at the start of the research project.

The process of moving back and forth between the materials under examination and the research questions and literature continues until it no longer serves to generate any further insight into what the researcher is exploring, a stage known as **theoretical saturation**. This is defined as 'the point in analysis when all categories are well developed in terms of properties, dimensions, and variations. Further data gathering and analysis add little new to the conceptualization, though variations can always be discovered' (Corbin and Strauss 2008: 263). When a researcher reaches the point where iteratively considering the research context and materials gathered – be it content analysis of news coverage of sexual assault in Silicon Valley, semi-structured interviews with fans of the *Wonder Woman* reboot, or observations of interactions enabled by a new fitness app aimed at teenage girls – only provides further examples of the patterns already observed, they have reached the point of theoretical saturation and can move forward with analysis and writing. Iteration in interpretivist research on the media is therefore open-ended and allows for a deep immersion in the materials and phenomena under examination as part of the process of analysis and theory-building. Grounding analysis in this way enables reflexive and situated feminist media critique.

Reflexivity – As noted above, when engaging in critique it is not possible to step outside of the power relations structuring the media, gender dynamics and their axes of oppression, or the social world. We may be looking at the materials in our media critique in a new way that does not resemble our casual viewing, playing, or reading as everyday media audiences, but that does not remove us from our subjective, embodied experiences. Our positioning does not make a rigorous critique impossible, but it entails being critical about the role we play in shaping the conclusions we draw in our projects, and how we design a study to begin with. Critically and thoughtfully considering the role of the researcher in the process of critique is called reflexivity, and is intended not to indicate 'bias', but instead to situate research and critique as social processes. As with other forms of research, the result of a feminist media critique is the production of knowledge, and our experiences, perspectives, bodies, and identities always shape how we engage in this process and its outcomes. Consider for instance how a universalized perspective on women's experiences, as reviewed in the previous chapter, elides significant differences between women based on their class, race, and sexuality. Reflexivity in research enables the analyst to understand how their work is always contingent on their social positions and relative privilege, so grounding and adding nuance to their analysis.

Researcher reflexivity allows us to intellectually grapple with the limits of our ability to understand a given situation and interrogate how our positions differently afford insight and access to particular communities and resources. For instance, an able-bodied researcher examining representations of embodiment and identity in the film *The Shape of Water*, which portrays a non-verbal female character in the main role, would do well to reflect on how their own embodied identity shapes their analysis. An intersectional approach recognizes that able-bodied people have privilege in power structures normalizing and pathologizing specific embodied ways of being in the world, and therefore that their approach to the representation of disability may be inflected with this viewpoint. When undertaking research on marginalized groups, it is important to reflect on the principle: 'Nothing About Us Without Us'. This slogan expresses the idea that research decisions should not be made without the participation of the groups and communities impacted, particularly marginalized communities, including people with disabilities (Charlton 2000). It is equally valuable for research on oppressed peoples and for considering who speaks for and about these groups. When selecting a research topic, site, or questions, it is essential to question one's relative privilege and power as a researcher and the ethics of engaging in analysis with those under consideration.

Reflexivity can be undertaken across the research and critique process, beginning with a discussion of one's research questions – for instance when a researcher's frustration at the lack of material on a topic leads them to formulate the questions they raise, rather than simply describing a literature gap. Reflexivity is also often productively included as part of the discussion of recruitment strategy. For example, it would be beneficial for a researcher to reflect on the decisions that have led to their entire interview sample being from a single racial group, even if race was not a feature of the study design. In cases where a researcher may be interested in a community or group they are a member of, reflexivity can serve to illuminate what language, norms, and practices they may not necessarily question because of their insider perspective. It can also highlight how membership of a group grants greater access to stakeholders, spaces, or types of knowledge. Other benefits would arise in the case of research by a non-member without such access, as each position enables different perspectives in the analysis. An outsider may find their distance enables them to observe and question taken-for-granted values, but at the same time hinders their ability to understand these with as much nuance as someone who is very familiar with the community or site. Reflexivity will shape the process of writing up the research, where, by necessity, the researcher will refer to themselves in the first person. In contrast to expectations of objective research emerging seemingly naturally from the page, reflexivity compels the researcher to reflect on their own subjectivity directly, which necessitates them referring to themselves in the write-up. In sum, reflexivity allows the researcher to develop a richer set of insights on complex phenomena as a result of a critical thought process about how power relations in our social realities might affect the research. Reflexivity is relevant to every step in the research process and can highlight what is always present in that process but is often obscured by the insistence on objectivity and neutrality – the role of the researcher in shaping not only the conclusions drawn but also the materials and phenomena under analysis and the patterns and relationships identified in the process of critique.

Situatedness – Closely related to reflexivity is the recognition that analysis is shaped by situated knowledges, limiting our ability to make an argument about the situations of others. Haraway (1988) argues that our understandings of the world are always only partial, as we cannot gain an omniscient, god's eye view on the truth of a situation, only an understanding that derives from where we and our participants and materials are located. In a later work, Haraway also posits the need for situated knowledges that consider different bodies and perspectives marked by race, gender, ideology, and ability. Regardless of our topic, we must recognize differentiated and contradictory social subjectivities in our cultural analyses, as 'a theory and practice of sisterhood cannot be grounded in shared positionings in a system of sexual difference' (1991: 147).

In other words, we bring into the research process our embodied realities, our differently politicized subject positions, and uneven access to power in the social systems we are operating in. Objectivity is an impossibility in research, and relative degrees of privilege and power will shape the meanings we make. This is intensified further when conducting research in international contexts or across axes of oppression, where the dynamics between the researcher and the researched may be further shaped by colonial histories of domination and control. Despite these challenges, Farhana Sultana (2007) urges us not to feel prevented from progressing with research despite what emerges from reflexive engagement with researcher positioning. Instead, looking at the work of those who have engaged in interpretivist research across different contexts and power dynamics can provide valuable guidance. For example, in her work on the sexual subjectivities of Afro-Surinamese women, Gloria Wekker (2006) discusses how she and her participants 'coproduced' the narrative detailed in her book. Her questions opened up the space for stories to be told and memories to be revisited. However, it is her participants that create what comes to be understood as the research. As she makes clear, she does not give these women 'voice', rather they grant her an audience for their life stories. Furthermore, as an Afro-Surinamese researcher herself, her engagement with these women enables a perspective allowing for the recognition of difference between people rather than a simplistic understanding of sameness based on shared nationality, language, and ethnicity. As this indicates, engaging in research, analysis, and writing *with* participants, rather than imposing the position of 'research subject' on them, is a good place to start in situated feminist media critique.

Texts on research methods offer competing techniques for assessing principles of rigour in interpretivist research. I highlight those outlined by Lincoln and Guba (1985) for how they complement the values of a feminist ethics of care and emphasize attributes in alignment with transparent and accountable research. As they note, collaborative or team-based research can be a useful way of encouraging both reflexivity and situatedness. By discussing the materials under review and the patterns identified from different positions, collaborating researchers can understand points of difference as well as assess the dependability of their conclusions. Sharing the findings with the participants of a study in cases where their words are part of materials examined, for instance in ethnographically informed research, can also test the rigour of an analysis. This allows the feminist media critic to check that the inferences drawn from interviews and observations resonate with those who have participated in the study, confirming their 'credibility' and 'plausibility' (Corbin and Strauss 2008). These practices aim to make the research process, including analysis, transparent, accountable, and more likely to reflect the perspectives and voices of those contributing the materials rather than the standpoint of the researcher.

In the remainder of this chapter we will consider a range of approaches undertaken in feminist media critique. The method selected will depend on the questions asked by the researcher, based on their engagement with the existing research on the topic as well as current affairs or emerging challenges that may motivate the study. In the following sections, foundational and contemporary examples of feminist media studies are showcased to demonstrate how a given method addresses questions asked about the phenomena under consideration. The examples provided do not, of course, capture the full range of feminist media critique, but they have been selected to demonstrate the multiplicity of research aims, approaches, techniques, concepts, and politics that may be explored as part of this interdisciplinary and intersectional field of inquiry.

Text-based feminist media critique

Feminist textual analysis

Scrutinizing how audio-visual texts frame and organize stories through their content and structure – including what they leave out – can reveal how we make meaning of our social world. For this reason, feminist media studies has had a long-standing investment in the method of textual analysis. Textual analysis consists of close readings of how media objects, from television to magazines to video games, represent the world. The ways gender and sexuality are typically portrayed make up an important part of this work, which we will investigate in greater detail in Chapter 3.

A foundational example of feminist textual analysis is Angela McRobbie's (1978) analysis of *Jackie*, a UK magazine aimed at teenage girls, first published in the mid-1960s. She examines the ideology of young femininity the magazine promotes, noting how its content naturalizes individualism and narrow interests in fashion, beauty, romance, and pop music, foreclosing other possibilities beyond the personal. By taking the media created for and consumed by young women and girls seriously, McRobbie's work makes a major contribution to the field of communication and cultural studies. Even the topic we select in feminist media studies can be a politicized decision, as some areas of focus are deemed marginal or 'low culture', while others are implicitly framed as more central, mainstream, and important. In McRobbie's study, it is the magazine itself rather than its readers, writers, or creators that constitutes the object of focus. She considers the meanings made within the magazine through an investigation of the text via **semiotics**.

Semiotics is the analysis of how meaning is made through signs and sign processes in communication, including the media. In the process of signification, we derive social meanings from the repeated combinations of particular images, symbols, and words – all of which are **signs**. Linguist Ferdinand de Saussure (1983) breaks the sign down into two components – the **signifier** and the **signified**. The signifier is the physical form of a sign, whereas the signified is the idea it represents. For instance, the word FIRE is a signifier, and the signified is the concept of hot flames. In relationship with each other, the signifier and signified make up a sign. When undertaking a semiotic analysis of the media, signs include words but also audio, interactive materials, and visuals, and exploration focuses on how they together make meaning.

In the case of *Jackie*, this includes the visuals and text of the publication, which represent not only literal and straightforward meanings (**denotation**) but also implicit and evoked meanings (**connotation**). As McRobbie notes, a semiotic analysis begins by identifying groups of codes structuring the message and then examining how 'these codes constitute the "rules" by which different meanings are produced' (1978: 11), whether in a film, a set of newspaper articles, or a social media campaign. Additionally, in relation to the broader cultural context in which the media circulates, semiotics can also provide the grounds for drawing conclusions about the way the text contributes to ideological notions, including in this case to gender and age norms. McRobbie analyses the text and codes of *Jackie* in conversation with industry and cultural norms, providing a contextual and holistic analysis demonstrating that the ideologies of young femininity in this magazine operate more broadly as well. Its emphasis on individualism and consumerism as key to an adolescent girl's development is reflected in the broader cultural environment, political ideology, and hegemonic gender norms. Interpretive analysis, even when focused on textual media, understands phenomena in its social context.

A more recent example of feminist semiotic analysis also demonstrates this. In a textual analysis of the representation of women in the UK-based men's magazines *FHM*, *Loaded*, *Zoo*, and *Nuts* over a two-month period, Mooney (2008) argues that the way women's bodies are posed, photographed and described normalizes the visual and textual repertoires of pornography, a move that is supported by the inclusion of 'real' women alongside professional models in the features and by the sale of these publications alongside other mainstream magazines. Furthermore, in their styling and layout there are clear parallels with the form of magazines aimed at women, including advice columns and a focus on banal consumerism and problem-solving. While the context and content of these lad magazines and *Jackie* are quite different – particularly in how they frame sexuality – both types of publication act as guides to everyday life in ways that are distinctly gendered and linked to normative heterosexuality. Overall, a close analysis of the signs, codes, and symbols of media texts and how they construct and represent the world provides a more detailed and nuanced understanding of the functioning of representation than simply asserting that the presence of images of particular people indicates fairness, equality, or justice.

Queer theory introduces further nuance to feminist textual analysis by challenging the tendency to overemphasize the denotative elements of texts and thereby affirm a reading of media representations as made for dominant groups of White, middle-class, and straight audiences. Queer readings of media texts for expressions of queerness are only alternative if we frame understandings of meaning 'within conventional heterocentrist paradigms' (Doty 1993: xiv). In the intersections between queer and feminist media critique the possibility of understanding seemingly straight stories in more critical and politicized ways becomes possible. However, as Doty notes, defining and fixing queerness can be a challenge. In his analysis of the sitcom *Laverne & Shirley*, which he reads as a lesbian show, 'the discussions of audience pleasure and character development that are connected to the textual analyses here gradually move away from the text as the source of queerness to find other sites of queerness in reception and within specific lesbian cultural coding and reading practices' (1993: xiv). Multi-method approaches to interpreting meaning-making in media, such as Doty's understanding of queerness as developing across its production, readings, uses, and reception within culture, are commonplace in the field. We will review approaches to the audience and industry below.

Feminist content analysis

In a study of 900 popular films released between 2007 and 2016, together involving more than 4,500 speaking roles, Smith et al. (2017) examined how many of these roles were acted by women, people of colour, people over the age of forty-five, LGBTQ+ people, and people with disabilities. The results revealed that heterosexual, White, able-bodied, and male characters were still over-represented in speaking roles in the popular films released in this decade. By looking at the intersections of identity longitudinally, these researchers provide a sense of the visibility and invisibility of certain kinds of characters, how representation has changed over time, and how proportionate or not the degree of representation is to the population of the US.

This example demonstrates that, in addition to engaging in qualitative analyses of media representation, feminist media critics may also adopt quantitative approaches which can provide important insights into more numbers-oriented questions. These may include, for instance, research on the number of women included in media texts, as above, but also on how many participate in media industries and communities. Content analysis is a quantitative approach that draws on a much larger sample of texts than does textual analysis, in order to understand how frequently types, figures, symbols, and other signs appear (or do not). Using this approach, the feminist media critic determines which ideas they want to examine across a given time period and an identified set of texts taken as a sample. Once these are determined, based on their research questions, the critic then develops codes for categories to understand where and how often a set type appears – for example, the number of positive or negative words used to describe an argument, figure, or location in a newspaper article. The codes need to be manageable and adequately simplified so that two coders can apply the same code in the same way.

Content analysis can be used to reveal absence as well as the ways that women are represented when they *do* appear in the media. This was the aim of Bathla's (2004) study of how English-language newspapers in India framed two female politicians in the run-up to the national elections in 1998. She conducted a quantitative analysis organized around four variables: type of story, placement of story, status of the subject, and status of the speaker. In tandem with a qualitative discourse analysis (discussed below), her study found that the candidates Sushma Swaraj and Jayalalitha Jayaram were associated with norms of 'good' and 'virtuous' femininity in the case of the former and 'bad' womanhood in the case of the latter. While Jayalalitha was linked to notions of corruption and disease, Sushma was associated with traditional customs and rituals through the pictures included in the coverage of her campaign. Bathla concludes that these ways of reporting favoured Sushma's conformity to dominant, patriarchal norms of feminine identity in India, while stigmatizing Jayalalitha's less conventional family life. As this example demonstrates, representation is therefore of interest beyond entertainment media – political communication as well as other forms of 'serious' media are shaped by relations of power, and content analysis can provide insight into how this operates across the media.

In sum, content analysis can reveal scales of presence and absence in identified texts, groups, and sites, as well as patterns of inclusion and exclusion. It is often complemented with interpretive methods including textual analysis and discourse analysis, which we review next.

Feminist discourse analysis

Language is as much a part of social practices and processes as bodies, communities, and institutions are. For this reason, the ways in which language functions and its relationship to power are of interest in feminist media studies and are examined using discourse analysis. Hall defines **discourses** as 'ways of referring to or constructing knowledge about a particular topic of practice: a cluster (or formation) of ideas, images and practices, which provide ways of talking about, forms of knowledge and conduct associated with a particular topic, social activity or institutional site in society' (1997: 4). Discourse can be analysed across a range of texts in the media as well as in the documents we produce in our research, such as interview transcripts. Discourse analysis examines language beyond individual sentences to investigate the meaning it makes within larger texts, considering its role in producing and reproducing social, cultural, and political ideologies, and how this is a dynamic, dialectical process between social actors, fields, and institutions. A subset of this approach – critical discourse analysis – focuses specifically on relations of power, considering how language contributes to ideas and belief systems that become common sense or hegemonic, and exploring 'the ways in which linguistic forms are used in various expressions and manipulations of power' (Wodak 2001: 11).

For discourse analysis, then, words have conceptual power and play a key role in processes of social transformation. Consider for instance the potency of terms such as 'freedom', 'terrorism', 'equality' and 'family' in political communications. These terms come to stand in for a range of ideological values and can be used to mobilize and justify an assortment of gendered practices and norms related to surveillance, border-policing, funding, and taxation. 'Feminism' as a concept also has discursive power conveying a range of meanings historically and across different groups, as we have seen. Discourse plays a key role in defining subject positions, from 'mother' to 'girl' to 'woman', as well as more pejorative notions such as 'slut', 'hag', and 'leftover woman'. Below we consider several examples of feminist media studies of the relationship between language, gendered power, and social systems to understand the range of approaches taken to discourse analysis and the insights that emerge from these examinations.

In his critical discourse analysis of television news in Morocco, Debbagh (2012) notes that growth in paid employment opportunities may indicate a shift in traditional media representations associating women with the domestic sphere. His analysis of news broadcasts on the two major national television channels focused on their reporting of women's issues over a four-month period. He examines this sample at two levels of analysis. At the microstructural level, he looks at the relationship between linguistic features of the news headlines, specific sentences used to describe women's issues, and the sources quoted. At the macrostructural level, he considers broader elements, such as the themes, story structures, and narratives of the news segments. The macrostructural discourse analysis also includes an exploration of how both levels taken together support a particular viewpoint about gender in Morocco. Debbagh identifies both empowering and disempowering features in the news discourse about women, arguing that as long as women's issues and activities align with governmental policy on development, the coverage is positive, but that this severely limits coverage of the diversity of women's concerns in the country. He concludes by making a key point about discourse analysis of the media, namely that there is no simple transmission of messages and their meaning from the media to audiences, but an active process of representation wherein 'the media choose one aspect of a communicative event (selection), frame it or highlight its defining characteristics from a particular point of view (structuring), and then establish it as the most easily recognizable image' (2012: 668). How the audience understands these frames is not the focus of discourse analysis, but it is important to remember that the production of certain meanings does not foreclose other possible readings.

While we often refer to media objects as 'texts', discourse analysis considers oral, visual, and interactive forms in addition to written language. This is important as so many topics of interest in feminist media studies extend beyond print media such as magazines and newspapers to include television, film, and social media, to name a few. For instance, in a study of posts on Facebook, blogs, and discussion boards, Sundén and Paasonen (2018) consider how Swedish and Finnish words historically used in a derogatory fashion to refer to women, racialized people, and LGBTQ+ individuals are reappropriated as powerful terms for self-definition in online feminist communities. They link this to the use of shame as a modality of online hate, and how shamelessness becomes a rallying cry in feminist resistance against xenophobic harassment and discrimination. As this study and others examining online incivility demonstrate, discourse is emotive and can gain power in the social field because of its relationship to feeling.

Indeed, discourses about inequality, oppression, and marginalization can be quite heightened in tone. Strong emotions and feelings accompany how gender is portrayed, how mediated content is consumed, and how media-making and feminist action are described. Feelings, both positive and negative, from love and joy to anger, guilt, and shame, are significant to feminist media critique, and **affect theory** provides a useful reference point for examining how these intensities manifest around gendered discourses, performances, and communities. Because so many gendered roles, such as those involving care, entail managing and performing emotions, the concept of affect has been an important element in feminist critique. This idea was introduced in the classic study of emotional labour by Hochschild (1983), which we will consider in more detail in Chapter 6. In the context of feminist discourse analysis, it is vital to note how affect can symbolically link communities together, particularly in the case of exclusionary discourses, as detailed in the work of Ahmed (2004) on racist White nationalism and Berlant (2011) on cuts to social welfare under neoliberal capitalism.

To conclude this introduction to text-based approaches to feminist media critique, it is important to note that what they share is an understanding of the complexity of the relationship between media messages and audience understandings. There are **dominant** but also **negotiated** and **oppositional** readings of mediated discourse, challenging the idea of passive audiences while also recognizing systems of power. As Hall (1980) notes in his discussion of the classic encoding/decoding model of communication, while dominant or 'preferred' readings will arise given the hegemonic social structures in which they are produced, these meanings are not predetermined as it is possible to decode discourses in other ways. Oppositional readings occur when the message is understood from another perspective, such as in a critical reading. A negotiated reading will occur when an audience member recognizes the broader common-sense worldview in which the message is encoded but also applies their own logic or rules to it. This is a blended and often contradictory reading that encompasses both dominant and oppositional readings. Feminist media critique aims to undertake oppositional readings of texts, on the basis that the status quo (re)produces unequal relations of power for women, people of colour, LGBTQ+ people, people with disabilities, and others facing oppression. This understanding of the polysemic nature of texts, and the significance of those who participate in the media in shaping meaning, informs the methods of media cultures critique we consider next.

Feminist media cultures critique

Audience studies

As Fairclough (2012) notes in his discussion of discourse and hegemony, what circulates as common sense in mediated semiotic sequences is not fixed but open and dynamically shaped by social interaction. Engaging in interpretivist research with and within media cultures can provide insight into how this occurs. To this end, early research in feminist media studies considered practices of media consumption to better understand relations of domination and resistance, media hegemony, and the everyday uses and practices of media audiences. The ground-breaking 'new audience research' of the 1980s included Ien Ang's (1985) study of soap-opera viewers and Janice Radway's (1984) analysis of romance-novel readers. These authors demonstrated that we cannot fully understand the significance of media messages without considering their audiences. Despite the originality of this research, it is possible to trace the focus on audience reception of texts intended for female consumers back to Herta Herzog's 1941 paper 'On Borrowed Experience', a study of female audiences of daytime radio series. Herzog asked women about their motivations for listening to soap operas, and challenged commonplace understandings of audiences as passive and susceptible to media effects. She thereby forged a tradition of research that sees audiences as active and understands their rationales for consuming media as premised on their **uses and gratifications**.

While the uses and gratifications approach tends to take an individualistic rather than socially situated perspective on people's uses of the media, we can understand it as paving the way for important feminist interventions into mass communications research, considering the activities and media texts of those previously left out of mainstream analysis. This includes women as audiences, but also popular culture and other disparaged media including romance novels and soap operas. In the process, feminist media studies has been foundational in establishing new areas of focus in media and communications, including television studies. Livingstone (1998) posits that feminist audience reception studies such as those of Ang and Radway challenge not only the conceptualization of audiences as either passive or active, but also the association of low culture texts with feminine audiences, the private sphere, and the passive reception of media messages, bringing new insight into a field that had previously foregrounded mass audiences and dominant culture. This work showcases negotiated and oppositional readings as well as the pleasures of media consumption. In the contemporary media environment, feminist audience studies shifts its focus beyond limited spaces of media consumption such as the home to consider how mobile, interactive, convergent, and ubiquitous media and their audiences interact in a context where media content is increasingly generated by audiences rather than media industries – dynamics we explore further in Chapters 5 and 6.

Overall, audience studies emphasizes the social processes of media use as well as audience members' own interpretations of their practices. This kind of analysis is important for complicating simplistic ideas about greater representation being necessarily positive for oppressed groups, as well as overdetermined critiques claiming that limited, stereotyped portrayals have a necessarily exclusionary or negative impact on viewers. For example, in his research on transgender audiences and their viewing of 'breakout texts' such as *Boys Don't Cry* and *TransAmerica*, Cavalcante (2017) moves beyond the celebration of these films for making transgender stories visible to consider their role in the everyday lives of the participants in his study. The transgender viewers he interviews articulate mixed feelings about these films – while they find the representations to be imperfect and at times problematic, they also feel it is important that these texts challenge the notion that films about transgender people appeal to insufficiently broad audiences to be financially viable. Furthermore, Cavalcante's participants express a range of perspectives on how the films play a role in their identity and sense of community. Such work from queer audience research offers feminist media studies insights into the relationship between heteronormative representations and oppositional queer readings (Doty 1993), including tactical engagements with media texts allowing for pleasure and desire (Muñoz 1999), and the affective power of the normalization of gay and lesbian characters for queer audiences (Griffin 2017).

In sum, feminist media critique that examines the interactions of audiences with media texts, universes, and genres can reveal a range of readings, meanings, and interpretations, which is particularly important when engaging with understudied or narrowly stereotyped texts and audiences. Feminist audience studies are typically designed using methods informed by the tenets of ethnographic research, discussed in the next section.

Feminist media ethnography

Given the centrality, pervasiveness, and persistence of media in our everyday lives and their key role in identity-making and community-formation, media ethnographies are an invaluable approach in the field. Ethnography refers to in-situ methods of studying media. Here, the researcher examines the contexts of media practices and cultures to map the relationships between social lives, media engagement, the processes underlying these relations, and the understandings and meanings consumers and producers of media generate from their practices. The aim is to produce a **thick description** of the observed culture through detailed documentation of the meanings described by people within the context (**emic** accounting) and those derived by the observer in as neutral terms as possible (**etic** accounting).

As a study of media cultures, ethnography typically entails deep immersion and long-term engagement with a community, entailing the methods of participant observation, interviews, and document analysis. The researcher focuses on the emotions, experiences, and actions of the participants, making sense of dynamic social processes in their context. As an active participant in the setting being studied, the feminist media critic must be especially reflexive about power dynamics and relations in ethnographic approaches. In addition to documenting the perspectives of participants with interviews (be they face-to-face, mediated by telephone or email, or in groups online or offline), the media ethnographer takes extensive fieldnotes and makes as many observations as possible about the context, including details about verbal and non-verbal communication, in order to better understand the lived experiences of the participants and their media use.

This approach is often adopted in feminist media critique when the research is focused on the experiences and locations of those under-represented in existing theory and critique. For example, Gray's (2009) ethnography of the new media practices of queer youth living in rural settings in the US addresses stereotypes about this group as well as their lack of access to institutional supports such as community services and health networks. Drawing on participant observation, interviews, and textual analysis of online discussions, Gray richly details their use of new media for accessing further peer groups and relevant support services, in addition to the ways digital technologies become modes of representing gender and sexuality for these young people, shaped by their race, class, and location. In taking an intersectional ethnographic approach, Gray's longitudinal study challenges a number of assumptions about LGBTQ+ youth, rural life, and uses of new media technologies.

Media cultures are not only representational and textual but also tactile, kinaesthetic, and affective. Sensory ethnography, a method developed by Pink (2015), addresses this by approaching media as objects, environments, and experiences that we perceive. In addition to this interest in examining the five senses, Alper (2018) argues, an inclusive sensory ethnographic study will consider the internal senses that allow us to understand where our body is in space – the vestibular (body movement) and the proprioceptive (body awareness) – as these will shape participation as well as exclusion in media practices. For instance, in her study of the use of media by children on the autism spectrum, this approach enables Alper to move beyond pathologizing and medicalized ways of understanding their practices, exploring instead each family's rituals and adaptations around media and how these enable them to accommodate the most pleasurable sensory experiences for their children. Her in-depth analysis thus demonstrates the potency of ethnographic work on media practices for challenging narrow understandings of audiences and their behaviours.

Media ethnographies of online media involve unique challenges as well as opportunities, including in how we enter into a community or culture for research purposes. Gajjala's (2004) 'cyberethnography' of the communities formed by South Asian women online examines the way virtual spaces allow these women to record their own narratives about their lives and experiences. Despite her status as a South Asian woman and active participant in these communities, Gajjala became an outsider when she revealed her interest in conducting research on one of the forums. As she details in her reflexive account of participant observation in the SAWnet discussion list (2002), the contributors to the list expressed concerns over their privacy in relation to the project and what risks it could pose to what they felt was a safe space. They ultimately refused to take part in the project, which we might see as a productive failure in so far as it challenges us to recognize how, in media cultures research, what is technically public or private, shareable or not, can be complicated by the norms of the community. Community values should therefore be discussed with potential participants rather than assumed. As will be discussed throughout this book, we cannot presume visibility and representation to be a universal desire of any group or community. As feminist media critics engaging in interpretivist research, our aim must be to engage communities and ascertain their preferences in this regard, in order to gain consent rather than making presumptions about their desire for us to 'speak for' or 'give voice to' them, or about our ability to do so.

Industry studies

Ethnographically informed methods in feminist media critique contribute grounded, contextually sensitive understandings of media uses, practices, and interpretations, complicating notions of media dominance and simple transmission models of media effects. This emphasis, however, should not suggest that media audiences have free reign to make any meaning at all in an open field of interpretation. As noted in the discussion of textual approaches, media are produced and disseminated in and through social relations characterized by an unequal power dynamic. An important element of this dynamic is how media-making is institutionally organized, and the material realities of who owns and controls the mode of production. The political economy of media and communication has demonstrated the ways that capitalist social relations and the concentrated ownership of media companies and platforms pivotally shapes how content is created, disseminated, and harnessed. As Cohen (2008) notes in her examination of Facebook, profit models in social media entail the commodification of user-generated activity and practices of surveillance that are initiated not only by the platform and third-party sites but also by users and communities. Turning the seemingly non-monetary activities of self-expression and social interaction into actions understood primarily in terms of their economic value means that what we might see as meaningful practices for users become a form of unpaid labour generating massive profits for the company hosting them. We will discuss in Chapter 6 how this is a gendered practice with uneven consequences for women in different positions, but here note that analysis of media industries across time demonstrates the complex interplay of power and how too heavy a focus on audience or user agency can risk overlooking the structural control exercised by a narrow group of individuals and corporations. Feminist media critique needs to consider these relations when researching media work, production, and industries.

A classic example of industry analysis is Julie D'Acci's (1994) work on the television series *Cagney & Lacey*, which aired in the 1980s and was ground-breaking in its representation of two women working in policing as the main characters. D'Acci's audience research contributes to our understanding of the meaning-making generated in response to these quite novel representations of gender in society, and she complements this work with industry analysis, including an examination of dynamics on the set, within production meetings, and in production files. Through this consideration of the culture and institutions involved in the show's production, D'Acci captures the tensions between the audience, the television industry, the team producing the series, as well as the press coverage, and their differing understandings of what representing women entails, in terms of both the characters and the viewers imagined for the series. Through this conversation between audience and industry studies, D'Acci illuminates not only the meaning-making of audiences but how industries shape gendered representations in conservative, delimited ways, demarcating how progressive these portrayals can ultimately be.

Research on media texts and cultures provides insight into how exclusions and inclusions based on gender and its intersections operate. In the next section we consider how the media can become an avenue for feminist action aiming to redress inequalities.

Feminist media action

Feminist archival work

Action-based approaches vary and can encompass a number of the research methods outlined above. What they share is that they derive directions for action from challenges and problems identified in previous exploratory research. As such, feminist media action is based on the conclusions and insights drawn from sustained, rigorous analysis rather than presupposed ideas or hypotheses about what a problem and its solutions may be. In this way, feminist media action is a form of what is called **normative research** aimed at making improvements, as it is intended not only to gather information and describe social phenomena but also to indicate directions for positive change. It thus involves an inherently evaluative perspective. This aligns well with a feminist politics, which aims to identify and transform inequalities.

Archiving as feminist media critique tackles inequalities related to the processes of collecting, documenting, and curating media materials in the creation of a record, and through this challenges what is considered history. The contents of an archive will include a range of materials, from printed matter such as magazines, newspapers, letters, and photographs to digital records such as tweets, online videos, memes, and websites. Archives have been used to preserve evidence of harassment, exclusion, heterosexism, transphobia, racism, and misogyny, as well as activities of resistance and organizing, creating a record of the work of activism often undocumented in history. As Rawson says of the online archives of LGBTQ communities, 'to argue that "everyone is a part of history" is an act of worldmaking and empowerment that attempts to deconstruct barriers separating the stories that are worthy of the historical record from those that are not' (2014: 51).

Online tools can provide the means for activists to undertake a do-it-yourself form of archiving, for instance using Storify, a tool enabling users to collect, organize, and save items such as tweets and forum posts for their preservation. Such resources can then act as pedagogical and research materials, allowing students, teachers, and scholars to learn from past events and debates that would have otherwise been lost or buried under more recent activity. For instance, Rentschler (2017) examines Storify archives related to intersectional feminist approaches to street harassment and justice, and finds that activists use this digital platform to provide the community with further reading and other resources on sexual violence and White supremacy. Feminist archiving can therefore intervene in dominant modes of documenting history and knowledge production as well as creating the grounds for community development and public education. The potential for digital media to support these practices is significant too in affording access to activist archivists. As Eichorn notes, 'for a younger generation of feminists, the archive is not necessarily either a destination or an impenetrable barrier to be breached, but rather a site and practice integral to knowledge making, cultural production, and activism' (2013: 3).

However, stories, voices, and materials do not simply wait to be archived, and archiving is not a neutral, value-free process (Dever 2017). What is included in an archive is determined in and through existing power structures, not least of which are the legacies of colonial and racist history and politics (Stoler 2009). Archiving the stories of marginalized women such as Black feminists is not simply a matter of posterity but 'a crucial strategy of survival: the transformation of information and communication into access, power, community, and visionary practice' (Gumbs 2011: 20).

As with all research practices, what is included in an archive, how it is framed, and what is left out need to be reflexively addressed. Feminist issues related to labour, visibility, reflexivity, sustainability, and access are raised by the practice of archiving, and by the digital technologies creating new opportunities for researchers and others to discover and peruse archived materials: *Who is responsible for the upkeep of the archive, and how is this work recognized, rewarded, and supported? How is access to the archive determined? Who determines what is included in the archive, manages permissions related to materials, and organizes the materials within it? How will these decisions shape what the archive looks like?*

Feminist media histories

As archiving undertaken as a mode of feminist media action reveals, how we document and narrate history is a political question. Another approach focused on intervening in the ways women are erased or marginalized in history is **media archaeology**, which looks beyond the chronological and success-driven narratives of media history, focused heavily on technological progress, to excavate failures and otherwise forgotten materials, institutions, communities, individuals, and events. For example, Nooney (2013) notes that commonplace modes of recounting the history of video games focus on male developers, hackers, and coders. She argues that we need to review this history not simply to add in accounts of women in the field, but to consider how 'our sense that videogame history as "all about the boys" is the consequence of a certain mode of historical writing, preservation, memory, and temporally specific affective attachments, all of which produce the way we tell the history of videogames' (n.p.). Our practices of telling stories in media histories play an important role in the process of **marginalization**, wherein certain individuals, communities, and actions are deemed to be less important and therefore pushed to the periphery, erased, and/or forgotten. Feminist media archaeology is valuable for considering the cultural and political motives for overlooking some groups. For instance, in Nooney's study, Roberta Williams, the most cited woman in game design history, disappears from that history as it shifts from valuing the storytelling she excels in to an emphasis on programming abilities and institutional connections. This indicates the evolving relationship between technological aptitude and gamer identity and its shaping role in how meaning is ascribed to historical events, in this case early games and their creators.

Another approach that can be useful for intervening in media histories is **oral history**. Oral histories entail interviewing participants, typically over a long period of time and across multiple sessions, about their memories and past experiences related to a particular topic. Feminist oral histories can be valuable for revealing the activities, perspectives, and challenges of groups of people overlooked in dominant historical accounts, particularly socially disadvantaged communities. For example, in her analysis of labour relations and policy in a Tibetan carpet factory, Zhang (2007) reveals the significant contributions of women weavers. She details how, as this kind of labour was legitimized in shifting relations between Tibet and China, women came to be left out of celebrations of the cultural heritage represented by Tibetan carpets. As this demonstrates, both ethnic and gender politics inform cultural policy, national heritage, and historical accounting. Oral histories can provide a thick description of experiences in the words of the people who lived them. While there is often no way of validating these stories, what is valuable in the analysis is how participants frame and interpret the histories they share (Wekker 2006).

Wreyford and Cobb (2017) note, however, that ethnographically informed methods such as interviewing have shortcomings in addressing historic marginalization because they typically only include those who have experienced some success in a given media industry. They argue for the use of data-driven historical methods to get a sense of the scale of exclusion and to make visible those who were not included. In their study of women in the UK film industry, they draw on a range of existing statistical and demographic data on the workforce as a complement to their interviews with women in the industry to demonstrate that gendered and racialized inequalities related to creative production have not shifted significantly in the last two decades.

In sum, as these different approaches to feminist media action via historical interventions should indicate, practices of collection, narrative sharing, and curation require the feminist media critic to engage with the principles of ethics and rigour detailed at the start of this chapter. There is no neutral way to create histories, even if they are focused on marginalized groups, and it is vitally important to reflect on the power structures influencing decision-making in feminist media action.

Feminist media action research

As noted above, feminist critique identifies not only challenges, problems, and issues but also possibilities for transformation through activism. To this end, feminist media critique draws on research approaches that merge inquiry with action in the form of activism-research. Here the focus is on creating change through the media, typically in collaboration with community members, key stakeholders, and other participants directly involved in the phenomenon or setting under examination. One example of such a method is **feminist participatory action research (F-PAR)**. Action research is practised in many disciplines and fields and refers to research designed to introduce interventions within social phenomena and examine the outcomes these produce. The 'participatory' element refers to the embedding of the researcher in the context they are researching, participating in the action alongside the stakeholders rather than observing it from outside. As this should indicate, attention to power dynamics between and within partners is essential, as the researcher will have an impact on the action and the context examined. Feminist participatory action research draws on the insights of feminist theory to inform the action, typically the recognition of how intersecting axes of oppression shape the social phenomena under consideration. F-PAR entails undertaking the entirety of the research process in consultation with the community, group, or organization under study, from identifying the issue or problem to be addressed, designing the research and action strategy, engaging in the action, assessing and evaluating the outcomes of the action and its impact on the problem, and developing new insight from these outcomes. This process is often repeated based on the insights derived from the action, as this can indicate the modifications needed and additional strategies for action. In this approach, researchers typically engage in ethnographic methods such as interviewing and participant observation, as well as textual approaches such as content and discourse analysis of documents including policy and news reports.

The Canadian-based Media Action Research Group is an example of a collaboration between feminist media scholars and activists undertaking work in this vein. This initiative draws on an intersectional and anti-authoritarian approach to activism-research, examining the use of grassroots media in social activism and movements. In their work, the authors critically reflect on their political stances and how they align with the commitments of the media activists they engage with, combatting state oppression, capitalism, racism, sexism, heteronormativity, cis-sexism, colonialism, and ableism (Jeppesen et al. 2017: 1058). The issues they identify are based on conversations with activists. Working from this, they deploy action-based approaches aiming to engage in advocacy, shape policy, and document and analyse the work of activists. As they indicate, the act of engaging in co-research with activist communities on their media practices plays an important role in ensuring that the knowledge produced is collectively and collaboratively developed, decentring academic institutions as the arbiters of research and knowledge.

Another example of F-PAR in practice is my own work with Stephanie Fisher. Drawing on the insight from existing theory that games production is a key site of inequality, we worked with women interested in making games and challenging exclusions to engage in action for change. After participating in a programme aimed at getting more women into games production, we collaborated with the participants to develop a lasting community group imagined, founded, and organized by women with an explicitly feminist agenda (Fisher and Harvey 2013). The women who participated in this longitudinal project on women-led games communities were not subjects but collaborators in action and knowledge creation. In turn, we engaged in practices of activism, including organizing, fund-raising, and resource development, to support the actions of these communities. As these projects indicate, F-PAR aims to intervene in exclusions in society as well as in research practices, challenging the power dynamics implicit in many methods of knowledge creation. This approach entails intensive reflection on the differences in experience, position, and privilege between researchers and communities, in order to ensure that the impact made in action research is not exploitative, harmful, or destructive in relation to what are often oppressed populations.

Popular feminist media critique

As the insights of F-PAR demonstrate, feminist media critique is not just the prerogative of academic researchers and authors. An abundance of popular feminist media critique is available, and valuable for considering how such critique can be created and shared in creative and playful ways. These materials can also be the topic of research, for instance in understanding what visions of feminism they espouse, examining their reception by audiences and critics, and investigating the labour practices entailed in their production and maintenance. They are also valuable for public education because they are often more accessible to broader audiences than academic materials. For example, Feminist Frequency is an online resource created by Anita Sarkeesian which includes a broad range of videos introducing terms and resources for feminist media critique through analyses of LEGO, video games, films, popular culture, and the internet. Another venue is Bitch Media, co-founded by Andi Zeisler, which produces print and online resources including a magazine, podcasts, and web articles showcasing feminist readings of the media and culture. Through such channels, Sarkeesian, Zeisler, and many others aim to introduce young and new audiences to feminist activism and the power of the media in defining and questioning gender and sexuality.

Indeed, a range of feminist magazines both past and present have generated popular critique and challenged the norms of publications typically created for young and female audiences, including *Spare Rib*, *The Vagenda*, *Hysteria*, *Boshemia*, *Shameless*, *Rookie*, and publications from the Grrl Zine Fair. Furthermore, there is a plethora of feminist media critique shared on Twitter, Facebook, and across other mediated and online platforms from a range of perspectives, playing an important role in bringing feminism to a wider audience and providing spaces for the multiplicity of voices therein.

To conclude, this chapter has delineated the rich, polyvocal field of work associated with feminist media critique based on its multi-method approaches and commitment to justice, equality, and inclusion. By examining both its history and contemporary examples, the chapter has given a clear sense of the intersectional and interdisciplinary interests of the field, its global purview, and its politicized ethos towards the act of knowledge production. In outlining a feminist ethics of care and the criteria of iteration, reflexivity, and situatedness for ethical and rigorous research, it also provides a clear direction for those aiming to engage in feminist media critique.

While feminist media critique is practised in a range of contexts, from academic institutions to archives to community groups and social media, it must as with all practices of knowledge-building be undertaken with care and critical thought. For instance, as Stacey notes, ethnography can risk the manipulation and exploitation of participants, as 'fieldwork represents an intrusion and intervention into a system of relationships that the researcher is far freer than the researched to leave. The inequality and the potential treacherousness of this relationship is inescapable' (1988: 23). This observation can be broadened to include the range of approaches and techniques undertaken in the field, and to remind us that, regardless of our good intentions, the process of producing knowledge through feminist media critique is deeply political, involving power and privilege. In our research we make some forms of knowing visible, while potentially obscuring others. In the next chapter, we explore visibility in more detail by considering the ways in which gender and its intersections come to be seen through representational regimes in the media. We remain attuned to care by also examining how celebrations of progressive or 'good' representations can overlook the dangers of visibility in the changing media landscape.

3   Representing Gender

In 1985, the popular comic strip *Dykes to Watch Out For*, created by the cartoonist Alison Bechdel, ran a piece called 'The Rule'. In the strip, two women discuss going to the cinema, and one of them explains her rule that she will only go see a film if it meets three criteria:

1) The film must have at least two women in it.
2) The two women must speak to each other.
3) What they speak to each other about must be related to something other than a man.

This rule, attributed in the script to a friend of the cartoonist named Liz Wallace, has come to be known as the 'Bechdel Test' – a simple but illuminating method for assessing the limited gendered representations available in film as well as other media (Resmer 2005). This is intensified when we include the refinements that have been added to the rule over the years – that the two female characters must have names and that their conversation should not focus on children. As the comic strip's conclusion indicates, with the characters ultimately deciding to go home and eat popcorn rather than see a film, the rule articulates basic criteria that many mediated stories do not meet. The ongoing use of the Bechdel Test as a tool to indicate the dearth of varied roles for women demonstrates that there remains much to critique when it comes to gendered representations in the media.

The fact that the Bechdel Test originated in a comic strip focused on lesbian characters suggests that the rule is attuned to the heteronormativity of gendered representations, such as the normalization of women's dialogue hinging on relationships with male characters and/or children. Since the 1980s, further 'tests' derived from Bechdel's original have been developed to examine representations of racialized characters. For instance, the 'DuVernay Test', named after the African American director Ava DuVernay and conceptualized by the film critic Manohla Dargis, gives a pass to films where 'African Americans and other minorities have fully realised lives rather than serve as scenery in white stories' (Dargis 2016).

Unlike those posed in the Bechdel Test, the question raised by the DuVernay Test is not one that can be easily addressed with a yes or no answer, and instead spurs conversation about how people of colour are represented, the depth of the stories told about them, and their relation in the text to White characters. It complements other variants of the test, such as the 'Shukla Test', devised by Nikesh Shukla (2013), which asks whether two people of colour speak to each other for five minutes or more about a topic other than race. Commenting on the White-washing of Oscar nominees, Latif and Latif (2016) suggest that a film would still pass the Shukla Test if it included two people of colour who only spoke to each other about a White character. They therefore propose to ask five questions: 'Are there two named characters of colour? Do they have dialogue? Are they not romantically involved with one another? Do they have any dialogue that isn't comforting or supporting a white character? Is one of them definitely not magic?'

The last question refers to a vitally important dimension of representation, which is that even when women, queer people, and people of colour appear in the media, they tend to be framed and portrayed in limited, repetitive ways, in stereotypical or otherwise oversimplified types of characterizations. This is also the case with the portrayal of people with disabilities, poor people, LGBTQ+ people, older people, refugees and people from the Global South. In the case of Black characters, in Latif and Latif's example, this includes the 'magical negro' stereotype as exemplified in the role played by Whoopi Goldberg in *Ghost* – that of a character with access to a mystical or spiritual world, used exclusively in support of the goals and growth of a White character. Representation is therefore not simply about presence and visibility, but also concerns the range (or lack thereof) of stories, dialogue, and lives that marginalized and oppressed groups are assigned in the media. Media portrayals reflect social norms and play a key role in circulating and perpetuating values about identities, communities, and cultures, which is why representation is an enduring topic of interest in feminist media studies.

This chapter contributes to this ongoing work by providing an intersectional perspective on the field's key concepts. Here we examine core terms and theories in order to better understand the representation of intersectional gendered identities in the media. Building on the textual approaches discussed in Chapter 2, we delve into quantitative and qualitative research on the frequency and types of male and female characters appearing in both fiction and non-fiction media. After exploring the common tropes, stereotypes, myths, and archetypes that typically frame gendered figures, we turn to the key concepts essential for an intersectional analysis of media representation.

By demonstrating the connection between representation and systems of power, this chapter delineates how media portrayals support and perpetuate inequalities in social life. As we will see, despite claims made about progress and greater inclusion in media culture, the constraints on how women's varied stories are told continue to be stringent. In addition to investigating intersectional gendered representations, the chapter analyses the active production of gendered identity on digital platforms to demonstrate how delimited representations are also created and reproduced by media users. These considerations coalesce around an emerging question in the field – the potential downside of visibility – a concern that is only intensified by normalized harassment and abuse in new media and digital culture. In order to understand the significance of questioning visibility, we will first consider quantitative research on representation in the media highlighting how rarely we see diverse women and girls in contemporary texts.

Where are the women and girls in the media?

It might seem that representational practices have shifted recently, with more visible roles for women in blockbuster films, big-budget television series, and triple-A video games, as well as a plethora of opportunities for women to represent themselves in self-produced media on YouTube, Youku, Tumblr, blogs, online fora, and other social media sites. Indeed, 2016 seemed like a year promising women screen-time on an unprecedented level, with actress Felicity Jones the first-billed actor on *Rogue One: A Star Wars Movie*, her face dominating ads for the blockbuster action film. Leading female characters were also promoted in the action film *Suicide Squad* and the animated movies *Dory* and *Zootopia*. Motivated by this apparent visibility of women, Thomas (2017) examines women's speaking roles in the top films of 2016. Despite the ostensible centrality of female characters, in her sample she finds that female characters speak only 27 per cent of the words in the films under review. Further analysis reveals that the majority of this small percentage of words are spoken by a single character rather than a range of women in each film. As this indicates, despite what appear to be more prominent roles for women in blockbuster films and other media, there are still inequities in terms of speaking parts and the inclusion of multiple non-male characters in these films (as well as a preponderance of animated rather than live-action female characters).

Including a singular woman (or otherwise portraying under-represented groups through a disproportionately small number of characters) is called **tokenism**, a gesture towards inclusion that is largely symbolic. While signalling an acknowledgement of critiques of inequality, this is often a tactic that results in the only Muslim, lesbian, or otherwise marginalized person in a story acting as a representative of an entire group or being set up as a foil to the 'normal' straight, White, male characters. It also means that people with intersectional identities, such as queer women of colour, appear in the media very infrequently. For instance, in the long-running Canadian-American television series *The L Word*, the lesbian characters featured are primarily White, able-bodied, middle-class, and heteronormatively attractive in alignment with the normalized standards of feminine beauty discussed below.

Thomas references several other studies over the last forty years examining speaking roles in film, all of which indicate a similar lack of diversity and equality in gender portrayal in films. Her meta-analysis of this research reveals that women had less than 35 per cent of speaking roles across all the films cited in these studies. The Annenberg Inclusion Initiative, Smith's research referenced in Chapter 2, and other quantitative analyses of the media further demonstrate the severe lack of diversity of characters played by women as well as people of colour, LGBTQ+ individuals, and people with disabilities. Film is of course not the only inequitable media form in terms of representation. For instance, the mission statement of the Geena Davis Institute on Gender in Media explains that its work on inclusion and representation is motivated by the fact that across children's media, girls and women are represented three times less often than boys and men (see https://seejane.org/about-us).

In video games, furthermore, female characters – as well as people of colour, older people, and children – appear with much less frequency than White male characters (Williams et al. 2009). Their portrayals also tend to be very narrow, with sexualized, often unplayable female characters and Black characters limited to the roles of criminals or athletes (Burgess et al. 2011). Research looking at the 571 games with playable female characters released between 1983 and 2014 finds that while the sexualization of these characters has decreased somewhat since 2006, there has been no increase in the numbers of female characters playing central roles in games. Sexualized secondary female characters also remain pervasive, particularly in fighting games (Lynch et al. 2016).

Research on television also indicates only very small increases in the number of women appearing in the media. The Center for the Study of Women in Television and Film produces annual reports on gendered representation in fictional television programming. The 2017 report (Lauzen 2017) notes an improvement in racial diversity, but still only 19 per cent of all speaking roles for women are played by Black characters, 6 per cent by Asian characters, and 5 per cent by Latina characters. Despite these relative improvements, the report finds that stereotyping of female characters remains a major issue. This is supported by Daalmans et al. (2017), who find that televisual content has increasingly become differentiated and directed towards gender-demarcated audiences. In their analysis of female- and male-branded Dutch TV channels they find heavily stereotyped roles for men and women in broadcasts intended for male audiences. For instance, while in both types of channels women are portrayed with a focus on their role as mothers, men are rarely represented as fathers, which we can understand as an example of how male characters are also impoverished in stereotypical representational regimes. Within non-fictional television texts these gaps in representation are also significant. The 2014 Latino Media Gap report notes that Latinos constitute 0 per cent of news anchors in top news programmes, and stories about them make up less than 1 per cent of news coverage, focusing primarily on criminal activities when they do appear (Negrón-Muntaner et al. 2014).

According to research by the Geena Davis Institute on Gender in Media and J. Walter Thompson (2017), women make up about a third of characters in advertising, with only a minimal improvement between 2006 (33.9 per cent) and 2016 (36.9 per cent). Where women appear, they tend to have four times less screen time and four times fewer opportunities to speak than men, and they are unlikely to be the only character in a commercial. Analysis of the spoken content in these ads indicates that dialogue uttered by men more frequently includes words associated with power and achievement. It is for this reason that voice and visibility must both be scrutinized in feminist media critique.

Overall, women are under-represented and portrayed in delimited roles across the media landscape, a trend that has not improved significantly over time. Women of colour, queer women, older women, women with disabilities, and women facing other forms of oppression are even less likely to appear in the media, and as the examples throughout this chapter reveal, representations of intersectional identities are restrictive and often subordinated to straight, White, able-bodied male characters. Explanations for the limited representation of women and girls across the media include the fact that the majority of industries producing mediated content are themselves male-dominated, with few directing, game programming, and animation roles filled by women or people of colour. This is important because films with female directors or writers are more likely to include female characters and experiences (Smith et al. 2014). A positive interpretation of this would be that diverse makers are more likely to tell different stories, including experiences that are more closely aligned with their own. On the other hand, it might suggest that women are steered into creating media targeted at female audiences, limiting their ability to choose what they produce, which Smith et al. suggest is supported by the preponderance of female-directed films in the genres of romance, comedy, and drama. We will revisit these ideas in greater depth in the discussion of gendered media work in Chapter 6.

Another rationale for low representation derives from assumptions made about both female characters and the broader audiences for these texts. Stereotypical understandings about audiences and what they consume prevail across the media industries and their marketing, including the idea that boys and men will not go to see films prominently featuring girls and women. While these presumptions are frequently belied by revenues – such as family films with female leads generating 7.3 per cent more profit than films with male leads, and films with people of colour as leading characters generating 15.4 per cent more revenue than those with White leads (Geena Davis Institute on Gender in Media 2016) – they continue to be invoked in explanations of representational inequalities, demonstrating the need for further audience research on this issue.

These quantitative analyses of the media in various national contexts and industries demonstrate the persistence of representational inequities and how the relatively few roles afforded to women are heavily restricted in terms of genre, relationships, and what kinds of women are portrayed. In what follows, we will consider the significance and qualitative nature of these limited representations. Drawing on feminist media studies and complementary scholarship from related fields including critical race theory, queer theory, and masculinity studies, the next section introduces long-standing and emerging questions and concepts related to intersectional gendered representation.

Representation matters

In this section we will look at how, as a site of the production and circulation of images, messages, frames, and narratives, the media reflect and reinforce key ideas about identity and the traits associated with groups of individuals. Through this, I will highlight the ongoing relevance and significance of these representational norms for gendered subjects.

According to the cultural theorist Stuart Hall (1995), the construction of race in the media is related to broader ideological struggles linked to identity. We can extend this argument to the construction of gender, class, and other forms of oppression. The ways subjects and groups are represented in the media serve to articulate hegemonic norms associated with them, presenting these norms as common sense and natural, and circulating them widely. The repetition of specific ideas about subjects means that they become self-evident and natural, easily recognized by audiences. For this reason, some explanations and stories become dominant sets of ideas, as in the example of images that portray feminists as angry, man-hating killjoys. More broadly, the media reinforce and perpetuate ideas of difference and problems associated with racialized groups in a process called **Othering**, which we will review in more depth below and in Chapter 4. In brief, this is the process of excluding those seen as outside a dominant social group, an action that the media supports by subordinating communities in their portrayal and characterization. While in some cases this is explicit and easy to identify as sexist, racist, homophobic, or otherwise discriminatory, in most instances, because of hegemonic norms related to these groups and conventional narrative devices, these portrayals seem unproblematic or common sense.

For instance, it is common in the media to encounter familiar **tropes**, which are devices that help viewers, readers, listeners, and players to identify with characters. These are culturally specific and therefore do not have a resonance on a global level, though as we will see some gendered tropes are quite dominant. For instance, a familiar trope in Western media is that of the Nerd, a typically heterosexual White male character supporting stereotypical ideas about hegemonic masculinity in his portrayal as lacking and insufficient. By focusing on the Nerd's deficiencies in social skills, athletic abilities, and sexual desirability, this trope bolsters the notion that appropriate masculinity is physically and socially aggressive (Quail 2011). You can likely imagine examples of this character easily. This is the purpose of tropes – they help media audiences quickly grasp the narrative role of characters and their relations with others. From a feminist media studies perspective, it is important to consider the enduring power of gendered tropes and how those related to women are primarily focused on sexual availability, care giving, and other relationships with men or children. Equally, the media contribute to the reification of delimited ideas of a singular correct masculinity, contributing to a gender order that normalizes violence, emotional detachment, and heterosexual desire for men and boys. Together these tropes contribute to ideas of irresolvable differences fixed in the body and a hierarchy of masculinity and femininity that subordinates and marginalizes attributes associated with women, care for the self and others (Connell 2005).

A historical basis informs these representational norms, as tropes can be linked to **archetypes**. These are broader common characters, traceable across historical and geographical contexts in a wide range of narratives, including the Hero, the Villain, and the Princess. In his study of Russian folktales, Propp (1968) identifies these and four other character types as predominating across the range of stories he analyses. For those interested in how we tell stories, the presence of such a limited range of character functions indicates the power of these archetypes in expressing common themes and subjects. Of significance for feminist media scholars is how these seemingly universal types are gendered. The Princess, for instance, serves as the prize motivating the quest of the Hero and signalling his ultimate success when he can marry her. We can derive two key observations from Propp's well-known archetypes: 1) the way we tell stories is deeply shaped by heteronormative patriarchal norms wherein men are primary actors and women are objects to be won, and 2) these archetypes, despite minor variations in how they are executed, continue to fundamentally shape gendered portrayals in the media to this day.

Another key term often used to discuss representation in the media is that of **stereotyping**. A stereotype, unlike tropes and archetypes, is not about narrative structures but is a broadly understood, socially constructed, oversimplified image or idea about certain 'types' of people. Stereotypes exist beyond the media but circulate therein in a manner that is not only easy to recognize but also further perpetuates narrow ideas about cultures, communities, groups, and identities. When typically negative stereotypes are inverted to shift portrayals in a more positive way they become **countertypes**, which themselves may develop into stereotypes should they circulate frequently, as we will see later in the chapter when we consider the figure of the **Strong Female Character**.

Taken together, we can understand this stereotyping and the overall lack of women's presence in the media as, in Tuchman's (1978) terms, '**the symbolic annihilation of women**'. By linking women primarily to domestic activities, the family, and private matters, rather than to positions of power and authority, the media **socialize** a view of women as dependent, inferior, and subordinate. We can see this in the predominance of roles for women as housewives, mothers, and romantic partners. It is also apparent in how working women or women in positions of power are consistently vilified or deemed to be unhappy, unfulfilled, or otherwise lacking because they have spurned traditional femininity.

Rather than being understood as either accurate or false reflections of the realities of groups or identities, representational norms should be understood as indicators of the perspectives of dominant ideologies. As with all hegemonic values, these norms are not fixed and can be challenged as well as reinforced in media representations. As Hall notes, representation cannot be understood simply as an expression of simple prejudice encoded into media by its creators, or as a channel of expression for an overtly sexist, racist, and otherwise discriminatory 'ruling class'. Instead, to understand how media representations contribute to ideological norms, we need to undertake a nuanced analysis of the complexity of these portrayals in their contexts of production. To explore this, Hall notes the distinction between **overt** racism, where explicitly racist perspectives and arguments are given favourable coverage in the media, and **inferential** racism:

> those apparently naturalised representations of events and situations relating to race, whether 'factual' or 'fictional', which have racist premises and propositions inscribed in them as a set of *unquestioned assumptions*. These enable racist statements to be formulated without ever bringing into awareness the racist predicates on which the statements are grounded. (1995: 20)

Rather than talking about stereotypes in this analysis, Hall refers to the 'grammar of race', a perspective that we can adapt to understand how unequal power relations are perpetuated by the circulation of limited gender portrayals, through archetypes, tropes, and stereotypes as well as other modes across the media – a potential 'grammar of gender'. Hall introduces three racialized figures: the slave (exemplified by the simple devotion of Mammy to the O'Hara family in *Gone With The Wind*), the native (an image of a primitive, savage, barbaric people posing a possible threat to the social order, illustrated by the horde-like Na'vi tribe in *Avatar*), and the clown/entertainer (an unserious figure portrayed as more physical and emotional than the rational, intelligent White character to which they are contrasted). Hall posits that these figures are presented for White eyes, and in their ambivalence (as they are linked to both positive and negative traits) they are used to reflect racist ideas about White, Western civilization and its opposite, racialized primitiveness. Through this, they contribute to the Othering of racialized people.

These three figures continue to circulate in the media, including in news media stories about Indigenous protest and conflict in Africa, North and South America, and Asia. They are apparent as well in entertainment media, in the representation of villains, dangerous settings, and sexually available but dangerous slave girls. In some texts these are overtly negative, and in others they are set up as fantasies for the White viewer, enabling the adoption of the symbols, activities, and other cultural features of oppressed groups by members of groups that have dominated them. Johnson (2015) highlights the importance of examining context and power dynamics when discussing this kind of superficial 'borrowing' – termed **cultural appropriation** – as it is a practice that supports rather than challenges stereotypes. One example is that of the docile, 'exotic' Asian woman, illustrated by White American pop star Katy Perry performing as a geisha at the

American Music Awards in 2013. Johnson notes that while the singer could remove her costume and enjoy the profits from her performance, 'Asian women ... have to deal with the racist and sexist social norms that Perry helped perpetuate, which is what happens when the only mainstream image of your sexuality is a negative stereotype reinforced constantly by cultural appropriation' (2015: n.p.). This practice therefore perpetuates racialized stereotypes – including those of the magical negro, the thug, the athlete, the evil wealthy Arab, the terrorist, the awkward Asian, and the sidekick – and because of the imbalance of power implicit in historical and contemporary relations of domination it cannot be seen as an equal exchange or harmless borrowing. In conjunction with the commonplace framing of non-White people in association with crime, either as perpetrators or police detectives (Noriega 1999), all of these representational norms reveal the centrality of the White male character as the primary positive figure in the media, and show how audiences are assumed to consume the media from the standpoint of the White gaze.

When we consider the intersectionality of limited gender and racial roles, we find that the positions available to women of colour are intensively restrictive. They are presented as caretakers to White families, welfare queens, confidantes listening to the problems of White protagonists, and as exoticized sexual objects to be used and discarded by White and Black characters alike, in texts ranging from music videos to James Bond films. As Smith-Shomade (2002) notes, these mediated roles consistently frame Black women as lacking subjectivity and agency, and Boom (2015) argues that such limited portrayals are indicative of the misogynoir prevalent in the media. She examines four predominant tropes, including the Sassy Black Woman, which demarcates humour as women's only personality trait, a stereotype Boom says 'dehumanizes us by presenting us as cardboard cut-outs with no depth of feeling or emotion' (2015: n.p.). There is also the Hypersexual Jezebel, perpetuating the idea of the persistent sexual availability of Black women that is a legacy of widespread rape in slavery; and the Angry Black Woman, focusing on disproportionate or unjustified rage and aggression as a character trait rather than a reasonable response to circumstances created by institutionalized inequality. The last trope, the Strong Black Woman, again focuses on a single facet of personality, and while it may seem positive, it again obscures the wide spectrum of emotions Black women experience and the origins of what might be a survival strategy in conditions of White supremacy.

As many of these ideas demonstrate, the media tend to put forth more inferentially sexist gendered portrayals rather than overtly hateful or discriminatory representations. However, such implicit subordination can be seen as widespread and insidious in how it is taken for granted as natural and common sense, demonstrating how normalized it is to trivialize, sexualize, and otherwise denigrate women's experiences. In what follows, we will build on Hall's points about race to explore an intersectional 'grammar of gender'. To do so we consider three key concepts in feminist media studies – the male gaze, the politics of feminine beauty, and the framing of girls and women as on top.

The male gaze

Laura Mulvey has linked the pleasures of film-viewing with normative erotic desire in social life. Arguing that film 'reflects, reveals, and even plays on the straight, socially established interpretation of sexual difference which control images, erotic ways of looking and spectacle' (1999: 833), Mulvey provides a key concept for understanding how patriarchy has shaped the structure of the film form – the **gaze**. This refers to the ways in which women in film are structured as objects to be seen and looked at rather than as active subjects. 'In a world ordered by sexual imbalance, pleasure in looking has been split between active/male and passive/female' (1999: 837), with the woman as the image to be gazed upon and the man as active subject who engages in the act of looking. Mulvey explains that the pleasure of viewing a film derives from **scopophilia**, the voyeuristic sexual pleasure of watching others while remaining unseen oneself, and **narcissism**, the viewer's desire to identify with the actor in the film. When a female figure appears in the filmic form, she is there to be consumed by both the characters in the cinematic narrative and the spectator viewing the film, thereby satisfying both voyeuristic and narcissistic desires. The viewer, regardless of their gender, is asked to identify with the active male character. This also shapes the representation of male characters – they cannot be objectified sexually as an object of the gaze (as, in this theory, the gaze is constructed for the pleasure of a heterosexual male viewer), and their role then is in taking action and propelling the story forward. Of course, many male actors are themselves normatively attractive, but they tend not be filmed as a spectacle to be consumed but as an ideal avatar the spectator can identify with. This figure is perfect – fast, strong, glamourous and powerful – and the conventions of camerawork enable the viewer to feel as though they are seeing and acting in the film's world through them. The female character then acts as a romantic and/or sexual opportunity for the male character and can be possessed by the viewer through this identification with the active figure in the film.

Mulvey's approach to understanding how gendered relations shape the ways that films are constructed draws on psychoanalytic theory and shares with other feminist media critiques an understanding that the language of cinema and its representations of men and women are shaped by dominant social relations. These societal norms structure what is pleasurable in what we see, and Hollywood as a successful media industry is premised on constructing visually gratifying experiences based on an understanding of patriarchal sexual desire. The film industry, like other graphic forms such as television and advertising, constructs and reproduces these gendered patterns, perpetuating and reifying what is classified as visual pleasure. Mulvey's argument about structured ways of looking focuses on how they are constructed within film, but the theory of the male gaze has become a concept applied in feminist media studies to a range of studies about gendered representation. Berger (1972) reveals how these trends in who sees and who is seen are found historically in classical art, wherein men, when they are present, embody power, potential, and capability, whereas women's presence is characterized by being seen, alone, by men. This serves to **objectify** women, making them the object of the gaze, a consumable, sexualized being existing only to be looked at. While it is important to consider how the unique affordances, technologies, and conventions of different media structure this relation between the male gaze and the objectified female body, it is striking how across our media (on a global level as well as historically), the objectification of women consistently entails them taking on the role of decoration, prey, and prize.

For instance, Mulvey describes how, under the male gaze, women's bodies are fragmented through close-ups. This disembodiment of female body parts is not exclusive to film but also a common convention in advertising, where headless bodies as well as disarticulated legs, lips, and torsos are used to sell anything from perfume to burgers, sneakers to cars. Of course, images of men are also used to market commodities, from watches to cologne to underwear. However, as Dyer (1982) notes, while men can be the subject of media images and presumably therefore an object of some kind of gaze, they are typically framed in these portrayals as engaged in or associated with action. Even when lying in a prone position their muscles are flexed, indicating that they are poised to be 'ready for action'. In their posing, framing, and overall portrayal, they are not configured as passive objects to be consumed in the same manner as women. Dyer also highlights distinctions between the representation of White male and Black male bodies, wherein the latter are associated more with Nature and animality, highlighting how the gaze is not only gendered but also racialized.

This is an insight explored further by hooks (1992), who observes that, as noted above, Black women's bodies are sexualized differently in the media. The Mammy figure, for instance, is rendered asexual, her body instead obediently in service of the care of White characters and households. As Collins notes, like other dominant media tropes, this acts as a 'controlling image' and may be understood as a justification for the exploitation of Black women in slavery and in low-paid, undervalued domestic labour, functioning as 'the normative yardstick used to evaluate all Black women's behaviour' (2008: 72). On the other hand there is the Black Jezebel figure, a hypersexualized character framed as aggressive, out of control and animalistic; and the Sapphire, an independent woman vilified through an emphasis on angry, 'sassy', and abusive behaviour. These representations serve to convey appropriate feminine behaviour and sexuality as located in the more restrained sexual availability and passivity of White women's bodies.

hooks also refines the theory of the gaze by exploring responses to the dominant gaze. While Mulvey's conceptualization of the gaze presumes a White, heterosexual, male viewer, hooks notes that viewing is enacted by a range of audiences in varying contexts and from different positions, including Black people in the US, who as spectators recognize the ways in which their media consumption has revolved around White actors, characters, and groups. As hooks argues, 'when most black people in the US first had the opportunity to look at film and television, they did so fully aware that mass media was a system of knowledge and power reproducing and maintaining white supremacy' (1992: 117). She describes the gaze of Black spectators as **oppositional**, in alignment with Hall's negotiated and contested readings, working as a mode of resistance against exclusionary representational regimes in the media.

The oppositional gaze reminds us that audiences, including those marginalized in the media, can develop strategies of resistance and derive pleasure from the act of undermining dominant messages, by engaging with them and therefore resisting their power. This can include the act of **reappropriation**, often associated with queer readings (Doty 1993) in which the heterosexual, White, male gaze is challenged, disrupted, or inverted by anti- or contra-straight and often playful and subversive responses. Examples of such readings can be found in Halberstam's (2011, 2012) analysis of media texts ranging from Lady Gaga's collaboration with Beyoncé in the music video for 'Telephone' to the animated television series *SpongeBob SquarePants*, which indicate the ways audiences can derive pleasure from contested positions that overturn or otherwise challenge a straightforward argument about an omnipresent White, heterosexual, male gaze. Queer readings also challenge the obfuscation of marginalized sexualities, contributing to the imagination of a 'necessarily and desirably queer world' (Warner 1991: 8). However, as Dyer (1984) argues, the problem with the stereotypes queer readings subvert is that they still allow marginalized groups to be defined by those in power, requiring those who are stereotyped to do the work of creating alternative representations and engaging in oppositional readings to counter seemingly natural dominant ideologies.

When considering representation it is important to avoid the trap of conceptualizing an overly simplistic cause and effect relationship between the norms of gender portrayal in the media and their impact on girls and women. As we have seen, the pleasure of media viewing articulated by Mulvey is not straightforward, and can be equally derived from oppositional, resistant viewings where meanings are made in different ways based on the active readings of audiences. As Holland writes of the topless Page Three girl discussed in Chapter 1, even within what seems to be a very classical image of a sexualized female body on display for a presumed male gaze, 'there is a struggle going on, a struggle to define and contain, a struggle for autonomy and resistance' (1983: 98). On the other hand, the pervasive objectification of female bodies across the media, and increasing similarities between visual norms in pornography and in mainstream culture, raises questions related to the ways women and men are portrayed within **the sexualization of culture**. This refers to

> a contemporary preoccupation with sexual values, practices and identities; the public shift to more permissive sexual attitudes; the proliferation of sexual texts; the emergence of new forms of sexual experience; the apparent breakdown of rules, categories and regulations designed to keep the obscene at bay; our fondness for scandals, controversies and panics around sex.
> (Attwood 2006: 78)

The dark side of this trend is referred to as **rape culture**, the cultural valuation of sexually aggressive masculinity and the normalization of sexual violence in the media, where stories of rape seem to circulate constantly without reference to a continuum of gender-based discrimination, exclusion, and violence under patriarchy.

Feminist media critique must be attuned to these contradictions in the media as a reflection of the social and cultural contexts in which representational regimes are embedded. In the next section, we will consider how the portrayal of women and girls is also linked to beauty, an aesthetic of the body that is typically young, White, slim, and, in contemporary postfeminist media culture, hot and sexy.

The politics of feminine beauty

In Chapter 1, we saw how the act of burning bras and other items associated with feminine fashion and beauty became a symbolic gesture linked to the second wave of feminist action. This image continues to be emblematically linked to both feminist protest and negative stereotypes about women seeking gender equity, indicating the political potency of resistance against, and feminist critique of, beauty and fashion. Beauty as a key consideration of feminist analysis was cemented in the third wave with the publication of Naomi Wolf's influential book *The Beauty Myth* (1990). Wolf argues that with the gains women have made in terms of power and visibility, the pressure to conform to unrealistic norms related to physical beauty has also increased. The subtitle of Wolf's book, *How Images of Beauty Are Used Against Women*, indicates the role of the media in contributing to these standards. The thin, toned bodies of models, actresses, and celebrities grace the covers of magazines, are used to sell a range of commodities in advertisements, and circulate across social media, leading to an overwhelming presence of such images communicating a normative social vision of an idealized form of beauty. In tandem, blog posts, advertisements, magazine articles, and news reports repeat the message that weight loss via dieting, exercise, or cosmetic surgery is a priority, be it to start the new year, herald the beginning of summer ('get beach body ready'), or to combat any number of woes from the end of a relationship to a job loss. Idealized images of feminine attractiveness and instructions on how to discipline and maintain one's own lacking body are omnipresent, circulating across platforms and fuelling entire subsections of media industries, from makeover reality television shows to fashion magazines and Instagram beauty accounts. Advertising in particular is an area of focus in the analysis of beauty and idealized femininity because it works as a 'commodity image system' that reflects not our realities but, perhaps more seductively, our dreams and desires (Jhally 2018). By emphasizing narrow and stringent standards of physical beauty, it defines and socializes cultural ideals related to appropriate gender performances located firmly within the body, promoting heightened expectations and aspirations for women related to their physical appearance.

The media emphasis on the body beautiful therefore acts as a form of discipline, generating impossible expectations related to physical appearance while obscuring other questions related to material, political, and social gains. In her book on the backlash against feminist action, Faludi (1991) argues that the emphasis in the media on idealized femininity is a technique deployed within popular culture to divert attention away from fighting for political and economic rights. This is partly evinced by media representations denigrating and mocking independent working women and positively framing those who are committed to the domestic sphere and traditional expressions of femininity such as motherhood and care. She notes in particular two trends that have generated much discussion within feminist media studies: 1) expectations around enduring youthfulness, through the popularity of 'girlish' clothing, and 2) the disciplining and punishment of women's bodies through restrictive fashion trends, from corsets to skinny jeans to Spanx. Staying forever young becomes an impossible injunction used to denigrate and dismiss older women based on their appearance, while also necessitating cosmetic surgery to target wrinkles, sagging body parts, age spots, and other signs of aging. At the same time, the emphasis on ever more youthful female figures in the media extends the pressure to meet unattainable standards of beauty to younger audiences, while also fetishizing and sexualizing images associated with girls and teens. Age is therefore a concern for feminist analysis and is one that is also changing in contemporary culture, as Jermyn's (2016) examination of emerging brands and marketing celebrating certain (White, slim) aging bodies demonstrates.

The choice to participate (or not) in these regimes of beautification is often a question that arises when discussing the disciplinary power of the media in relation to feminine beauty standards. This is particularly resonant in postfeminist media culture, wherein participation in beauty practices is positioned as a self-selected activity, one that is not only pleasurable but also skilful and supportive of personal expression and freedom (Lazar 2011). As Lazar's analysis of beauty advertising in an English Singaporean daily newspaper demonstrates, the idea that participating in the beauty industry is linked to agency, autonomy, and emancipation holds out the promise that femininity and a feminist consciousness can be compatible. Indeed, the strategy of associating dominant norms of beauty with personal power through a knowingness about feminist critiques has been a successful marketing campaign for the Dove Beauty brand, which emphasizes 'real beauty' by portraying more diverse female bodies (including those that are older, freckled, less curvy, dark-skinned, or larger) as part of their advertising, referencing both the normalization of unattainable beauty standards and its impact on self-esteem. Despite the seemingly feminist message of this campaign, Murray argues:

> 'Real beauty' is an oppressive ideology that reinforces the value of female beauty and its pursuit by garnering women's agreement with its values of ideological and material consumption. At its core is a paradox: while apparently decrying it, 'real beauty' embraces conformity to hegemonic

beauty standards through both corporate instigation for brand attachment and women's striving to be part of what they may feel is a positive beauty ideology. (2012: 98)

The linkage of normative beauty ideals with feminine power and freedom is often articulated through a connection to personal, individual attributes such as positive thinking and self-confidence, eliminating any need to consider the influence of social forces, cultural norms, or collective struggles. The 2018 film *I Feel Pretty*, starring comedian Amy Schumer, is but one recent example of how beauty standards are perpetuated while the barriers faced by women are framed as being rooted in a simple lack of confidence on their part. Rather than staging a critique of the unrealistic norms of contemporary beauty (including airbrushed images and ideals linked to White bodies), this film, along with a range of texts in postfeminist media culture, presents individual women as having only themselves to blame should they feel lacking. Overall, within the discourse of consumerism upon which advertising is premised, the pursuit of fashion, beauty, and fitness is no longer a form of bodily discipline imposed on women by men, but, as Lazar argues, a right in and of itself.

If the power to choose to opt out of these beauty standards is available, why do so many continue to engage in the labour and pay the high costs of attempting to adhere to them? If this is a choice that women freely make, what other aims are sacrificed in pursuit of this all-consuming beauty project? What are the consequences in terms of voice and visibility for those who eschew the attainment of these beauty norms? Given the freedoms on offer, why is the beauty ideal still so narrow and so pervasive? While many people derive pleasure and enjoyment from the accoutrements of feminine beauty, from sparkly nail polish to pastel hair dye to high-heeled shoes, it is important to balance these forms of engagement, pleasure, and desire with an acknowledgement of the structural power of the media industries in constructing social reality. In many cases, it is productive to consider who benefits from these norms and who suffers from them.

Wolf concludes her book with the argument that the social pressure placed on women to pursue a narrow, unrealistic vision of beauty has serious consequences, including eating disorders, the rising consumption of pornography, increased demand for cosmetic surgery, and a fixation on body image and weight loss. Others argue that the objectification of women in advertising, including in the circulation of images of unrealistic body shapes and sizes, contributes to their infantilization and dehumanization, while normalizing masculine aggression as well as violence against women (Katz 2011; Kilbourne 2010). Such direct media effects are difficult to measure, assess, and evaluate. However, it is clear that the emphasis on choice and self-development through fashion and beauty imposes limits on appropriate feminine subjectivity and contributes to rigid forms of scrutiny and judgement focused on women's success and failure (McRobbie 2007a).

Those engaging in feminist media critique of beauty must be attuned to the historical and cultural specificities that shape these standards. Expectations about body size and shape, length of hair, and skin colour are shaped by societal norms over time, and can be linked to racist and classist prejudices against people of colour. In their cross-cultural analysis of advertising in nine women's magazines published in the US, Taiwan, and Singapore, Frith et al. (2005) find that advertisements in the latter two contexts emphasize the face via beauty products and cosmetics whereas the American magazines focus on the body via fashion and clothing. Media analyses like this one can reveal how many of the attributes of the perfect woman discussed by Western critics examining the politics of beauty (and other norms of femininity in gender portrayals) are contextually specific and not applicable across the globe, while also revealing others that are more universal, indicating the potency of globalization in shaping the media. Frith et al. conclude that a major implication of these differences is that within the Taiwanese and Singaporean magazines White women are more overtly sexualized than Asian women, who are portrayed in a more culturally appropriate, demure manner. As this indicates, theories of the gaze and of any kind of overarching beauty ideal may reflect a Western perspective that does not align with other media systems and cultural norms – which is itself a topic worthy of further analysis.

In the last two sections we have seen how women's bodies are represented in narrow ways in media cultures, in accordance with norms that have endured over many decades. The next section considers 'progressive' trends in representation that position girls and women as powerful agents. We examine how these seemingly positive representational practices maintain inequalities in insidious new ways.

Girls and women on top?

Despite the statistics mentioned at the start of this chapter, it is very common to hear the claim that things are improving for girls and women in terms of both representation and status in society. While there is pervasive evidence of beauty standards holding sway, the ubiquitous presence of sexualized female bodies, and enduring stereotypical framings of women and girls, there are also notable examples of more positive and inclusive portrayals of gender, race, and sexuality in particular. For example, in the television series *Grey's Anatomy*, *Scandal*, and *How to Get Away with Murder*, the Black American showrunner Shonda Rhimes features intelligent, independent, successful women, including women of colour, gay women, and women of different sizes and shapes, in leading roles. The media has lauded Rhimes for her development of stories based on Strong Female Characters, though she is critical of this framing and of the notion that these women are exceptional rather than the norm (Kinane 2017).

Further evidence for this argument about progress would include the trend towards reworking male- and White-dominated mainstream media texts to feature diverse casts. Examples include the 2016 remake of the *Ghostbusters* movie with an all-female team, the 2018 release of *Black Panther*, a superhero film featuring primarily Black actors in the main roles (including four major roles for Black women), and the 2018 movie *Ocean's 8*, a spinoff from the *Ocean's* trilogy based on a female crew planning a heist. Storylines about transgender characters also appear to be proliferating, with the television series *Transparent*, reality programmes *I Am Cait* and *I Am Jazz*, and notable roles on shows such as *Orange is the New Black* and *Sense8*. If we include here the rise of the trope of the Strong Female Character, exemplified by Katniss Everdeen of *The Hunger Games* and the leads of *Buffy the Vampire Slayer*, *Atomic Blonde*, and *Lara Croft: Tomb Raider* – rejecting the Princess archetype and inverting the norm that it is always a male character who plays the Hero – an impressive list begins to accumulate in support of the argument that we have moved beyond racial and gendered inequalities towards the normalization of more progressive mediated representations.

But feminist media studies as a field is concerned with examining the nuances of such inversions, especially given that they often entail a sort of gender- and colour-blind approach to casting that does nothing to alter the structural properties of standardized narratives. As we saw with the array of tests for assessing media representations at the start of this chapter, there are a number of questions we might ask to complicate straightforward celebrations (or dismissals) of these portrayals. For example, Gomez and McFarlane analyse the representation of race and gender in the above-mentioned television show *Scandal*, a programme centred on the character of Olivia Pope, a Black woman in a position of influence and power in American politics. While race, gender, and feminism are discussed across the first three seasons of the programme, the authors argue that 'these ostensibly progressive politics only serve to refract the material realities that both Olivia and many women of color often face' (2017: 363). By refraction, they are referring to the contradictory and simultaneous readings one can have of a text such as *Scandal*. The show is both progressive and depoliticized in how it represents gender and race, including in how it embraces but also challenges familiar tropes such as the slave mistress and the Jezebel, acknowledging and denying both sexism and racism. Gomez and McFarlane conclude that 'refraction thus exposes the lack of progress cloaked in progress narratives' (2017: 374). As this example demonstrates, ascertaining whether contemporary trends in media representation are progressive is not a simple question, and perhaps not really the most important one. Rather, it is more fruitful to interrogate such representations in the context of postfeminist and 'post-race' assertions that we have moved beyond the concerns of feminism and critical race theory. *What ongoing inequalities are obscured or erased when we claim that progress is being made?*

The idea that patriarchal forces have weakened their hold on representation is not new. In a 2005 study, Tasker and Negra describe how the acknowledgement of feminism (including critiques of the sexualization of women and the disciplinary force of beauty standards) began in the 1990s to be associated with texts aimed at female audiences. These texts showcase self-aware female characters who reflect on 'having it all', the challenges of balancing family, career, and love, and the disciplinary forces of beauty regimes. In romantic comedies such as *Bridget Jones's Diary*, television programmes focused on female characters such as *Sex in the City*, and so-called 'chick lit' books aimed at women readers such as *Shanghai Baby*, there is an obvious visibility of the postfeminist thematics discussed in Chapter 1. These include an emphasis on personal agency, choice, and freedom, and reproduce traditionally feminine motifs (beauty, weight loss, shopping, child care, cooking and other domestic labour, heterosexual romance and marriage). The key difference is that participation in these gendered activities is framed as the desire of the characters rather than imposed and disciplined by social norms in a system of inequalities based on gender. Women are represented as choosing to engage in hegemonic femininity because doing so makes them feel happy and fulfilled. Tasker and Negra argue that these thematics are found more broadly in genres and texts aimed at female audiences, with a growing trend towards recognizing and commodifying feminist ideas by emphasizing empowerment through consumer practices and individualistic narratives, rather than focusing on structural inequalities or topics such as economics, politics, or health. In the case of Strong Female Characters and otherwise empowered women and girls, despite their power to choose, we still find widespread compliance with the standards of idealized beauty and the satisfaction of the male gaze. Media texts representing diverse gendered subjectivities, including women of colour, often execute these stories in a manner that removes these subjectivities from their social context and the dynamics of power that oppress them. To return to the case of Olivia Pope in *Scandal*, this character potentially obscures the historical and widespread structural barriers to women, particularly women of colour, entering politics in the US.

The acknowledgment of feminist concerns in these media representations therefore does not equate to greater critical awareness of sexist and racist stereotypes or reductions in discriminatory portrayals. As we saw in Chapter 1, **irony** is a core element of postfeminist representations. Within our contemporary media culture, sexist and racist stereotypes are often represented in a knowing manner, recognizing that such portrayals can be identified as exclusionary or offensive but claiming innocence in this regard because they are invoked for a laugh or not meant seriously. The figure of the killjoy is typically deployed when critiques are made in this context: because these representations are intended to be humorous, so the argument goes, feminist critique is simply the product of someone who doesn't get the joke. These ironic representations are discussed by Douglas (2010) in her book *Enlightened Sexism*. She contrasts the media representation of women in powerful professional roles, what she calls 'embedded feminism', with the rise of 'ironic sexism', illustrated by reality television programmes such as *The Bachelor*, where retrograde representations of women in fights with each other, fixated on beauty and shopping, and obsessive about relationships are the norm. The latter portrayals, Douglas argues, are premised on the idea that feminism has succeeded, and that media representations of women on top have mischaracterized the gains made by feminism in framing it as a completed rather than ongoing project. Levy (2005) notes that the regressive sexist trend towards the objectification of female bodies is an active process in which women also take part in their own sexualization, in what she calls **raunch culture**. This is exemplified by the normalization of *Playboy*, stripping, and porno chic across media and popular culture in the early 2000s, including the rise (and fall) of so-called lad magazines such as *Maxim* and *FHM*. The dominant rationale for these kinds of representations, so similar to those critiqued for objectification and unattainable beauty standards, is that there is now a widespread societal understanding of feminist critique and that women are choosing to participate in these texts because doing so empowers them.

Critiques of the role of women in contributing to ironic or enlightened sexism through self-sexualization have reignited debates about sex positivity. *Is the embrace of one's own sexuality a liberatory move? Is it an example of **false consciousness**, wherein the limits on the autonomy of subordinated women in a patriarchal system go unrecognized? Is the expression of female sexuality within a sexist media culture actually a much more complex proposition?*

Dobson (2011) provides some insight into this issue in her examination of the social media site MySpace and the ways young women between the ages of eighteen and twenty-one represent themselves in their profiles. While in some ways their images might seem to conform to the expectations of the male gaze, and in particular heterosexual pornography, Dobson explores how the self-produced nature of these profiles challenges the idea of the gaze, and whether these practices may be playing with raunch culture rather than endorsing it. Indeed, as she notes elsewhere (2012), the emphasis on examining sexualized self-representation online can overlook other common traits of these forms of identity performance, including expressions of individuality, self-worth, and personal strength. For this reason, Dobson argues that interpreting these self-representations as necessarily oppressive is too simple, demonstrating the need for more nuanced analyses of online representation as well as its audiences. Taking a structural view on these performances, including the ways that hardcore pornography has become more 'everyday' (Boyle 2010), indicates that the sexualization of women's and men's bodies, be it in mainstream or DIY media, is not an individual choice but part of an ongoing shift in popular culture. Furthermore, as Gill (2009) demonstrates, this is not a neutral process, as how bodies are sexualized is shaped by gender, race, and sexuality as well as age and class.

These insights also apply to the self-production of media in digital culture and how representational norms may be shifting with the apparent democratization of media-making. The promise is that social media users can construct and control their representations, potentially enabling greater identity play and, possibly, more diverse and inclusive gender portrayals. Banet-Weiser (2011) examines the amateur production practices of girls via content analysis of videos and comments on YouTube. Despite the promises of democratization afforded by the ability to 'broadcast yourself' (YouTube's former slogan), Banet-Weiser identifies a norm emerging across these creations, with an emphasis on and normalization of entrepreneurial self-branding practices and postfeminist articulations of individual empowerment. Thus, while it is tempting to see online identity-making as a creative and open practice allowing young people the opportunity to subvert traditional gender portrayals, Banet-Weiser finds that a postfeminist ethos shapes the internet and its uses, particularly in the way that 'the dissemination of discourses about freedom and equality provides the context for the reentrenchment of gender norms and traditional gendered relations' (2011: 283). The comments on these videos in turn serve to shape the performances of media-makers, from the reification of the need for sexual desirability to the objectification of female bodies to the dismissal of girls' self-presentations. Similarities in representational norms across media forms, including those authored by DIY media-makers, underline the ongoing significance of social norms in shaping gender portrayals.

We can read these forms of self-representation in the context of the broader cultural emphasis on female empowerment and success – 'progressive' discourses we consider in detail in Chapter 4. As McRobbie notes, such discourses imply that gender equality is a universal and normalized goal in neoliberal capitalism, which shares with postfeminism an emphasis on individualized efforts and successes. In this context, 'the visual (and verbal) discourses of public femininity ... come to occupy an increasingly spectacular space as sites, events, narratives and occasions within the cultural milieu' (McRobbie 2009: 60). Here, the focus on individual talent, determination, desire to win, and the attainment of qualifications in both education and employment obscure structural inequalities related to gender, race, and class. Female participation becomes vital to the new economy as labour participation over women's lifetimes reduces reliance on welfare and revitalizes consumer culture. At the same time, these visibilities afforded to women are defined through commercial activities, and maintain pressures related to motherhood and reproduction. McRobbie (2007b) refers to this subject position as that of 'top girls', and we can see parallels with Harris's (2004) 'future girl', Projansky's (2014) 'spectacular girl', and Banet-Weiser's (2015) discussion of the figure imagined in 'girl empowerment organizations'. While each of these analyses focus on distinct contexts, from celebrity culture to international development initiatives, they all highlight processes where girls and women become visible in media cultures, often based on the linkage between empowerment and commodification. Within these processes, appropriate feminine performance is frequently tied to an entrepreneurial spirit, self-discipline, and a conventionally attractive body, and a collectivist ethos is supplanted by an emphasis on the individual and her responsibility for success in a seemingly meritocratic, level playing field. Importantly, Banet-Weiser points out that while the media visibility of girls is a form of power, it does not guarantee access to power. These subjectivities remain intensively exclusionary, with the resources necessary to participate in media-making limited by race, age, and class. Opportunities for girls to become visible are often restricted to slim, White, able-bodied, heterosexual, and middle-class bodies, which, McRobbie concludes, 'exacts a violent exclusion of diversity and otherness thereby resurrecting and solidifying gendered racial divisions in the cultural realm' (2009: 70).

In sum, what these critiques highlight is that while it can be tempting to cite seemingly more progressive gender portrayals and intersectional representations as evidence of change, it is vital for the feminist media critic to read these texts in their broader contexts and reflect on trends in the media cultures and socio-political realities in which they circulate. It is important to critically assess even the most progressive representations. The Strong Female Character, for example, is frequently lauded for her physical power and her feisty attitude, but, as McDougall (2013) points out, 'strong' can become its own limiting frame. Male characters are rarely referred to in this way, and are allowed to be more complex and multifaceted, something not often afforded to this trope for female characters. As this critique indicates, even a positive countertype is still a delimited containing force hindering the portrayal of complex identities in the media.

Our task is not to judge media representations as either 'good' or 'bad', correct or inappropriate, but to understand their qualities, how they function, and how they challenge or contribute to broader norms. The objective of feminist media studies is not to dismiss viewers as passive dupes of these messages, ignorantly succumbing to regressive sexist values, nor to present them as beyond the systems of power in which they operate as audiences, oppositionally and critically reading every text they encounter. Instead, gendered representations, whether created by digital media users or professional media companies, need to be analysed in their structural contexts. *Where are these representations created and shared, and how are they shaped by this milieu of production?* In the case of digital media, this would include examining the structure of the platform to understand their affordances and logics as well as their cultural norms (we review these ideas about the shaping role played by platforms in more depth in Chapter 5). *Who is responsible for creating these representations and what degree of relative autonomy do they have?* For instance, in the case of growing opportunities for women in comedy to star in their own films, such as *Bridesmaids* and *Trainwreck*, we must consider the supporting role played by the powerful Hollywood producer Judd Apatow (questions of power in the industry are examined further in Chapter 7). As these questions highlight, feminist analysis of media representations, from the most retrograde to the most progressive, must remain attuned to the economic, political, social, and cultural forces shaping gendered portrayals.

Critical race and masculinity studies as well as queer theory indicate an equally important direction for the field, which is to engage in critical readings of portrayals that complicate narrow and normative understandings of the intersection of gender, race, and sexuality. As Gray notes, a key challenge to dominant ideologies in the media is the analysis of 'nonnormative masculine performances enacted by those performing and residing at marginalized masculinity' (2018: 11), including men of colour and queer men, as this allows the contours of the presumed norm of White heterosexual masculinity to become visible as an identity rather than as the default. Such analyses therefore serve the purpose of decentring and denaturalizing common-sense and commonplace understandings of gendered identities and relations, bringing to the fore how patriarchy, heterosexuality, and White supremacy become normative ideologically and institutionally.

The dark side of visibility

We began this chapter with a discussion of the Bechdel, DuVernay, Shukla, and Latif and Latif tests for assessing media representations. These tests provide a simple means of demonstrating what a wide range of quantitative research has substantiated – that women in all their diversity are not portrayed with the same vividness as men in our mediated worlds. However, such tests and other numerically focused studies tell only part of the story, especially when it seems that women, people of colour, LGBTQ+ people, and people without class privilege are appearing in the media more often and in more visible roles. Qualitative, interpretivist analyses of media representation show that these tests do not necessarily reveal the rich range of experiences and narratives available (or not) for gendered characters. For instance, the 1998 movie *Run Lola Run* would not pass the Bechdel Test, but as Latif and Latif note this is a film with a powerful feminist message. The tests also only focus on a singular text, which can indicate the exceptional rather than the commonplace. Nguyen (2018) proposes the idea of 'narrative plenitude' to describe the robustness of some kinds of stories, such as accounts of the Vietnam War, and its opposite, 'narrative scarcity', to describe how Asian people are deprived of a range of stories representing their lives. Discussing the heightened expectations for the 2018 film *Crazy Rich Asians*, he argues that the limited number of films about people of colour are held to a higher standard because of their rarity, and that greater narrative plenitude would allow space for exceptional but also mediocre films to be made about diverse people.

With the growth of new media and digital culture globally, greater opportunities for visibility for diverse people would seem apparent. However, as this chapter demonstrates, the interactivity of these sites can impose its own disciplinary mechanisms. Cases of online harassment painfully underline how being seen does not equate to inclusion. Leslie Jones, the Black actress who plays one of the four main roles in the *Ghostbusters* reboot, for instance, was subject to a campaign of vitriolic racist and misogynistic abuse by those who took offence at the inversion of the norm of male-dominated films.

As Lawson (2018) notes in her discussion of Jones' harassment, the social media platforms enabling these attacks also allowed the actress to make her experience visible to a wider audience. This example demonstrates the contradictions of visibility. New roles for women in the media can lead to a violent backlash enabled by participatory new media. In turn, marginalized people can deploy these media forms to publicize hitherto privately experienced gender- and race-based harassment. In these processes, it becomes visible to all how gendered media portrayals always circulate in a broader social context shaped by relations of power. Therefore, while visibility in the media is an important consideration for feminist media studies, so too is the examination of where it can be dangerous or otherwise undesirable. We discuss the challenges of increased, digitally enabled visibility in Chapter 5.

This chapter has demonstrated the necessity of critical close readings attuned to social norms – rather than a cursory counting and superficial assessment of intersectionally gendered portrayals – in order to understand the kinds of cultural values these representations perpetuate, circulate, and challenge. These values are specific to their contexts of production and consumption, requiring the analyst to draw on the principles of iteration, reflexivity, and situatedness discussed in Chapter 2. In the next chapter we explore a globally focused approach to the field, considering how historical legacies of exploitation and oppression shape visibility for women in the media, and mapping the concepts and challenges that form part of a transnational feminist media studies.

4 Transnational Feminist Media Studies

In 2012, a group of young activists from Syria launched Refugees Not Captives (RNC), a social media-based campaign 'to protect Syrian women' by raising awareness of women sold into forced marriages in refugee camps, encouraging mobilization amongst the Arab youth they were being married to, and networking with international stakeholders and funders to support marriages between Syrian men and women. As Alhayek (2014) notes, despite RNC being led by Syrian activists and labelled as feminist, the initiative generalizes and renders invisible the actual experiences of female Syrian refugees, essentializing and vilifying Arab men while constructing Syrian women as victims without agency. In this case of mediated feminist organizing, social media amplifies the voices of those with 'economic and educational privileges … who reflect the language of Western hegemony in understanding the Arab and Muslim world' (Alhayek 2014: 699), making visible only the oppression, rather than the agency, of the women the campaign aims to protect.

This example highlights the significance of two recurring ideas in this book's mapping of intersectional approaches to feminist media studies – voice and visibility. The importance of these concepts was crystallized in the exploration of the presence (and absence) of particular perspectives in feminist action and thought as discussed in Chapter 1; in the power relations implicit in the knowledge production entailed in designing and executing feminist media critique explored in Chapter 2; and in the mixed blessings of gendered portrayals in mediated representations examined in Chapter 3. The case of RNC indicates the importance of broadening these discussions of the power to be seen and heard in both media and research through a transnational approach to the field. As we will see in this chapter, a range of mediated stories, initiatives, groups, and debates direct our gaze to so-called 'developing' countries and to the actions of their female populations in particular, necessitating a critical grasp of the myriad power dynamics at play in such forms of visibility. As discussed in Chapter 2, this also entails an examination of how research and knowledge production practices contribute to hegemonic ways of understanding the world and gendered subjects, and in particular how power, agency, and choice operate.

The focus on girls and young women in the Global South, including Africa, South America, and developing nations in Asia, tends to emphasize opportunities to address sustainable development, including but not limited to peace-building, ending poverty, achieving gender equality, and improving health, education, employment, and the environment. Initiatives such as Technovation's #WorldPitch (where girls propose to develop apps aimed at 'solving global problems') and the Women Deliver Young Leaders Program (in which young people are trained as advocates, particularly using the media, for gender equality) foreground communication tools and platforms for delivering solutions to significant global challenges. While these programmes hinge on the seemingly inclusive premise that investment in girls and women will lead to a more equal, fair, and safe world, a feminist media studies approach needs to consider who has the power to set the agenda of these projects, determining the global problems they address, and measuring their success. Of particular importance is how the media frames these gendered subjects and defines 'empowerment'. This chapter contributes a much-needed synthesis of interdisciplinary concepts from diverse scholarship in postcolonial, Indigenous, and critical race theory to support the exploration of these questions via transnational feminist media studies.

Given the emphasis throughout this book on taking an intersectional approach to addressing axes of oppression and differential privilege, the focus on the Global South here entails considering global relations of power related to citizenship, ethnicity, race, religion, and class, among other inequalities. Recognizing these dynamics is essential to the future of feminist media studies and its **decolonization**, which refers to the act of addressing and dismantling the effects of colonialism on our practices of knowledge production. This aim, as this chapter shows, is not peripheral but fundamental to feminist aims of equity and justice.

The term 'Global South' originates from transnational and postcolonial theory, where it was introduced to replace metaphors such as the 'Third World'. It is intended to address the histories and present realities of political, economic, militaristic, and social dominance and subjugation perpetuated by what we refer to as the West through colonialism and imperialism. While the Global South is an important concept for referencing broader geopolitical networks of power and the relative degrees of autonomy and suppression within them, when undertaking feminist media critique it is essential to refine our focus and examine the nuances of the contexts that make up this broad concept. The Global South is neither a fixed entity nor a blanket region south of the equator with identical inequalities, histories, and relations to the West. As Mignolo explains, 'the Global South is not a geographic location; rather it is a metaphor that indicates regions of the world at the receiving end of globalization and suffering the consequences' (2011: 184). If we remain attuned to the relations of power and domination this indicates, the concept enables us to reflect on the dynamics of gendered global power and flows, migrations, and movements across borders shaped by material and symbolic inequalities.

In this chapter, we explore several concepts and examples to understand how we might 'think transnationally' (Dosekun 2015: 964) in feminist media studies. Dosekun argues that research on postfeminist media cultures has not adequately captured how women living in the Global South are implicated and incorporated in postfeminist cultural logics and figurations. Drawing on the work of Grewal and Kaplan (1994, 2001), she argues that the terms Global South/North, Western/non-Western, and Developed/Developing are categorizations applied to spaces produced through colonial histories and imperialist actions. She therefore uses the term 'transnational' to refer to a way of thinking that does not frame global inequalities as an essential truth, and that better encapsulates the ways discourses and imagery move across arbitrarily demarcated borders and boundaries.

Thinking transnationally as an approach to feminist media studies means accounting for the asymmetries and complexities of how cultures, practices, ideologies, and migrating bodies move across the lines we draw around nations and areas in gendered ways. This approach also recognizes how such boundaries still have very real consequences and are therefore not nullified by movement and circulation, and indeed how migration is an uneven experience depending on context and relative privilege. For example, I am a Canadian woman teaching at a British university, and therefore my experience of migration and movement differs in a multitude of ways from that of the Syrian refugee women interviewed by Alhayek. Migration is an uneven process. As such, a transnational approach endeavours to go beyond simplistic framings of 'the local' and 'the global' (and awkward neologisms such as 'the glocal') in order to critically understand the complexity of movement, with specific attention paid to intersectional and gendered power relations. As Dosekun says, 'the transnational implies asymmetries and incompleteness, flows not fixity, cross-cutting rather than uni-directional linkages' (2015: 965).

A decolonizing transnational perspective also makes a needed intervention into the politics of knowledge production and citation in the field. It challenges the emphasis in feminist media studies and action on researchers and texts from English-speaking nations, with colonial histories often unacknowledged in theorization, particularly in the US, the UK, Australia, and Canada. Gender-based oppression is a global issue with significant contextually specific nuances to consider, so it is imperative to broaden feminist media studies beyond a Western focus in terms of the scholarship we engage with, the theories we draw on and develop, and the sites and texts we consider in our research design. At the same time, it is pivotal that we avoid judging the practices, policies, and problems of other nations from a Western or otherwise 'universal' perspective. Sensitivity to cultural norms, specific social and economic challenges, and historical forms of marginalization is vital in a critical feminist media studies approach. Considering opportunities for mutual benefit and respect, in cooperation, exchange, and relations between groups, and how global problems can be addressed in a way that acknowledges their origins in racist and colonial domination, is also vital for transnational feminist media studies.

Such an approach is critically important but still relatively under-explored in the field. To address this gap, this chapter draws on a wide range of scholarship to set out key concepts and questions for transnational feminist media studies. We consider examples of research engaging in this form of critique and the insights such studies generate. In the process, we explore the interaction of feminism, politics, and the media in a range of texts, and deal with questions about reflexivity and positionality that are especially poignant when thinking transnationally, as we are all implicated within these global systems of power. Consequently, we will return to questions of method and power raised in Chapter 2, paying attention to how systems of knowledge production are inextricably shaped by social and historical structures. Gunaratnam and Hamilton (2017) highlight how common metaphors for describing research (such as mapping, extracting, and journeying) mirror the gendered colonial quest narratives of privileged White European explorers on an expedition to '*see* the world' (recall here how the gaze is not innocent). The use of such metaphors can indicate a lack of mutuality and recognition of systemic inequalities, and remind us of the necessity of reflecting on the relationship between the researcher and those implicated in the research.

A transnational feminist media analysis does not exclusively entail looking at 'non-Western' media texts, audiences, platforms, or industries. Dosekun's (2015) critique of the field's emphasis on Western women is influenced by Butler's work on women of colour in postfeminist media culture, in which she argues that, 'despite the increasing visibility of women of color in contemporary popular culture, the processes by which they are incorporated into media representations may, in fact, reproduce hierarchies of difference and dominance' (2013: 49). Transnational flows move across, through, and within the West, where the representation of non-Western, non-White, and Indigenous women, and the relationship between gender, race, religion, class, and migration status, necessitate feminist media analysis as well. Overall, what this chapter aims to demonstrate is how an awareness of and reflection on transnational relations and decolonizing approaches enhances all feminist media studies research. Decolonization of the field is a vital move in challenging contemporary cultural politics informed by both neoliberalism and postfeminism with their emphasis on specific definitions of choice, empowerment, and freedom. Focusing on transnational feminist media studies enables us to envision and create new forms of solidarity between women on a global level. In the next section, we examine the concepts essential for beginning this project, and in the sections that follow we consider some enduring challenges in transnational feminist work before looking at alternatives and future directions for the field.

Conceptualizing the 'transnational' for feminist media studies

The context for the analysis of movements and flows is the idea that we live in an increasingly globalized world, and that gender relations and the media are both shaped by processes of **globalization**. Most broadly, this refers to economic trade and exchange on a worldwide level, enabled by information and communication technologies as well as national policies and international organizations supporting business operations that cross borders. Such technological, economic, and political incentives have significant social and cultural implications, including the outsourcing of work to nations with cheaper exploitable labour forces, the internationalization of Western brands, cultural products, and media texts, and migrant workers supporting families from abroad, to name a few. Sassen (1999) demonstrates how globalization's impact deepens inequalities, particularly for women and immigrants typically working in industries where dangerous working conditions and low wages predominate. Gender shapes the unequal redistribution of reward and recognition under globalization, with women's care labour, ever more essential under neoliberalism's dismantling of the welfare state, becoming increasingly less visible and valued (Nagar et al. 2002). Overall, within the friction-free flows of globalization, wealth concentrates around major corporations and creates new patterns and ideas of identity, power, labour, migration, and cultural contact, all of which are significant when considering gender and the media. And yet, as Harp et al. (2013) demonstrate in a mixed-methods study of US news magazines *Time* and *Newsweek*, women are often made invisible in media discourse on globalization, the exception being in discussions of its impact on traditional domestic roles, a transnational dimension of the symbolic annihilation of women discussed in Chapter 3.

Despite these deepening inequalities and relations of dominance and subjugation under globalized capital and trade, the dominant discourse about globalization tends to be apolitical, framing these relations as natural and universally beneficial. This discourse normalizes thinking of the world in terms of the 'West and the Rest', with the dominant world powers at the centre and the Global South at the periphery, reducing the complexity of these global relations to simple economic formulations within bordered nation-states. We can easily critique this perspective by noting how the media for the most part do not circulate within borders, and neither do the cultures in which they are produced and consumed. Cultures and media instead move between and across local villages, face-to-face conversations, multicultural cities, groups of migrants, displaced workers, diasporas, nation-states, and families, in what Appadurai refers to as '**global cultural flows**' (1990: 296). Appadurai's conceptualization of these flows enables an understanding of how economic, political, and cultural relations operate through asymmetrical transnational movements of people, ideas, media, technologies, and capital. Subsequent research indicates that affect also circulates in global cultural flows, creating shared sentiments of belonging and alignment across borders, about topics including celebrity deaths and terrorist attacks (Döveling et al. 2018). We can see the value of the concept if we return to the example of RNC discussed earlier, where the global expansion of platforms such as Facebook and YouTube elicits emotional responses of outrage and concern from those with the greatest economic privilege in response to mediated Western ideas of 'backward' gender relations affecting migrant women. As Appadurai notes, global cultural flows are neither stable nor static but dynamic and shifting, and transnational feminist media studies needs to be concerned with these transformations and their implications for gendered subjects.

This emphasis on flows, however, does not contradict the importance of considering the specificities of the locations we examine. Flows have unique resonances that are dependent on context. One way to understand this is through what Appadurai (1990) refers to as **deterritorialization**, where ideas, capital, individuals, and cultures become less embedded in place. For example, Dosekun's (2015) analysis of highly educated Nigerian women living in Lagos demonstrates that these women cite familiar discourses of choice and individual expression when explaining their investment in costly beauty and fashion rituals, demonstrating that postfeminism is a deterritorialized logic. However, in this context, access to a postfeminist subjectivity is limited to those occupying a class-privileged position, an insight that underlines how economic disparities are local within given sites and not exclusively a relation between the West and non-Western nations. Therefore, as much as global cultural flows emphasize circulation and movement, we need to remain attuned to the specificities of local contexts in which ideas are adopted, media are engaged with, financial practices occur, technologies are deployed, and people move.

Furthermore, in undertaking a transnational approach, it is essential to consider the relations of exploitation and inequality underpinning global cultural flows. As Katz (2001) points out, global trade and movement are not new or emerging phenomena, but globalization is a name given to recent relations premised on historical patterns of domination. Therefore, attention to the contemporary shape of situated local practices needs to be balanced with an attunement to the past and to how life and social realities on a global level are the by-product of hundreds of years of relations of control, occupation, appropriation, and domination. This set of practices, referred to as **colonialism**, is often traced back to Classical Era Greece and the conquests of the Roman Empire, but from a critical perspective it refers to modern colonialism, specifically that of Western European countries including England, France, The Netherlands, Portugal, and Spain, in parts of Africa, the Americas, Asia, and Oceania. Colonial practices are not simply events from history, but a set of relations that continue to impose and maintain inequalities, particularly for Indigenous people who were invaded and occupied as part of these missions, and for racialized people who were enslaved, tortured, imprisoned, raped, and otherwise dehumanized to support the growth of industrial sectors within these occupied settlements. As this indicates, an understanding of colonization is essential for undertaking an intersectional approach to both theory and method in feminist media studies.

Histories of colonization are also germane because the occupation of territories claimed as the possession of another nation is a form of **imperialism**. This is an ideology that understands a state's power as supreme and that justifies the subordination of others, including through military action, economic and physical exploitation, colonization, and other forms of control and domination. The pursuit of colonialism and imperialism is intrinsic to the project of constructing an **empire** for the dominant force, enabling its political, economic, and military authority over others. The prefix neo- is attached to both colonialism (**neo-colonialism**) and imperialism (**neo-imperialism**) to refer to contemporary extensions of these historical relations, including the perpetuation of relations of dependency between the Global South and dominating empires, such as those enabled by globalization. The histories and legacies of colonization and imperialism, as we will see throughout this chapter, are deeply gendered and racialized, and notions of the differences between men and women were key to the colonial project's definition of 'civilization' (Lugones 2010). The hierarchies of humanity established within colonial relations continue to inform the experiences as well as the representations of Indigenous and settler communities to this day (Arvin et al. 2013). This is apparent in the media coverage of missing and murdered Indigenous women in Canada, which draws on colonial stereotypes of sexual deviance and criminality, contributing to a 'politics of ugliness' framing these women as deviant (Morton 2018). It is also illustrated by how the contributions of Navajo women in early computing circuit assembly are erased from histories of cultural production and digital media labour, even as their initial inclusion was premised on racial stereotyping about the character and innate abilities of Indigenous peoples (Nakamura 2014).

The media demonstrably plays a key role in framing, spreading, and reifying colonial legacies and ideologies, understanding Western ways of living, doing business, and producing knowledge as superior acts that vindicate the system of domination and exploitation entailed in colonialism, as part of the pursuit of 'progress' and 'civilization'. Racist assumptions about the lives, societies, and cultures of Indigenous people are used to justify colonial actions, and linger within the lived realities of both settler-colonial inheritors and Indigenous and racialized people today. Ideas of superiority, for instance, normalize educational curricula taught by middle-class White European male scholars employing research methods that do not recognize the validity of Indigenous forms of knowledge production. Our ways of researching and understanding the world, our methodologies and epistemologies, are informed by colonial relations. The university as an institution producing and sharing knowledge is shaped by this history and continues to perpetuate colonial values, including in the field of communication, where analysis of publication and citation statistics demonstrates a glaring absence of non-White scholars in the canon (Chakravartty et al. 2018). As researchers, we need to be concerned with what Santos (2014) refers to as 'cognitive injustice' and with the ways we can contribute to social justice in our research practices – issues we consider in the last section of this chapter.

Histories of colonial violence therefore do not remain at a distance from our social lives but have shaped our cultural, intellectual, economic, educational, religious, political, and physical systems. Spivak (1988) refers to this as **epistemic violence**, through which Indigenous ways of knowing the world are destroyed in the process of colonization, robbing colonial subjects of self-expression. Fanon (1963) argued that the negative repercussions of colonization are enduring, as those who have been colonized and subjugated, mentally and materially violated, are consistently framed as less than human. Colonization therefore impacts not only physical structures and institutions but also the mind and the body. Settler colonialism is furthermore not just a regrettable history. It is an ongoing structural form of exclusion demonstrated by the persistence of 'the triad relationship among the industrious settler, the erased/invisibilized Native, and the ownable and murderable slave ... evident in the ways in which the US continues to exploit Indigenous, Black, and other peoples deemed "illegal" (or otherwise threatening and usurping) immigrants' (Arvin et al. 2013: 12). For this reason, transnational relations cannot be incidental but must be central within an intersectional feminist media studies concerned with identity and subjectivity, affect and embodiment, and cultural oppression and resistance.

A key conception that has framed relations between dominant powers and subjugated populations and places is an understanding of people from different parts of the world as essentially different from each other. As Said (1978) argues, an 'us' and 'them' dynamic conceptually divides Western nations from the rest of the world. Whereas the West is framed as the progressive, enlightened, rational core, those outside this constructed centre, the varied societies, cultures, and populations that inhabit 'the East', come to be characterized in delimited stereotypical ways – as servile, romantic, tribal, mysterious, exotic, feminized, and ultimately subordinate and inferior to imperial powers. **Orientalism** is the term used to refer to these homogenizing stories and images circulated in the West about the cultures of non-Western peoples. This kind of knowledge of the 'Other' becomes the justification for control via imperialism and colonialism, contributing to the dehumanization described by Fanon. We saw examples of how this occurs in Chapter 3, and we will examine others below. Spivak (1988) uses the term **subaltern** to describe those groups and people whose voices have been removed from sanctioned, Western discourse; it is not meant to encapsulate all forms of oppression but rather the precise ways in which non-Western people's knowledge, thought, and language are delegitimized. Despite the manifold harms, such actions have been framed in the rhetoric of humanitarianism, as 'civilizing' and 'helping' the Other, not only necessary but also morally correct. This racist, philanthropic impetus used to justify colonialism and empire is termed 'The White Man's Burden', after a poem by Rudyard Kipling, and can be discerned in many of the media-based initiatives targeting women and girls in the Global South.

In practical terms, of course, there is no such thing as the Orient/the East, as the cultures, social structures, and histories of Africa, Asia, the

Americas, and Oceania are thoroughly heterogeneous. So too, of course, are the peoples of Western Europe and other nations grouped as 'the West', particularly given historical patterns of migration, but these constructs manufacture a sense of cohesion and similarity between disparate groups, while also supporting notions of difference and Otherness in relation to the rest of the world. These cultural stereotypes shape how we understand – to name a few examples – religion, freedom, and social relations in the Middle East; traditional dress and feminine behaviour in Asia; and spirituality and relations to nature in Indigenous communities in Australia, the US, and Canada. Such stereotypes not only overstate difference but are used to rationalize domination and inform prejudicial ideas about entire peoples and parts of the world. We need only to revisit the example of the RNC to see how the stereotype of Arab men as threatening predominates. Indeed, media portrayals of Muslim and Arab people largely depend on stereotypes of the religious fanatic, the oil-rich despot, and the terrorist. How such stereotypes are used to support Western military interventions and tightened immigration regulations is evidence of the ways in which limited Orientalist images inform political, economic, militaristic, social, and cultural ideas and practices.

Orientalism is a core concept within postcolonial theory and is valuable for examining the gendered framing of global relations in the media. In addition to binaries such as rational/irrational, strong/weak, and civilized/primitive, the East has been framed in feminized terms in contrast to a masculine West. The reverberations of these gendered relations can be widely seen in mediatized representations of non-Western peoples; for instance, in the media portrayals of East Asian men as effeminate, weak, geeky, and awkward, or, in the case of physically powerful martial arts masters such as Bruce Lee, Jet Li, and Jackie Chan, as ultimately sexless. Representations of South Asian and Muslim men focus on the policing of sexuality, as in the media coverage of 'honour killings', or on sexually aggressive masculinity, with narratives framing these men as pathological sexual predators, as in the case of the RNC. This demonstrates the importance of considering mediations of masculinity as part of feminist media studies, as colonial relations contribute to the construction of hegemonic masculinity (Connell 2005).

In parallel, women from heterogeneous non-Western contexts are framed in Western media as constrained by traditional (backward) customs, in narratives revolving around intergenerational conflict between young women and their parents (for example, Jess in the film *Bend it Like Beckham*, fighting with her Indian parents about her playing football, or *Coronation Street*'s Rana in estrangement from her Muslim parents because of her homosexual romantic relationship). In these texts, cultural and religious customs are framed in opposition to female empowerment through choice, with the West portrayed as progressive, open, and female-friendly. At the same time, non-Western women are represented as highly sexualized, as observed in a range of James Bond films fetishizing East Asian women, and in the emphasis on the erotics of the exotic exemplified by the treacherous African priestess Citra in the *Far Cry 3* video game. As these examples demonstrate, the gendered implications of global relations of domination based on colonial histories and their impacts today deeply inform the types of gendered representations discussed in Chapter 3. Furthermore, as Alhayek (2014) indicates when discussing the Syrian-led RNC campaign, orientalization is a process that people from the Global South can contribute to for their own purposes. As such, alongside other deployments of East/West stereotypes impacting on visibility in social media, 'self-orientalization' must also be a key concern for transnational feminist media studies.

As with the claims of progress discussed in the last chapter, there is a common discourse that these relations are just a matter of our past history, and that we now live in a more hybrid, fluid, open world with great opportunities for cultural exchange. Such **cosmopolitanism** would seem to negate difference and domination, fostering transnational world citizens with equal access to global cultural flows. However, as the examples we have seen so far demonstrate, a cosmopolitan perspective is not equally available to all. It is shaped by privilege related to class and citizenship status, as Calhoun (2003) notes, as well as gender, as argued by Grewal (2005). Rather than a solution to colonial violence, cosmopolitanism is a direct product of these global relations of power and reaffirms certain nations and subjects as progressive with others as backward, provincial, and parochial. Furthermore, in many ways this cosmopolitanism is based on the linkage of democratic citizenship to consumer practices. Grewal (2005), for instance, examines how the purchasing of American cultural products by women in India becomes an expression of empowerment. Indeed, access to media, technologies, and commodities associated with Western life informs many engagements with 'problems' in the Global South.

For example, one dominant method proposed for rectifying global inequalities via access is **ICT4D** (Information and Communications Technologies for Development), an **international development** project aimed at modernizing so-called developing nations by resolving economic disparities through information and communication technologies (ICTs). This approach to global challenges includes addressing what is known as the **digital divide**. The United Nations emphasizes the use of ICTs as an important force in pursuing social and economic equality, and therefore access to these technologies, and correcting disparities between the 'haves' and the 'have nots', are major priorities. Reports indicate that differential access is a reality across the world – less than half the world (48 per cent) has access to the internet according to the UN Broadband Commission for Sustainable Development (2017).

However, there are several issues raised by this approach to dealing with global inequalities, including the actual site of disparities. Despite attention to places like sub-Saharan Africa in ICT4D projects, Western nations including the US (Anderson et al. 2018) as well as the UK and Sweden (Helsper and Reisdorf 2017) are characterized by digital inequality linked to age, race, gender, class, education, and location. Furthermore, as the UN report points out, on a global level internet usage is stratified according to gender, with men outnumbering women in use, a statistic that is perhaps a surprise given the dominant stereotypes about young women using social media to post selfies. Access is also further determined by structures heavily influenced by colonialism and imperialism, including English language literacy and competency, demonstrating the legacy of empire within these sites of ICT4D attention. This legacy is rarely addressed within techno-utopian discourses of technology for good, whether historically (as demonstrated by Fernández 1999) or more recently (for an example, see the UN's focus on big data for sustainable development). The structural features of many less- or non-connected places cannot be addressed by individualized projects such as the One Laptop Per Child initiative – a project led by futurist and digital optimist Nicholas Negroponte which seeks to transform education in developing nations by distributing sturdy, low-cost, hand-cranked computers to children. Rather, we must critically reflect on the origins and ongoing basis for poverty, unreliable infrastructure, and unequal educational opportunities, as well as the unique contexts for diverse sites of disparity, including digital but also educational, economic, and social inequities. Furthermore, the focus on access often overlooks questions of concern regarding the barriers to participation faced by women and girls, including harassment and gender-based exclusion in digital spaces, which we discuss in Chapter 5. Therefore, 'solutions' need to take a more nuanced approach not only to access but also to questions of participation, ownership, and control over production, all of which are shaped by location, age, gender, economic and educational privilege, and ability.

Still, individualistic approaches inform a range of activities focusing specifically on the power of young women to initiate and enact positive social change as noted at the start of this chapter, often within what

Banet-Weiser (2015) refers to as 'girl empowerment organizations'. Here we can see continuities with the depoliticized attention to feminine subjects in postfeminist media cultures and neoliberal ideology discussed in Chapters 1 and 3, perhaps demonstrated most plainly with the UN-backed Project Everyone's remake of the Spice Girls' music video for the song 'Wannabe'. With this initiative, 'girl power' is revisited and harnessed to address UN global goals related to gendered inequalities such as violence against women, child marriage, pay gaps, and access to education. The inclusion of transnational artists, from India, Nigeria, and South Africa, alongside those from the UK, the US, and Canada, and the call for girls and women to contribute ideas for change via the hashtag #WhatIReallyReallyWant, returns us to the theme of female empowerment with a focus not on cosmetic individual differences but on a vision of the universality of what women 'really really want'. This emphasis on girls' empowerment sidesteps the numerous ways these global challenges are embedded in colonial systems of power disproportionately disadvantaging female subjects. As Gajjala and Mamidipudi (1999) note, top-down approaches such as development projects focused on the internet will fail in the pursuit of empowerment unless they support women's self-determination and the creation of spaces of dialogue, coalition-building, transformation, and resistance.

Postcolonial theory is a key field of engagement for feminist media studies, as it is generative of approaches challenging the consumerist and depoliticized concepts associated with cosmopolitanism, empowerment, and development. For example, Bhabha (2004) argues that to transcend ideas about imaginary totalities we should be attuned to **hybridity**. This refers to the interrelations between colonizer and colonized, which result in emergent cultural identities that are neither pure nor a straightforward matter of exchange, given power imbalances and ongoing inequalities. Focusing on hybridity rather than diversity or multiculturalism can be a productive way of thinking about how culture works in the 'in-between' spaces between peoples, groups, and social structures. While this is a contested concept, in her analysis of Latina American pop star and actress Jennifer Lopez, Shugart (2007) concludes that hybridity offers a challenge to Whiteness that popular culture works to contain in order to neutralize its threat, demonstrating its interest to feminist media studies.

In this section we have explored a number of concepts and debates from beyond feminist media studies to inform a transnational approach to our research. Feminist media studies requires an attunement to power, to its historical legacies as well as its contemporary developments, and to the intersections of gender with a range of structural inequalities contextualized in local lived realities and histories. Embracing the complexity of cultural flows, including hybridity, entails rejecting simplistic notions such as 'us' and 'them' while still holding in tension the global relations of power. In the following sections, we will look at debates in transnational feminist critique highlighting two of the challenges faced when engaging in this type of critique from a Western standpoint: saviour discourse and cultural appropriation. These challenges remind us of the importance of considering power when celebrating not only voice and visibility but also notions of freedom, choice, and progress.

Western women as saviours

In 2017, a mobile application developed by a team of five Kenyan high school girls called 'The Restorers' made international news. Supported by a local mentor, they created an app for Technovation's #WorldPitch initiative mentioned at the start of this chapter. The app, called iCut, aims to provide support and tools for young women facing female circumcision, or what is more commonly referred to as female genital mutilation (FGM). The removal of external female genitalia for non-medical reasons – a highly disputed practice conducted mainly by communities in Africa and Asia – has become a global cause of concern, often revolving around arguments put forward by the philosopher Martha Nussbaum (1999, 2000) about choice, the universality of rights, and human capabilities. International feminists frame FGM as a practice of gender control, wherein women's sexuality is curtailed to uphold local cultural values related to feminine modesty and beauty. Since the 1970s the procedure has been the subject of global activism aiming to end the practice and its deleterious impacts on health, well-being, and social status. Some critics argue, however, that this intervention is an example of **cultural relativism**, wherein the traditions and norms of one culture are transposed onto another, which is then judged without attention or value given to differences. Nussbaum (1999) refers plainly to her analyses as 'judging other cultures', and given that feminist approaches are normative about the existence of systems of gender inequality oppressing people and groups, action against practices like FGM that would be illegal in the Western world would seem logical and appropriate.

Transnational feminist media studies, however, must hold in tension the insights of postcolonial theory reviewed in the previous section and reflect on how these conversations and actions related to FGM, or other topics of Western feminist concern, reflect new discourses of 'us' and 'them'. Binaries of primitivism/progress, traditional/enlightened, ignorant/educated are all too familiar from the historical practices of imperialism and colonization. The practices and relations of global domination reviewed above were historically justified largely by an understanding that the territories being occupied and the Indigenous people living within them were undeveloped, uncivilized, and primitive (because their lands were not deemed property or were not farmed in the same way as those in Western European nations). Due to these differences in norms, forced settlement of land and the regulation of Indigenous people were seen as positive and even benevolent actions, enabling 'progress' in accordance with the values of the colonizers. As we will see in this section, such ideas still inform perceptions of the Global South and the need to 'save' women and girls outside of Western contexts, including feminist approaches to working with individuals, groups, and communities therein.

The support of the iCut app by Technovation, which is sponsored by Google, Verizon, and the United Nations, indicates that, at a global level, Western values will inform which kinds of action on gender-based oppression are deemed important. For this reason, despite the central role of young girls in developing this app, it would be worthwhile in a feminist media analysis to examine the strategic and managerial leadership of such projects, as well as their sponsors, in order to understand the complex association of corporate interests, governmental and non-governmental bodies, and grassroots and community groups participating in global gender activism supported by ICTs. Equally pressing is the need to probe why it is that some global issues rather than others – such as domestic violence, workplace sexual harassment, and the negative effects of beauty standards – tend to be highlighted within these global feminist media projects.

The practices criticized within international feminist movements, such as FGM and child marriage, share an emphasis on the victimization of women based on systems of racialised sexual difference and male dominance (Mohanty 1984). In the case of FGM and child marriage, a core feature of the argument is the age of the girls impacted – too young to give consent and therefore unable to make a choice. However, in the case of another contested practice – the wearing of the hijab – we can observe a tension in this logic indicating that age is not the sole determinant in perceptions of a lack of autonomy and agency within international feminist action. Rivers (2017) examines the activism of the European feminist collective Femen, who went topless to protest women wearing the veil in France, a secular society that she notes is more accepting of sexualized women's bodies than of expressions of religious devotion. As she argues, the veil is worn to express modesty, but in a range of mediatized texts the veiled body becomes a symbol to represent submission, docility, and repression. Despite Femen's bold references to 'sextremism' and the 'bravery' of using bare female breasts as a tool of activism, we can see in their organizing a paternalism similar to that of the Western saviour discourses of the White Man's Burden that enabled colonization, only in this case atheism is positioned as the path to liberation. This example also highlights how, in contemporary action, the 'burden' of bringing about progress is spread across White men and women.

Mahmood (2011) notes a tension between feminism, as it has been developed in the West, and discussions of religion, particularly Islam. When discussing women's participation within Islam, the dominant discourse frames it in terms of oppression within a patriarchal system. Mahmood argues that this indicates the rooting of Western feminism within another political system, that of liberalism, which assumes the universal desire to be free from social norms and traditions. **Liberal feminism** attributes agency and empowerment to those who resist local customs, which are framed as universally submissive to male power regardless of history or context. Such a simplistic framing, Mahmood contends, needs to be challenged when discussing gender in global, non-Western, and transnational contexts, and critiqued for its stereotypical framing in a range of Western media. These arguments raise a number of important points for transnational feminist media analysis and critique. Power, agency, choice, and autonomy are complicated ideas, and a rigorous feminist media critique will explore their complexities rather than making simple arguments about oppression and resistance, especially when discussing cultural contexts that differ from that of the critic. Addressing the liberal feminist analysis of Arab Muslim women and their wearing of the veil, Mahmood says that 'agency ... is understood as the capacity to realize one's own interests against the weight of custom, tradition, transcendental will, or other obstacles (whether individual or collective)' (2011: 8) – another instantiation of the emphasis on individual choice that is so common in Western expressions of empowerment.

These frames around women's agency, which universalize desire and a specific vision of freedom as normative, contribute to a politically prescriptive approach that diagnoses non-Western structures and customs as patriarchal, oppressive of women, and necessarily to be resisted. In contrast, Mahmood argues that we need to separate the idea of agency from progressive political work, and see freedom, autonomy, and agency as emerging in context, with a focus on how norms are lived. Mohanty (1984) notes that this includes the meanings and values associated with social structures in context, as well as an attunement to local configurations, ideologies, institutions, and differences based on class, culture, race, ethnicity, and religion.

In sum, a key challenge faced by transnational feminist media studies is that of falling into the seductive trap of framing Western thought as more 'progressive' or 'modern', and Western women as saviours of non-Western women and girls. There are many problems with this viewpoint, including how it frames women living in diverse contexts as unified objects of victimization (Mohanty 1984). These ways of looking at and understanding the relationship between the Global North and the Global South replicate historical patterns of domination, and do not adequately account for the complexity of transnational relations or of local arrangements. Despite the increasing attention paid to girls and women living in the Global South, too often we see a contemporary neo-imperialist framing of feminine subjects in the North as empowered and of those living in the Global South as only to be benefitted by their liberation from patriarchal systems through the rhetoric of a sort of 'missionary girl power' – or what Sensoy and Marshall refer to as 'newly emergent discursive strategies that construct first world girls as the saviours of their "Third World" sisters' (2010: 296).

In contemporary media texts and initiatives, from #WorldPitch to #WhatIReallyReallyWant, we can observe traditional types of paternalistic saviour discourse aligned with girl power, which is linked to both Western subjects enlisted to 'help' non-Western girls and women, and increasingly to girls from the Global South themselves in how they are hailed to conform to Western popular feminist discourses in order 'to break the cycle of backwardness' (Sensoy and Marshall 2010: 301). Missing from these visions, as Dosekun (2015) observes, is both the plurality of women's experiences and the possibility of local feminist practices in the Global South, such as campaigns against gender-based violence and oppression pre-dating Western interventions. Indeed, Spivak (1999) notes that the turn towards young women in the Global South typically serves to highlight their potential and power for social change while displacing feminism as a collective, intergenerational political project. Furthermore, as McRobbie (2009) argues, this creates a disarticulation between women in the West and women in the Global South, setting up barriers to solidarity and political ties across cultures by falsely contrasting the empowerment of White Western women (who are offered the vision of a post-racial society in postfeminist media culture) with those living under ongoing systems of colonial domination (but whose victimization is delimited to sexual constraint).

The media coverage and social media activism that accompanied both the Nigerian #BringBackOurGirls campaign and the shooting, recovery, and educational activism of Malala Yousafzai demonstrate the persistence of this framing. In the case of the kidnapping of 300 schoolgirls by Boko Haram in Nigeria, Loken (2014) argues that the rhetoric of property – 'our girls' – infantilizes these young women and serves to decontextualize the event from its racialized colonial reality. Khoja-Moolji (2015a) finds that the cultural discourses and tropes associated with Yousafzai serve to affirm two universal narratives – that of the oppression of Muslim women by Muslim men, and that of White men (and now women) saving brown women from brown men. Overall, as Mohanty (1984) notes, this dominant approach to stereotyping women and girls from the Global South contributes to the process of Othering by framing them as the objects of victimizing male dominance and of Western saviour work – trends increasingly linked to girl power discourse. As we will see in the next section, this objectification also occurs through consumption practices in media culture, where the Other becomes something to be celebrated, but in a fetishistic manner reminiscent of the male gaze.

'Eating the Other'

In Chapter 3 we reviewed the critiques levied at White US pop star Katy Perry for dressing as a geisha during an awards show performance. This is not the only case of Western celebrities becoming the targets of controversy after being accused of cultural appropriation. Victoria's Secret model Karlie Kloss walking down the runway sporting a Native-American-style headdress and moccasins, musician Selena Gomez including the Hindu bindi as part of her look during a show, and singer Justin Bieber styling his hair into dreadlocks, are all high-profile examples of a practice that has also been defended as a form of cultural appreciation or fusion. The logic of exchange, however, is belied by the asymmetries of power in the cultural contacts between racialized, Indigenous, and colonized groups and those who have historically benefitted from their exploitation in the West. In addition to decontextualizing these varied cultural objects from their traditions and peoples, Kloss, Gomez, Bieber, and other high-profile figures in Western media have been critiqued for using the cultures of others for the purposes of self-expression and garnering a more edgy, hip image, capitalizing on racialized others without addressing the systemic inequalities they face. As Banet-Weiser details in her discussion of Mattel's short-lived Flava doll line, race in a postfeminist context 'is just a flava, a street style, an individual characteristic, and a commercial product' (2007: 202), putting forth a vision of a multicultural society where race no longer matters and can therefore be unproblematically commodified. In this way, the idea that we have moved beyond gendered inequalities has its parallel in a vision of a post-racial world where racism is no longer a problem either.

The (mis)use of hairstyles, garments, accessories, traditions, and symbols from other cultures by Western subjects is a form of what hooks (1992) refers to as 'eating the Other', wherein cultural difference becomes something that can be tried on and discarded by privileged groups, an aesthetic pleasure rather than a part of a meaningful, cultural tradition. These practices are rooted in historical performances of Otherness, including American minstrel shows where White people applied Blackface and circulated stories perpetuating damaging racial stereotypes. There are ongoing debates about the racism of 'dressing up' and performing as a person from another racial group, from Halloween costumes to the Dutch practice of celebrating Christmas by dressing up as Zwarte Piet, or 'Black Pete'. Wekker (2016) argues that claims of 'innocence' in these discussions become a means of obscuring rather than addressing and making restitutions for colonial histories and racist legacies.

Eating, as a synonym for consumption, is deployed more broadly in hooks' critique to refer to the social relations between the most dominant in society and those they have subjugated to establish their power, including racialized groups, Indigenous populations, and peoples from the Global South. As the examples of cultural appropriation in fashion, beauty, and music demonstrate, 'within commodity culture, ethnicity becomes spice, seasoning that can liven up the dull dish that is mainstream White culture' (hooks 1992: 21). In her analysis, hooks considers a range of ways in which the Other becomes constituted as a consumable object, including the persistent sexualization of non-White bodies as exotic and different. As we have seen in the examples from Chapter 3 and earlier in this chapter, this occurs through the stereotypical fetishizing of women of colour's bodies, from the Hot Latina stereotype to the docile, unthreatening Japanese woman to the hypersexualization of Black women's bodies. Racialized women become the locus by which to elevate one's sexual experiences, articulated through fantasies of and desire for 'contact with the Other' (1992: 22) that are fundamental to White supremacy in how it affirms the White, Western, colonizing status quo.

Fashion imagery, as hooks notes, also incorporates racial difference as a way of playing with Otherness – perhaps best exemplified by the advertising of the United Colors of Benetton brand, but increasingly common in fashion and beauty promotional materials. For example, in a controversial 2015 fashion shoot called 'The Migrant', by Hungarian photographer Norbert Baksa, a model is portrayed wearing a headscarf and being detained by a security officer near a fence. Coverage of the negative reception of this campaign highlights the power dynamics that make such portrayals an issue, for example Hungarian law has changed to support militarized force in combating migration (Jackson-Edwards 2015). As hooks also highlights, travel and touristic narratives and images in media culture continue to perpetuate colonial fantasies of the Global South, a trope we can see at play in Taylor Swift's 2014 video for the song 'Wildest Dreams', which features no African people even though the storyline is set on the African continent. Travel romance narratives in films such as *Eat, Pray, Love* and *Under the Tuscan Sun* mobilize stereotyped figures of the Other as objects of support for the enlightenment of the White female leads – women in crisis who 'serve as fantasy ambassadors sent beyond US borders to be schooled in appropriate forms of international relations in an age of imperial politics, advanced consumer capitalism, and anxiety about immigration' (Marston 2016: 4). Within such mediated travel stories, foreign nationality becomes key to White women's empowerment (Negra 2001), further objectifying and homogenizing racialized, Indigenous, and non-Western people. As hooks observes, 'in mass culture, imperialist nostalgia takes the form of reenacting and reritualizing in different ways the imperialist, colonizing journey as narrative fantasy of power and desire, of seduction by the Other' (1992: 25). In this way, media culture romanticizes colonial histories while continuing to contribute to the dehumanization of those this system has dominated.

Whitlock (2007) refers to this as 'the alterity industry', wherein cultural difference is commodified in ways that serve to support Western, capitalist ideologies despite their inclusion of discourses and products from the periphery. In addition to the consumption of the cultures and bodies of non-Western people within media, this is evidenced in the growth in popularity of stories about them, such as the novels about Muslim girls and women analysed by Sensoy and Marshall (2010). Such narratives focus on the poverty of non-Western female subjects in need of rescue, and therefore serve as a consumable pleasure while also grounding the saviour discourse already discussed. In these trends we see how 'the very celebration and recognition of "difference" and "Otherness" may itself conceal more subtle and insidious relations of power' (Morley and Robins 1995: 115).

These examples demonstrate the fundamental inequality within these moments of cultural contact, and how they conform to the discourse of cosmopolitanism rather than the practice of respectful exchange. While they may seem to have moved beyond racist taboos, indicating a greater pluralism, they constitute a form of cultural imperialism in how they follow the logics of extraction, collection, and theft characterizing colonization. As Joseph (2009) points out, post-racial discourse posits that racial inequalities were eradicated by the civil rights movement and that race can therefore become an individual trait rather than an object of structural oppression, enabling justifications of cultural appropriation, among other imperialist actions. Consumption of commodities and mass culture does not require White Westerners to relinquish or even question their privilege, only to enjoy race, ethnicity, and culture as well as the bodies of Others as a source of pleasure, 'constituting an alternative playground where members of dominating races, genders, sexual practices affirm their power-over in intimate relations with the Other' (hooks 1992: 23). As Lazar highlights in her analysis of postfeminist thematics in advertising in Singapore, models from various ethnic backgrounds are often included in order to demonstrate both internationalism and local specificity, indicating a kind of 'a global consumer sisterhood' (2006: 515). This empowerment of the global woman, however, is predicated upon the purchase of consumer goods and conformity to a uniform beauty ideal – slender, symmetrical, able-bodied, and heterosexual, often with whitened or lightened skin tones; 'membership in the global sisterhood of power femininity, therefore, is premised upon certain criteria for inclusion' (Lazar 2006: 515). The cultures and bodies of others become a matter of taste and choice in consumer practices, further objectifying and fetishizing non-Western, Indigenous, and racialized peoples.

Transnational feminist media studies must be attuned to the prevalence of such discourses and images, especially given the temptation to claim, as discussed in Chapter 3, that the increased representation of women in all their diversity within media cultures is a positive sign of greater inclusion and progress. As hooks argues, taking pleasure in racial difference by turning cultures into items for selection from a figurative menu is not adequate cultural contact. Instead, contact between the dominated and the dominant requires a recognition of the history and presence of White supremacy and its relations of power. 'Mutual recognition of racism ... is the only standpoint that makes possible an encounter between races that is not based on denial and fantasy' (1992: 28). Approaches that further serve to universalize, decontextualize, dehumanize, and essentialize women from other transnational contexts will fail to meet this standard. In the next section, we consider alternatives and future directions that aim for this mutual recognition.

Future directions for decolonizing feminist media studies

In this chapter we have seen several ways in which colonial legacies shape the objects, subjects, and approaches of feminist media studies, demonstrating how women's bodies and subjectivities become a site of negotiation of global difference (Shome 2006). In this final section we consider work that, by introducing a decolonizing approach, challenges these inequitable systems of power and how they inform the field. Such a project aims to undo the impacts of colonialism on ways of knowing, assessing, seeing, and theorizing the media from a feminist perspective. Decolonization refers to the reclamation of spaces and institutions that have been colonized or created by colonizing forces. As we have seen throughout this chapter, decolonizing research, teaching, the classroom, and our own minds is an equally important part of this project, as we are all impacted by global histories of domination and their effects today, and need to actively engage in action supporting liberation, self-determination, and reclamation. Feminist theory, including in its application to the study of the media, popular culture, and communication processes and technologies, has a role to play in challenging epistemic violence, putting an end to the silencing and erasure of the work being done by those who have been marginalized, and reclaiming Indigenous ways of knowing (Tuhiwai Smith 2012).

One important technique within the project of decolonization is the consideration of our **citational politics**. This entails examining which thinkers tend to feature in our reading lists, syllabi, and bibliographies, and what we have normalized within our disciplines and fields as legitimate approaches to critique. Student-led campaigns seeking to decolonize university curricula demonstrate a growing recognition of how the canons of many disciplines and fields are 'male, stale, and pale' (Woolcock 2017), delegating the authority to speak about the world to a narrow group of individuals privileged under White supremacist colonial patriarchy. As feminist media scholars, who we cite is a deeply political question, and an important step in decolonizing our work is to research broadly, read more widely, and cite voices and perspectives marginalized in knowledge production. That marginalization has often included overlooking or erasing the existence of feminist thought within other fields (Ahmed 2013), but in pursuing feminist media studies we might think of how we can be more inclusive and supportive of Indigenous and native liberation from colonial thinking in our research, and indeed draw on the scholarship of Indigenous thinkers themselves. This does not mean simply adding more racialized thinkers to our bibliographies and carrying on as usual; decolonizing feminist media studies entails rethinking the normative frames we bring to the field, including the colonial legacies of racial power (Chakravartty et al. 2018). Mott and Cockayne urge 'a conscientious engagement with the politics of citation that is mindful of how citational practices can be tools for either the reification of, or resistance to, unethical hierarchies of knowledge' (2017: 956), demonstrating the centrality of citation politics in feminist media studies' attunement to power and ethics.

Another tactic for decolonizing feminist media studies is to resist any simplification in our engagement with difference from our own situated perspectives, including seemingly positive narratives such as the power of the 'Third World Girl' to save the world. In her 2009 TED Talk, the novelist Chimamanda Ngozi Adichie discusses 'The Danger of a Single Story', both in terms of those we tell and those that are told about people from the Global South. She recalls how, as a child growing up in Nigeria, she only read stories about White children with blue eyes playing in the snow, and how when she began to write these were also the stories she told, because they were the only ones she knew. When she went to university in the US, her roommate also thought she knew Adichie's story – one to be pitied, one that she assumed to be wholly different from her own and what she recognized as common humanity. As Adichie argues, 'flattening experiences' into single stories – typically those of poverty, victimization, suffering, and catastrophe, which are not necessarily untrue but are truly incomplete – contributes to the stereotyping and dehumanization of those we do not see as like ourselves. This echoes Lorde's point about intersectionality and how we do not 'live single-issue lives' (1984: 138), requiring of our feminist media analysis an attention to the complexity and multiplicity of experience. *How in our critique can we capture both our shared humanity and the contextual and paradoxical factors shaping situated experiences?*

One answer can be found in Dosekun's analysis of the postfeminist logic operating among the women she researched in Lagos, Nigeria. She did not simply conclude that postfeminism is universal nor that the expression of this media culture is experienced identically in Lagos as it is, for example, in the UK. Instead, she found that only those with a great deal of capital, be it material, discursive, or imaginative, are able to buy into postfeminism, and that postfeminist logics come before feminism for some women in her site of study. As this demonstrates, transnational postfeminism 'engenders contextual and contradictory, localized, and hybrid interpretations, as well as new cultural formations and subject positions' (Dosekun 2015: 966), presenting a complex and nuanced picture of gendered media culture and participation in this context.

A further strategy for decolonizing feminist media studies is informed by Projansky's (2014) call for the field to look beyond and challenge 'dominant' representational norms, particularly those emphasizing White and Western women and girls, and to research media texts outside of this regime. This can highlight differential configurations of gendered media relations, as for example in Reddy's (2006) analysis of the discursive framings of 'the body beautiful' in the South Asian magazine *Femina*, and how they link to hybridized valuations of nationalism and globalization. Similarly, Parameswaran (2004) notes a blending of tradition and modernity rooted in class relations that frame representations of Indian beauty queens in the print media. Broadening the scope of our analysis in this way enables a better understanding of postfeminist and post-racial media culture and its operation in transnational contexts marked by unique configurations of gendered relations. This includes differences in the relations between men and women, as in Gwynne's (2013) analysis of male-authored Japanese manga. A transnational view also enables an understanding of how the dominance of Western values and global capitalism is reified in the context of China, as Chen (2012) demonstrates in her discussion of chick lit. As these examples highlight, the representational regimes discussed in Chapter 3 are contextually unique and require critical attention to understand how they flow and are deterritorialized in potentially hybrid ways.

Decolonizing feminist media studies, however, entails not only looking at texts produced outside the Western world but also examining the constitutive feature of Whiteness in the texts we commonly study. As Springer notes, it is a common conclusion that postfeminist media culture is a racialized representational and discursive regime, but 'the analysis seems to stop there' (2007: 249). A decolonized feminist media studies seeks to widen the focus of its research, recognizing and examining the racial privilege of White characters and the impact of both the presence and absence of people of colour in media culture, and challenging the framing of Whiteness and Western-ness as neutral and default. Our task further includes countering the marginalization of women in some types of analysis. For instance, while women and girls are placed at the centre of some narratives, as described above, in others they are notably absent. Take the example of the 'Arab Spring' uprisings in 2010 and the #BlackLivesMatter activism in response to the acquittal of George Zimmerman for the murder of Black teenager Trayvon Martin in 2012. The role of girls and women in these actions has been under-reported, leading in the case of Black Lives Matter to the use of the #SayHerName hashtag to highlight violence against Black women and to challenge its invisibility in the media coverage. Decolonizing our work includes delving deeper into cases where visibility is uneven, challenging the totalizing and repetitive narratives applied to women and girls the world over. Our task is not to 'give voice' – as though non-Western and Indigenous people never spoke before and speech were a gift to be bestowed by the privileged – but to actively combat the erasure, silencing, and marginalization of voices within structures of gendered and racialized settler colonialism (Mohanty 1984), recognizing the knowledge, insight, and perspectives that were always present but actively hidden, including by feminist scholars, within Western discourse.

These cautions are not simply reserved for the analysis of media representations, as audiences and producers are also shaped by global flows of capital. As Parameswaran (2013) argues, audience studies research needs to be undertaken with an eye to the relationship between global media and systems of power wrought by colonialism, imperialism, hybridity, and the interplay of nationalism, gender, and class. As Cavalcante et al. note, 'transnational audience research can illuminate the gendered dimensions of globalizing media networks at the same time as posing methodological challenges that illuminate structures of power that underpin local customs' (2017: 7). All of this points to the care and consideration required of a transnational feminist media studies as well as to the necessity of undertaking such examinations across different objects of analysis.

Ozkazanc-Pan asks, "'for whom do 'we' produce knowledge?" and – "what are the consequences of such claims of knowledge?"' (2012: 582). As the good intentions of feminist saviourhood demonstrate, it is vital that we reflect on the risks of taking a paternalistic approach in our media critique, particularly in defining priorities for others (Amos and Parmar 1984). Mohanty (1984) notes that a common methodological pitfall in feminist scholarship is to adopt an additive approach, taking a wide range of examples of a practice as evidence of its universality, without considering historical, material, and other contextual factors shaping the meaning and value attached to the act. The universalizing of the lives of women in the Global South acts to discursively colonize their lived realities, and feminist scholarship is therefore not apolitical, value-free, or innocent of global systems of power. To cultivate a methodology attuned to heterogeneity and power relations, we need to return to the principles of a feminist ethics of care and in particular the tenet of reflexivity discussed in Chapter 2.

Decolonizing approaches to feminist theory and media studies must address Spivak's (1988) critique of epistemic violence and its legacies today, and pay greater attention to the critical, creative, and activist work undertaken by diverse women in a range of transnational contexts. As Anzaldúa (2015) writes, women of colour face a number of dangers and barriers in writing, but self-expression is a method by which to challenge dominant power and its oppressions, combat complacency, and foster solidarity within feminist movements. In alignment with this, the documentary filmmaker Aishah Shahidah Simmons (2002) posits that creative expression and media-making help to heal wounds, combat racism, sexism, misogyny, classism, homophobia, and sexual violence, and challenge the silencing and stereotyping of Black women's histories. Bailey (2016) affirms that for trans and queer people of colour, independent digital media-making enables the creation of health resources and support for communities marginalized within existing medical systems. Films like Abeer Zeibak Hadad's *Women of Freedom* and Eylem Atakav's *Growing Up Married* centre the voices of women, challenging the common single stories of victimization, suffering, and saviourhood reviewed above. These examples demonstrate the necessity within a transnational feminist media studies of considering not only how women consume media and are represented but also the media-making practices of diverse women around the world.

Furthermore, we need to investigate the national policies and laws shaping media and communication and feminist action alike. For example, in China, media are highly controlled, and censorship of the internet is a lived reality for those using social media such as Sina Weibo and WeChat. Feminism is a highly contentious and politicized topic here, as demonstrated by the arrest of the so-called Feminist Five in 2015 for protesting gender-based violence and inequalities such as the differential treating of unmarried women over the age of twenty-seven as 'leftover women' (Hong Fincher 2018), and by the closure of the Feminist Voices online forums in early 2018. In China, then, the expression of feminist sentiments has a distinctly different resonance than in North America. The well-known #MeToo hashtag campaign has been very popular in China, but its origins, key figures, digital technologies of sharing, and cultural response are very different from the American context in which it originated. The hashtag is associated in China with the sexual harassment of a student by her professor and with abuses of power in the university more generally. When the social media site Weibo blocked the use of the hashtag after it grew popular, users began using #RiceBunny and images of rice bowls and bunny faces as a workaround. When spoken out loud, the words rice bunny sound like 'mi tu', allowing for ongoing public debate despite monitoring, censorship, and incarceration – practices that do not mirror the realities of #MeToo activism in other places. As Zeng (2018) writes: 'it is naive to expect women in China to follow a Western trajectory to achieve gender equality. But as the #RiceBunny hashtag on social media shows, even under political pressure activists continue to use their creativity to circumvent the system.' As this example reveals, while topics of interest related to media and gender are global in scope, significant institutional and cultural factors need to be analysed in transnational feminist media studies.

The ways in which different media are implicated in global histories of (neo-)imperialism and (neo-)colonialism will shape the questions we can ask about visibility and voice. For example, in their analysis of the newspaper coverage of two high-profile cases of rape in 2012 – of young female students in New Delhi, India, and in Steubenville, US – Patil and Purkayastha (2015) argue that the differences in visibility in these cases can be traced to the colonial histories of the newspaper as a media form as well as to neo-colonial discourses of modernity versus tradition in relation to gender. Historically, newspapers are linked to the formation and reinforcement of societal and national values; in the era of globalization they are shaped by power relations between the Global South and the Global North, with a great deal of content generated by Western nations, resulting in negative or non-existent coverage of non-Western nations. In their content and discourse analysis of the *New York Times* and the *Times of India* reports on the two rape cases, Patil and Purkayastha find that the US coverage of the New Delhi rape emphasizes rape culture and broader issues of gender-based discrimination in India, portraying this as an issue of 'incomplete modernity' (2015: 608), while the Indian newspaper focuses on protests and other responses to the tragedy. In regard to the Steubenville rape, the *New York Times* limits the context to local football culture, in contrast to the national framing it takes in reporting on the New Delhi case – a scaling down that serves to frame the US as a place where violence against women is an outlier phenomenon, unlike in 'disordered' places such as India. In contrast, the *Times of India*'s reporting on the Steubenville case draws parallels between the two cases, with no hierarchizing of them or of rape culture in either country. Patil and Purkayastha's analysis thus demonstrates the centrally important role played by transnationalism in questions of visibility and the framing of media coverage. As they argue, these differences in reporting cannot be divorced from 'larger histories of colonialism, imperialism and neo-colonialism which have produced a civilizational narrative in which states in the Global North are always and inevitably further along on the scale of progress regarding democracy, freedom, and gender and sexual equality compared to states in the Global South' (2015: 611). For this reason, transnational media analysis must consider the interplay of nationalisms, feminisms, and histories in shaping visibility. Understanding these relations will help us to better understand how moments of violence against women and girls may (or may not) enable new forms of solidarity by linking global issues (see Keller and Ryan 2018).

As the insights and examples considered throughout this chapter demonstrate, the purpose of transnational feminist media studies is not simply to replicate approaches or confirm the existence of particular formations such as postfeminism or femininized consumer culture across different contexts. Thinking transnationally entails exploring how gender is framed, configured, and disciplined in particular ways shaped by these contexts.

It means considering how identities become visible and what remains invisible (Hegde 2011), and how these figurations intersect with axes of power according to nationality, migration status, and religion, as well as specific relations of race, sexuality, and class in each locale. This chapter has mapped the concepts and the pitfalls to consider when engaging in this work and demonstrated how a transnational perspective and decolonizing approaches to feminist media studies are essential to the field's future. Our challenge is to 'actively seek alliances in which differences are respected and issues of land and tribal belonging are not erased in order to create solidarity, but rather, relationships to settler colonialism are acknowledged as issues that are critical to social justice and political work that must be addressed' (Arvin et al. 2013: 19). In the next chapter, we consider how solidarity may be supported as well as challenged by an increasingly digital global media landscape, raising new questions about activism, resistance, and visibility.

5   Feminist Digital Media Studies

Throughout this book, we have considered issues and challenges for feminist media studies across a range of forms, including digital media, the umbrella term used to refer to computationally enabled technologies and platforms, from mobile phones to streaming services to video games to social media. This chapter drills down into the implications of the growth of digital media for the field, considering issues that arise based on shifts in how some parts of the world interact with media as well as in how we envision the power of these forms for resistance, action, and change. For some readers, digital media will have been a part of their lives for as long as they can remember. Or perhaps you fall into the group of people who can remember when digital media began to grow and spread. As noted in Chapter 4, there is also a large, geographically dispersed set of people for whom digital media is not an everyday reality because of an absence of reliable infrastructures to support universal access. In each case, it is very common for discourse to deploy hyperbolically positive or negative terms about digital media, referring to sweeping changes and the broad implications of these 'new' media for communication, education, information-seeking, and socialization, as well as matters of public concern, from 'fake news' to access to porn to increased narcissism and anti-social behaviour. Our so-called digital life is characterized by heightened rhetoric about the power of social media, the sharing economy, and the rise of the network society, as well as concerns about online hate and harassment, surveillance capitalism, and data discrimination, among other social blessings and ills. As we will see in this chapter, these promises and problems are shaped by pre-existing power dynamics and are experienced differently depending on gender and its intersections with race, class, and age.

Broad claims of societal change and threats to the moral order have accompanied new mediated forms across history, from the creation of the alphabet to the printing press, up to and including the rise of the radio, the television, video games, and the internet (Baym 2010). Each new form of communication enables not only a unique means of reaching out, but also plays a role in the reorganization of our social lives (see for example Williams' (1974) analysis of the rise of television). Digital media such as mobile phones and social media are only the most recent additions in a long history of humans either fantasizing or being concerned about the social impact of emerging communication technologies on their lives. Media that are at one time new become habitual, embedded in and structuring parts of our everyday lives until the next update (Chun 2016). Therefore, it is important that we do not overstate what is new or different when we analyse digital media, and that we resist the urge to argue that shifts or changes are either wholly positive or negative. We socialized, communicated, watched, shared, protested, argued, and played well before the spread of what we call digital media, and there are often concepts and perspectives from research on the histories of other mediated, cultural, and social forms that can help us to understand these practices rather than assuming they are wholly unique, different, or transformative. Contrary to hyperbolic claims about digital revolutions and ubiquitous usage, access to new and networked media remains limited, uneven, and stratified on a global level, and therefore gendered encounters with these technologies and platforms are not universal.

While fetishizing the 'new' in media and communication is a historical trend, as feminist media scholars our task is to be critically attuned to the continuities of the interactions between media and culture as well as the unique features and elements of each form, including those of digital media, as we will focus on in this chapter. The digitization of media has created the grounds for a range of new practices, opportunities, technologies, and environments, with specific impacts on gendered, racialized, and otherwise marked bodies and subjectivities depending on location. For this reason, the rise of digital culture requires the analysis of media forms, activities, and opportunities in their unique contexts, as well as how these can enable the visibility and circulation of gendered ideas and feminist and antifeminist voices, as we will discuss below. This chapter therefore highlights the continuities of our digital lives with the ongoing challenges presented by visibility and voice discussed throughout this book, showcasing how emerging media may deepen and contribute to inequalities for marginalized people as well as create opportunities for resistance and subversion for those with access. To do so, we begin with an overview of the foundational questions, concepts, and debates relevant to feminist digital media studies, contributing insights drawn from feminist analysis of the gendering of technology, the history of the internet, and science and technology studies. We then turn to two active areas of feminist media research – hashtag activism and selfies – which encapsulate both long-standing and emerging matters of theoretical and methodological concern for the field in relation to visibility, power, and resistance. The chapter concludes by examining feminist action based on digital media and mapping intersectionally focused alternatives and interventions in the field.

Gendering technology

As soon as the internet was launched for commercial use in the West, enabling communication for those beyond the military and elite education contexts in which it was developed, scholars raised questions about the relationship between information and communication technologies (ICTs) and gender, race, and class (Gajjala 2004; Nakamura 2002a; Shade 2002; Stone 1994). These analyses were informed by an extensive array of previous research showing that technologies have been differently associated with identity, contributing to uneven power dynamics in gendered systems of oppression. Consider the user that comes to mind when you think of the following technologies: washing machines; video games; 3D printers; stilettos. Ponder also what these technologies are associated with – the public sphere or the domestic realm? 'Active' production or 'passive' consumption? While these technologies are not based on particular biological attributes associated with a person's sex, they and others have an entangled relationship with gendered and otherwise embodied subjectivities, contributing to some familiar tropes such as the female housewife and the White male scientist. Stereotypes and common discourse do not necessarily reflect actual use, practice, engagement, expertise, or interest, as we will see, but they contribute to the cultures of particular digital media and can therefore shape participation in important ways. Technological forms contribute to the construction, performance, and disciplining of gendered subjectivity and its intersections through their development, deployment, and socialization. The work of Cockburn (1988), Cowan (1985), de Lauretis (1987), and Wajcman (1991), among others, provides nuanced analyses of how, contrary to the visions of depoliticized yet progressive technological change ushered in by new forms such as the internet, technological artefacts and systems are socially shaped and in turn play a role in shaping society, with gendered repercussions.

In the case of the internet, its basic infrastructure was developed within institutions characterized as sites for the production and reification of masculinity, control, and mastery over technology, contributing to its ideological values as well as how it is designed, promoted, institutionalized, and regulated. These sites include technology companies, military institutions, and university laboratories, all historically dominated by men. Furthermore, networked communication systems are run on programming languages requiring the hard mastery skills traditionally associated with masculine identity, including planning, logic, technical ability, and abstract thinking. As Edwards (2003) notes, in Western ideology, soft mastery (interaction, intuition, and creativity) has been linked to women's skills in nursing and child care while hard mastery is allied to computers, sciences, and men, relations reinforced in the popular media as well as in scientific journals, textbooks, and conferences. Such stereotypes do not reflect the realities of female participation in these practices, as indicated by the erasure of women from histories of game development and circuitry discussed in previous chapters. However, the embedding of hard mastery in the language and systems of the microworlds of the computer, as well as in artificial intelligence and simulation research, has meant that tools for the creation and modification of tech have been culturally framed as the appropriate domain of male subjects. Indeed, computing and its standards of dispassionate, context-independent, logic-oriented work have become a master trope in the construction of gender and technoscience. Narratives about the development of computers, networks, and the internet highlight men upheld as paragons of technophilia – emotionally isolated, competitive, rational, and seeking control – akin to contemporary stereotypes of hackers, hardcore gamers, and Silicon Valley engineers and programmers (Turkle 1984).

Consequently, stereotypical notions of feminine technophobia due to the association of hard mastery skills with masculinities have informed how we use computers from the earliest days of its domestication (Lupton 2000) to today. Companies address anxieties about computer technologies by personalizing software and hardware with characters such as Microsoft Word's animated paperclip character 'Clippy'. The conception of the mechanics and look of computers as 'scary' to female consumers, in particular, shapes the marketing of devices inscribed with human values such as friendliness, as for example in the feminized marketing of the Google Home Mini smart speaker, with its cosy fabric mesh design and references to it being 'donut-sized' (Gregg 2018). Technology is not only marketed using gender-based tropes but designed with gender in mind.

This does not, however, mean that we must think of digital media technologies as deterministically sexist, racist, or unequal, but that we should consider how they are shaped by historical social forces that can contribute to inequalities. Consider for instance how computing, like other technical pursuits in the sciences, engineering, and mathematics, has been associated with the masculinized stereotype of the nerd, along with the male-gendered subject positions of hacker, gamer, and geek. Kendall's (2011) examination of media forms including music videos, advertising, and corporate websites indicates that gender as well as race continue to shape this trope, linking computer proficiency to Whiteness and marginalized masculinities. Historical analyses by Abbate (2012),

Ensmenger (2010), and Hicks (2017) demonstrate that, contrary to these hegemonic narratives, a large number of women played a significant role in the development of computing, including the hardware and software forming the basis of our contemporary digital media and networked communication. We can see the erasure of women's participation from the history of computing, in tandem with its growing cultural, economic, and political significance, as part of how this technology has been gendered, a dynamic process normalizing and naturalizing the idea that masculinity is linked to the realm of technical ability and production, whereas femininity is more passive, emotional, and oriented towards consumption. These notions about women's abilities and interests continue to inform initiatives designed to encourage more women into technological education and careers, often with the presumption that they require special individualized incentives to do so, rather than recognizing how they may be deterred by historical and ongoing structural exclusions.

Engendering the internet

How technologies are gendered and otherwise stratified by race, class, location, age, and ability requires an analysis of the social histories of technological developments and the actors, institutions, and industries that contribute to them. Consider the early history of the internet, a time when access was dependent on a phone line and a modem, and limited to a very small number of people in the Western world. As with all new media and technologies, the internet was described in the early days of its introduction to consumer markets using vivid metaphorical images: as an 'information superhighway' or 'cyberspace' that users could 'surf', passing through 'gateways' and 'portals' if they were not blocked by 'firewalls'. As these examples highlight, spatial visions of what was rather abstract and complicated provided a way of grounding the internet in familiar ideas and images. The use of recognizable tropes and practices when introducing new communication technologies is common practice; reflect on how artificial intelligence agents such as Siri and Alexa are humanized and designed to speak with a female voice, or how we engage in computing in 'the cloud', an image much more accessible than that of the enormous, fortress-like data servers in often remote locations. Of interest is how these metaphors and tropes become linked to the kinds of fantasies and anxieties we associate with 'new' media, and how they can obscure the processes, actors, and stakeholders involved, as well as important questions about the consequences and impacts of digital media. In her analysis of the materiality of seemingly immaterial cloud-based data, including wireless technologies and data centres, Hogan draws attention to the environmental and gendered consequences of processes of digitization and datafication that often go undiscussed, highlighting the implications for surveillance and labour and asking the important questions: 'just what are we progressing towards, and to whose benefit?' (2018: n.p.). As this indicates, metaphors and myths about ICTs and their uses often serve to hide more than they reveal; it is therefore important for feminist media studies to critically examine how they may contribute to or potentially subvert unequal relations of power.

Looking at the early days of the internet's formation provides insight into how the use of metaphors to express large-scale change and ideological beliefs have long-lasting repercussions. Mosco and Foster (2001) analyse how discourse, funding, and policy-making in relation to the internet were shaped by political and commercial actors invested in spreading the vision that this communication technology would usher in the end of traditional institutions and ways of being. From this **techno-utopian** perspective, the internet's structure as a non-hierarchical web of connections rather than a top-down chain of command and control would enable greater individual freedoms, creating a break with historically tiered systems such as government, religion, corporations, family, as well as the social limitations imposed by embodied differences such as gender and race. It would therefore bring about an end to racism, sexism, and other forms of discrimination by bypassing the body entirely. In this positive vision of change based on technological development, networked communication enables barrier-free access to information and self-sufficiency, spreading power across networks rather than solidifying it at the top of a vertical structure as has been the historical norm (with kings, patriarchs, CEOs, presidents and other powerful heads). The end result promised by this reorganization is absolute freedom, a compelling promise for those who have been relatively powerless and oppressed in hegemonic social, political, and economic structures. This blue-sky vision of radical societal transformation ushered in by the possibilities of networked communications became the subject of a range of manifestos and documents calling for widespread change.

Such possibilities informed the early thought of **cyberfeminism**, most notably Sadie Plant's *Zeroes and Ones* (1998), which proposes a sexual revolution based on networked computing. Plant argues against hegemonic masculine cultures of computing and posits an affinity between women and computers. As evidence, she points to the work of the programmer Ada Lovelace and the homosexual artificial intelligence scientist Alan Turing in the development of the technologies underlying the internet.

As with the Indigenous women building electronic circuits discussed in Chapter 4, and the contributions of female media workers discussed in the next chapter, this participation has been obscured in histories of computing and has required the kinds of feminist historical action outlined in Chapter 2 to make it visible. Utopianism about the possibilities afforded by new networked communication technologies is also present in Haraway's influential text 'A Cyborg Manifesto' (1991), a playful invocation of the human-machine figure of the cyborg as a means of de-essentializing gender and other dichotomous associations made in relationship to technology on a global level.

Yet, a number of considerations for feminist media scholars arise from even the most seductive visions of the digitally mediated future. While it may be very attractive to imagine the possibility of escape from the bodies, institutions, and geographies that lead to oppression, we must also critically consider the actors promoting these visions of change, and how they propose to actualize them. What kinds of values are espoused and which become less visible are clearly matters of concern when considering the promises and pitfalls of digital life. This is particularly relevant to feminist media studies if we consider which people, groups, and communities are implicated, consulted, marginalized, and silenced in these discourses. As we saw in Chapters 1 and 4, terms such as freedom are ideologically loaded and can be enacted in a range of ways, which means that the kinds of equalities and freedoms promised by early internet proponents need to be examined in depth.

We might also scrutinize how these promises and beliefs – what we might understand as myths of digital media – envision historical social structures and relations of power, especially given how technology is so closely entangled with ideological notions of progress and civilization that facilitate practices of colonialism and imperialism, as we saw in Chapter 4. Such legacies inform technological expansion to this day, exemplified by the neo-colonialism of Facebook's 'global community' (Shepherd 2017). As Mosco and Foster (2001) note, when examining such myths in communication the point is not to prove that they are falsehoods but rather to trace how such stories allow us to make meaning despite contradictions between events, influences, effects, motivations, and outcomes in the world. Our feminist critique must focus on how myths about digital media and communication, such as the claim that they will free us from gender- and race-based inequalities, become a form of 'congealed common sense' (Mosco and Foster 2001: 219), depoliticizing our discussions of these forms and naturalizing certain relations between social actors, their actions, and the dynamics of power.

Early internet myths

In terms of the internet, this includes examining how key actors such as technology companies participate in lobbying against the regulation of their activities through arguments about electronic freedom. From AT&T's 2017 Statement on Internet Freedom to Google's claim that 'a free and open world depends on a free and open Internet', tech companies demonstrate a clear interest in 'freedom'. Freedom from what, for whom, and to what ends are questions for researchers to consider. Mobilizations for freedom from regulation have historically played a shaping role in practices that are normalized today, including the relatively weak legal oversight of communication on online platforms (Citron 2016) and the widespread network surveillance of users (Andrejevic 2007). Digitally enabled harassment with relatively few mechanisms for protecting oneself is but one example of the consequences of this lack of regulation.

Despite the promise of redistributing power and creating new individual freedoms, power tends to coalesce anew around particular groups and organizations who then play a key role in articulating and circulating myths about the internet. Consider the 1994 manifesto written by the Progress and Freedom Foundation (PFF) entitled 'Cyberspace and the American Dream: A Magna Carta for the Knowledge Age', which promised that power would be redistributed amongst individuals via ICTs, shifting away from monolithic institutions towards a newly revived public life premised on virtual spaces and interests no longer limited by traditional institutions, politics, and social relations. However, rather than a liberation from social exclusions, the kind of the freedom articulated in this document more closely resembles neoliberalism's emphasis on entrepreneurialism: the PFF advocates for reforms of government regulation to facilitate a more friction-free relationship between ICTs and capitalism (Mosco and Foster 2001). The emphasis therefore is on supporting capitalist aims rather than an orientation towards social justice.

The PFF was comprised of powerful interests, including the chair of the Internet Corporation for Assigned Names and Numbers (ICANN) and board members of tech companies, and was financially supported by organizations with vested interests, including AT&T, IBM, AOL, Microsoft, and Netscape. The 'freedom' celebrated and sought by these social actors is thus specifically one found in self-government and the privatization of public life, culture, politics, and economics, with technological code the only needed regulatory force. The internet is framed as a natural friend of liberal democracy precisely because of its networked structure, with equality and freedom supposed to follow naturally from this design. As we will see throughout this chapter, a **technologically deterministic** approach promises that technology will drive equality. This is belied, however, by the myriad ways in which technical features of the internet contribute directly to exclusions, in part based on the commercialization of networked ICTs and the ways that interactions of all sorts, including harassment, are profitable for platform owners (Shepherd et al. 2015). In other words, the freedom and equality promoted so heavily in internet history is not available to all, and can lead directly to inequalities for women and girls.

Another manifesto, 'A Declaration of the Independence of Cyberspace', written by Electronic Freedom Foundation (EFF) founder John Perry Barlow in 1996, highlights early myths about the power of the internet's decentralization and its impacts on gendered subjectivities even more explicitly. Barlow proclaims that the internet is 'the new home of the mind ... not where bodies live'. This idea of fundamental differences between online and offline life has informed ideas about divisions between 'the virtual world' and 'real life' for two decades, despite their ever-increasing interconnectedness and mutual influence. For example, in his research on MySpace, chat sites, YouPorn, and Dutch blogs, van Doorn finds that 'users mobilize the socio-technical possibilities of these platforms to reinforce, rather than experiment with, established boundaries that designate the "appropriate" place for bodies and technologies, leaving the changing conditions of embodied gender and sexuality largely uncomplicated' (2011: 583). Despite these continuities and connections, the myth that subjectivities are wholly reinvented online, rather than extended in actions there, still persists. This articulation of the separation of the mind and the body resembles the stereotypes previously discussed linking masculinity to rationality and logic and femininity to the embodied, natural world. In Barlow's vision, progress and civilization is associated with those who can opt to leave behind their bodies (no mention is made of those who do have the access to this possibility). His vision of the utopian internet values a realm where matter does not matter, where all voices can be heard and all sentiments can be expressed, and where the only ethical regulation is the **Golden Rule**. This refers to the moral principle according to which one must treat others as one would like to be treated, an approach that emphasizes self-regulation and that intentionally avoids making a clear statement about how people are expected to behave because it assumes altruism across all participants. In practice, however, it also legitimates the sending of sexist, racist, and homophobic slurs to others by people who claim not to be bothered if such abusive comments are sent to them.

Visons of online-offline divides and the possibility of shedding the body pervade popular culture, not only in science fiction films but also in everyday discourse. This is best exemplified by the widely shared cartoon published in *The New Yorker* in 1993, in which a canine at its desktop computer tells another pooch: 'on the Internet, nobody knows you're a dog'. The reference here is to how the early internet was primarily text-based, with users of chat rooms and other virtual communities describing themselves in ways that could range from the honest to the exaggerated to the outright fictional. Nakamura (2002b) explores the promises of identity play and bodily escape by examining the text-based virtual world LambdaMOO. She finds that the promise of the free performance of identity online often translates into heavily stereotyped representations of gender and race, with users performing as sexualized geishas and 'exotic' samurai. Through this tokenization, Othering, and co-opting of racialized and gendered identities, the affordances of the online community allow its White male users to engage in **identity tourism**. This is a performance aligned with the colonial fantasies of cultural appropriation, where users play with and therefore reify the idea of the exotic Other. Dibbell's (1993) report on 'A Rape in Cyberspace' revealed how the manipulation of LambdaMOO's affordances, involving a contested but possible use of the site's features, allowed one user to render another's avatar unusable and then inflict sexual violence upon her while she was immobilized. These examples demonstrate how the body continues to matter online, while reflecting ongoing inequalities related to gendered and racial privilege.

As these analyses demonstrate, gender- and race-based violence and discrimination have been a feature of networking communication from the earliest days of the internet. From a feminist media studies perspective, it is pertinent that the mythic nature of the internet is characterized by visions of freedom from identity and context, and centres on the valuation of equality rather than justice. However, the routes to this freedom are determined by particular groups with pre-existing social power in terms of gender, race, and class privilege in particular. Furthermore, these freedoms are premised on capitalist forces rather than on social change, ignoring the existing power asymmetries that may inform one's experience online, or indeed whether one can access such experiences at all.

Feminist critique of online 'freedom'

Feminist media scholars delineate how such definitions of freedom, extended in other forms of mediated discourse about the internet including advertising and policy documents, have unique consequences for oppressed groups. For example, Hobson (2008) demonstrates how discourses framing the internet and digital media as the cure for social problems, and access and digital divides as the main social justice concerns, are premised on racialized and gendered assumptions about technological advancement. As with the colonial discourse discussed in the previous chapter, progress related to technology is associated with masculine, White, and middle-class identities, while paradoxically indicating that networked communications can create a social world where these markers become meaningless. Hobson quotes Fusco, who notes that the erasure of the concerns of identity politics in internet discourse conveys the message that '"we" don't need to be concerned with the violent exercise of power on bodies and territories anymore because "we" don't have to carry all that meat and dirt along to the virtual promised land' (2001: 188). Fusco's emphasis on a universal subject – 'we' – indicates how such visions of freedom are articulated without reference to ongoing effects of structural and historical inequalities shaping both access and experiences in these spaces. A further contradiction within this myth lies in how, despite the supposed egalitarianism of the internet, people of colour are framed transnationally in digital culture as outsiders, a norm that Hobson highlights is being challenged by artists, bloggers, and other women of colour engaging with digital technologies.

In *Digitizing Race*, Nakamura (2008) details how early policy discourse about the internet in the US was premised on the vision that this digital media environment would be colour-blind and non-discriminatory, a perspective that she argues overlooks both the ways that educational and class privilege shape access as well as how the internet as a textual and then increasingly audio-visual environment represents race and gender, in avatars, advertising, and memes for example. For instance, in the advertising for the internet she analysed, the Other is used as an image to represent cyberspace as a 'technological utopia of difference' (Nakamura 2000: 25), reinscribing imperialist narratives of progress. In sum, the myths of the internet as a value-free space of progress and technologically enabled liberty revisit and reify familiar ideologies, including colonial fantasies and the association of masculinity with technological progress.

The idea that embodied and situated selves, marked by race, gender, class, age, ability, and sexuality, could be erased in a virtual world where all are equal may be compelling. However, these promises are largely espoused and then enacted into policy by powerful middle-class White and Western men such as John Perry Barlow and the board members of tech companies. Given these origins, it is perhaps unsurprising that the erasure of the body has not been actualized in a manner that might be envisioned by those who have experienced inequalities and can speak to how they operate. As Wakeford (2000) argues, the origins of the internet in university-military partnerships, and in association with the discourse of neoliberal, techno-utopian boosters, contribute to its historical gendering as a White, male space. Even Wikipedia, self-defined as a 'free' encyclopaedia to which in theory anyone can contribute, is characterized by editing practices that define some content as intelligible at the expense of other forms of knowledge (Raval 2014). Digital media technologies are therefore neither neutral nor value-free but distinctly marked by power dynamics, including those related to gender, race, and class.

Socio-technical approaches

As this brief history of the gendered and racialized forces shaping the development of networked computing and communication indicates, feminist media studies of digital media and cultures entail a consideration of the dynamic, mutually shaping relationship between social forces and these technologies, including their technical features, the industries they are part of, and the institutions they are imbricated with. We must begin by rejecting any suggestion of a linear cause and effect, such as that digital media have led to increased feminist activism. We must also resist the opposite perspective of **social determinism**, where technologies are seen as empty tools imbued with power solely in their use. This perspective permeates conversations about the possibilities associated with interactivity and **participatory culture** in considerations of digital media. Instead, we need to consider an array of elements when looking at our objects of interest in digital media research, including power relations, discourse, ideology, and systems of meaning.

The field of science and technology studies (STS) is a valuable source of conceptual and methodological insights when examining digital media, as it demonstrates how technological artefacts are political (Winner 1980) rather than simply the product of industrial innovation, value-free scientific endeavours, or fantastic moments of individual genius. However, as Joerges (1999) argues, technological artefacts are not fixed and can change; they can be interpreted and used in various ways, and are contingent on uses and meanings beyond their designer's original intentions. Our aim then must be to address the mutuality and reciprocal nature of the relationship between the technical and social by looking at these technological artefacts as **socio-technical**. Bruno Latour, writing under the pseudonym 'Jim Johnson' (1988), notes that the inseparability of technologies from human relations becomes clear when we consider how we delegate responsibilities and actions to technologies (what he calls nonhumans) while prescribing behaviours and human actions based on them, which is where ethical and moral questions arise. Noble (2018) exemplifies this approach in her analysis of Google's search engine algorithm, a technical, mathematical artefact to which we delegate responsibility for finding the best, most accurate and credible information based on the search term we enter. In her research, Noble found that when she searched for 'Black Girls', 'Asian Girls', and 'Latina Girls', the massively popular search engine exclusively returned pornography in the top results. The seemingly neutral technology of the algorithm therefore contributes to the misrepresentation and marginalization of women of colour and, overall, to the amplification of certain voices over others. As Noble concludes, this is because of the social forces underpinning the technology, including the key role of advertisers. There is a clear consequence for civil life and marginalized groups in particular as we delegate more information-seeking and curation to this corporate tech company, with fewer resources distributed to public utilities such as libraries.

These insights from STS and critical analysis of digital media indicate some useful questions for undertaking a socio-technical approach to understanding digital media. *What would we need to do if the technology under examination was not present? How are behaviours and actions changed as a result of this replacement of human labour or effort? In what ways do these technologies then expect particular actions or behaviours on the part of the user? How might these changes and expectations impact in different ways on different groups, leading to discrimination or exclusion? What are the* **affordances** *– what is enabled or allowed for users – and* **constraints** *– what is made impossible or very difficult – of this technological form?* Affordances and constraints may not be hard-coded and can also be interpreted and given meaning in diverse ways by users (what Nagy and Neff [2015] refer to as 'imagined affordances'), which demonstrates why a deterministic approach is too simple, and how we might find dominant, negotiated, or contested uses when we research digital media practices (Shaw 2017). For feminist media scholars, a productive investigation of digital media will examine the intended and unintended consequences of design features, as well as who decides on and who benefits from them.

Feminist considerations in digital media

The uses and consequences of technological design, whether anticipated or unforeseen, raise a number of questions for feminist research. Perhaps most prominently, this includes instances demonstrating the anti-social nature of social networking and online communities. Jane (2014) proposes the term 'e-bile' to refer to a wide range of uncivil practices online, demonstrating that the affordances of the technology underpinning our digital media, including **anonymity**, **interactivity**, and the rapid **spreadability** of content across sites, can cause harm. As she highlights, a historical review of internet scholarship indicates that these affordances have consistently been mobilized for exclusionary ends over time and across media and platforms, with pronounced impacts on women, people of colour, queer people, and other subordinated groups.

However, given the indeterminacy of affordances, it is perhaps no surprise that women and girls who have access to the internet have engaged in a range of communicative practices online, despite this harassment and incivility. As networked technologies become domesticated in everyday life, they are used for community formation, civic participation, self-representation, and creative expression through participation in forums (Gajjala 2004), web design (Kearney 2006), blogging (Keller 2015), games (Gray 2013), and on social media such as Tumblr (Kanai 2017), often subverting hegemonic portrayals of women and girls, including through critical reflections on feminism and intersectional oppressions. That digital media enable such connections and visibilities has elicited in turn many deterministic 'nightmares' about the dangers of online and mobile technologies for girls in particular, including panics about sexting (Hasinoff 2015), solicitation by paedophiles (Cassell and Cramer 2008), and cyberbullying (Mishna et al. 2018). Here, girls in the West are framed as being especially vulnerable and endangered by new digital media, particularly by sexual victimization, and as lacking any agency, savvy, or resilience.

In addition to the overtly sexist and racist practices noted above, as well as these gendered framings of young women and girls as potential victims, feminist analysis of digital media finds that networked communication technologies can serve to reinforce and reproduce normatively gendered relations of power. This includes the reinforcement and disciplining of traditional beauty ideals in social networking and selfie creation (Chua and Chang 2016), the migration and intensification of antagonisms related to appropriate mothering strategies in the so-called 'Mommy Wars' (Abetz and Moore 2018), and the extension of feminized caring responsibilities entailed by the adoption of mobile devices in South Korea and China (Lim and Soon 2010) and digital games in Canada (Harvey 2015). Contrary, then, to offering wide opportunities for subversion and resistance, research shows that the experiences, practices, and uses of digital media are shaped in significant ways by social relations related to race (Nakamura 2008), sexuality (O'Riordan and Phillips 2007), location (Gajjala et al. 2010), migration status (Leurs 2015), ability (Ellcessor 2016), class (Marwick 2015), and their intersections with gender (Noble and Brendesha 2015), far beyond the simple digital divide discourse discussed in Chapter 4.

In the research we have reviewed, the impact of unequal power relations on digital media is understood from a socio-technical perspective, traced through both the specific design features of a given platform as well as the socio-cultural norms that shape interaction on and across digital media sites. Consider for instance the affordance of anonymity, a feature of online communication that has been celebrated by privacy advocates but that becomes less attainable with shifts in online platform design and governance. As internet platforms and sites have become increasingly visual, both anonymous identity play and discussions of the utopian potential of the internet for the body have become less prominent. With the rise in social media linked to our local communities, professional networks, and personal profiles, anonymity and identity play is consigned to the domain of more niche sites such as 4chan, Reddit, Tumblr, and online gaming. On many platforms this consistency between online and offline identity is a normalized expectation, and in some cases, such as Facebook, it is imposed as a requirement through both design and policy.

The significance of the latter is demonstrated by Bivens' (2015) analysis of modifications to Facebook's gender selection option over a ten-year period, changing from non-mandatory gender identification with three available options (male, female, undisclosed) to mandatory binary gender selection with myriad customization options available depending on language. Looking 'below the hood' at the application programme interface (API) for the site, Bivens finds that, despite the appearance of gender fluidity, at the level of code these selections are coded back as binary classifications. As she argues, 'this technique maintains public-facing progressive politics while bolstering hegemonic regimes of gender control' (2015: 6), for the purposes of providing granular data about gender to marketers and advertisers in the binary form they desire. Embedding hegemonic values such as binaristic gender into code is a technique of power, maintaining a 'natural' gender order in the pursuit of profit. Haimson and Hoffman (2016) link this to how Facebook's founder Mark Zuckerberg rhetorically constructs 'authenticity' through the enforcement of the real-name policy, algorithmically and via community reporting, linking safety to being able to find a person in the Facebook directory rather than to the option of remaining invisible or untraceable, which is an important consideration for many marginalized people. This element of 'context collapse' (Marwick and boyd 2010) across multiple sites of identity performance, produced through the entanglement of invisible code, visible interfaces, site policy, community norms, and public discourse can have deleterious impacts on those for whom anonymity or using a different name is a matter not only of pleasure but of safety and survival. 'Default publicness' has unique implications for queer youth (Cho 2017), as well as for transgender and genderqueer users and abuse survivors, among others (Electronic Freedom Foundation 2015).

As this overview of the socio-technical forces shaping digital media should indicate, a feminist analysis of digital media practices necessarily entails a critical and careful approach attuned to politics, discourse, technical design features, and actual practices. We must balance the opportunities afforded by new media that may seem to democratize communication against the challenges posed by corporate ownership of these platforms and how economic, political, and social norms influence their design and functioning. It is compelling to think that digital media enable marginalized people to express themselves and have their voices heard. A wide range of feminist media studies of social media platforms from Twitter to Tumblr, YouTube to Facebook, highlight these practices. It is important to note that this critical work focuses as much on the content of this activism as on the form of the digital media technologies enabling it. For example, in her discussion of the #handsoffaboriginalkids hashtag in protest of the treatment of Indigenous Australian children in police custody, Verity Trott (2018) considers how the tweets of feminist activists challenge post-racial discourse and the Whiteness of postfeminist new media cultures by engaging in explicitly anti-racist critique. While Twitter is the context where these utterances are written, shared, and read, what makes them a feminist intervention is their content. Overemphasis on the platform itself simplifies the nature of engagement with the media and can lead us into the trap of technological determinism. On the other hand, attributing all agency and power to users and their social practices can fail to account for the often-invisible power of the platform in shaping our engagement – an example of social determinism.

A critical feminist digital media studies approach thus requires attention to the mutually shaping relationship between technologies and social forces and actors. To return to Trott's analysis, she highlights how Twitter, rather than Facebook, is the preferred tool of Indigenous feminist activism because of the different features of each platform. In the case of Facebook, the community standards and policies related to nudity led to the removal of images of women breastfeeding or participating in Aboriginal ceremonies, a decision premised on the sexualization of women's bodies. As Trott says, 'social media sites such as Facebook thus embody White attitudes through the enforcement of community policies that are developed and sustained within a cultural and social context in which a post-identity ideology is dominant' (2018: 150). Twitter has become the site of this activism because it has less stringent policies on moderating content – an attribute that can be useful for such activism but also oppressive in the case of harassment campaigns.

In what follows, we will look at feminist digital media scholarship on digitally mediated feminist action and selfie production to consider how the interplay of the socio-technical has been analysed in practice. Throughout this discussion, I draw attention to the tension between promises of empowerment and fears of victimization in relation to women and girls' engagement with digital media, often centring on recurring questions of visibility.

#Activism – Analysing digitally mediated feminist action

Despite the long-standing gendering of computational technologies as areas of masculine expertise, digital media has been highlighted as a key feature of the rise of fourth wave feminism as we saw in Chapter 1. Indeed, it seems that in recent years most feminist campaigns have come to be linked to a hashtag, from addressing rape culture with #YesAllWomen, #BeenRapedNeverReported, and #MeToo, to challenging street harassment through #YouOKSis? and #bystanderintervention, to demonstrating the persistence of sexism in daily life using #distractinglysexy, #croptopday, and #everydaysexism. The use of the hashtag symbol before a phrase referencing an event, campaign, concern, or slogan filters content and can link together diverse users across multiple platforms, creating what has been called a **hashtag public** (Rambukkana 2015). Such purpose-focused, often temporary groupings can raise awareness, rally support, educate and inform, and create affective connections, among other aims. The affordances of the hashtag for activism and the formation of networked publics is due in no small part to how they allow discussion and interaction to be distributed across wide audiences of users who do not need to be previously connected to each other on a site, as 'followers', 'friends', or via other forms of platform-specific linkage. The use of multiple hashtags can also connect diverse sets of users, creating a conversation across them. This enables the formation of ad hoc communities of interest traversing physical geographies and social locations, largely through affective connections and intensities in relation to the topic under discussion.

The publics formed through hashtag use can serve the dual purpose of creating communities and engaging in broader advocacy, both of which can be meaningful for marginalized groups. For example, Jackson et al. deploy network and discourse analysis to examine the formation and growth of the #GirlsLikeUs network, noting that use of the hashtag included posts ranging from the political and activist to the mundane, but that these tweets 'work to both center trans politics and normalize trans lives' (2018: 1883), which is vitally important in a context where the exclusion, violence, stigmatization, and incarceration of trans people is prevalent. However, while ad hoc community formation enables activists to foster linkages and open up a dialogue about specific issues, it also facilitates the participation of other users who may have a different affective response to the topic. For example, while discussion around the hashtag #SolidarityisForWhiteWomen can connect those who are critical of feminist approaches or theories lacking an intersectional perspective, it can equally invite counter-discourses in the form of accusations of reverse racism or indeed antifeminist rhetoric, which seems to regularly follow the rise of feminist hashtags. The value of the hashtag for feminist organizing, then, is complex and at times ambivalent, and must be carefully analysed alongside other digital media affordances in terms of the opportunities and challenges they create.

For instance, one challenge within hashtag feminism is the prominence of certain causes, particularly Western-based topics, over others. Guha (2014) notes that feminist hashtag activism originating in India does not have the same impact as that originating in the US, because nations with lower digital participation are more dependent on mainstream media coverage for reaching and influencing those with the power to make concrete changes. This highlights not only the ways in which hashtag activism may reflect particular forms of privilege in participation, but also how this digital media practice is not an end in itself but a means by which to enact change. As Rivers (2017) notes in her analysis of digitally mediated action, its impact is not assured, and in some research the effectiveness of these feminist hashtag campaigns for policy, law, institutions, and broader society is unclear.

Therefore, while such activities represent a new direction in feminist media studies and organizing, it is vital that we do not overestimate or overinflate their role. Equally important is turning a critical eye to how technologies work, particularly in terms of what they allow and what they do not, and how their use can contribute to oppression rather than liberation. Consider the example of Hollaback!, one of the best-known feminist organizations focused on street harassment, which has received tremendous positive attention from both mainstream media and feminist scholars. However, it faced a great deal of criticism in 2014 when the New York chapter released a video entitled '10 Hours of Walking in New York' (Rentschler 2017), featuring a young White woman being subject to street harassment while walking down city streets. Critics noted that the harassment portrayed in the video was almost entirely perpetrated by men of colour. This led to some chapters of Hollaback! in other cities splitting from the organization and forming new groups to examine street harassment from an intersectional feminist perspective. These splinter organizations, which include Feminist Public Works, the Safe Hub Collective, Safer Spaces Winnipeg, Collective Action for Safer Spaces, and the People's Justice League, also emphasize in their mission statements the need for greater engagement with communities beyond the online sphere, which demonstrates how digital feminist media action such as hashtag activism is not the only site for this work, nor even the most important.

A corollary critique to be made in this case concerns the way that the Hollaback! website and app operate through a pinning feature allowing users to tag harassment sites on Google Maps. As Rentschler observes, this contributes to larger 'racist geographies of fear' (2017: 575), where certain neighbourhoods are framed as undesirable and dangerous and therefore assessed differently by the police, the government, and real estate agencies. In this way, these uses of digital media by Hollaback! can be viewed as participating in a White feminism insensitive to the issues and lived realities of people of colour, who experience these forms of mapping negatively. Anti-oppression is therefore not apparent in either the explicit representations of street harassment (highlighting only men of colour as harassers of White women) or in the implicit use of mapping technologies (contributing to the mapping of often low-income and racialized neighbourhoods as dangerous).

Rentschler's work on feminist action through hashtags, websites, apps, and locative media demonstrates the interplay between politics embedded in communities and digital technologies, highlighting racist logics in particular, and more generally the necessity of considering carefully how feminist organizing plays out using digital media. Feminist digital media activism can also evince neo-imperialist logics, as demonstrated by Khoja-Moolji's (2015b) analysis of the #BringBackOurGirls hashtag campaign. Tweets with this hashtag were shared in response to the kidnapping of hundreds of schoolgirls in Nigeria, with the aim of stimulating government action in both Nigeria and the US. But, as Khoja-Moolji notes, 'through the practices of hashtagging and (re)tweeting, the participants become part of a collectivity that seems to have certainty about the lives of girls in the global south as well as its own role in alleviating their suffering' (2015b: 348), thereby simplifying local politics and histories while drawing in particular on the trope of the Muslim terrorist and the discourse of the White feminist saviour. As Khoja-Moolji concludes, this perpetuates epistemic violence against women in the Global South, as discussed in Chapter 4, extending its purview within contemporary feminist organizing and discourse via digital media. As these two examples demonstrate, the power of hashtags and other digitally mediated feminist action requires close attention to the dynamics of oppression that can be too easily supported by networked communication technologies.

These critical points about the socio-technical character of digitally mediated feminisms are not intended to dismiss the potential of these forms of engagement nor the importance of engaging in their study. A growing body of research demonstrates how these digital networks contribute to the process of creating cultural change in their questioning of oppressive tropes, practices, and norms such as rape culture (Keller et al. 2016). Hashtag activism enables the formation of peer-to-peer networks of witnessing, care, and support (Rentschler 2014), and the establishment of counter-publics allowing for alternative formations of public life for those marginalized in mainstream forums for debate, and therefore for new political subjectivities (Keller 2011). The explorations in this chapter should indicate the importance of taking a nuanced approach to any feminist media study of digitally mediated organizing. This includes recognizing how digital feminism is diverse not only in its aims but also in its politics and approaches, reflecting the plurality of feminist thought and action as well as, at times, its points of disagreement and tension such as the debates around #SolidarityisForWhiteWomen and #FemFuture discussed by Loza (2014).

Furthermore, as Fotopoulou (2016) argues, our approaches to feminist activism within digital networks must include a focus not only on its socio-technical features but also on the significance of both the symbolic practices of identity and community-formation and the material practices of infrastructure-building, including women's labour in setting up these networks. Forging solidarity, creating connections, caring, testifying, and witnessing – these all entail work, often of the affective and emotional kind that is frequently devalued, as we will examine in Chapter 6. We can avoid the trap of positive technological determinism by recalling how the media have played a role in feminist organizing historically. Remember too how the celebration of digital and social media's 'accessibility' cannot be justified when we consider the transnational inequalities related to participation. Finally, as we will see in the next section, when women's participation in digital culture becomes visible, it is often subject to harsh scrutiny of its legitimacy.

Taking selfies seriously

Some technologies, as mentioned at the start of this chapter, are associated with gendered subjects regardless of actual practice. Perhaps the most obviously feminized digital media practice in contemporary culture is that of taking and sharing selfies. While self-portraiture using a mobile device to capture one's image for the purpose of posting it on social media is a commonplace practice, it is framed as a distinctly gendered digital media activity. Associated with young women in particular, it has been the topic of moralizing hype and dismissed as narcissistic, vain, apolitical, and frivolous, as books like *Selfie: How We Became So Self-Obsessed and What It's Doing to Us* (Storr 2018) indicate. Dobson (2015) argues that this common denigration of selfie production and the girls and women who engage in it is experienced as a double-bind. These dismissals coexist with the expectation within digital culture that we must be visible, intimate, authentic, and open in our social media use. They furthermore sit alongside the judgement of selfies according to gender norms about appearance, and the harassment of those who create them for any perceived failure to conform to these multiple, contradictory expectations. We can see therefore how it is that social and cultural norms become affixed to a technologically mediated practice, in this case selfies, and serve to reaffirm the association of masculinity and technological expertise despite the widespread participation of women and girls in digital culture. As Burns notes, 'by repeatedly devaluing selfie takers, the discussion of selfies not only acts as a cloaked expression of sexist attitudes but also defines and stigmatizes a specific group of subjects' (2015: 717). For feminist scholars of digital media, assessing which activities are deemed legitimate and which are seen as without virtue or less valid is an important exercise in understanding how digital media practices contribute to histories of gendered technology and the dismissal of feminine activity, a pattern linking digital media to other media forms such as soap operas and romance books.

Taking selfies seriously reveals numerous important topics of interest for feminist media scholars, as they are not merely self-portraits enabled by the affordances of front-facing cameras on mobile phones and social media for sharing. Senft and Baym (2015) note that, for media critics, selfies are simultaneously objects, cultural artefacts, social practices, and gestures, conveying affect in relationships as well as various meanings to a range of audiences depending on the community as well as the platform. They also point out that, despite the emphasis on the agency of individual users in making a selfie, these images 'are created, displayed, distributed, tracked, and monetized through an assemblage of nonhuman agents' (2015: 1589). Consequently, analysis must go beyond the cultural hype around selfies to focus on the multiple features and processes entailed in this everyday practice of self-representation. This may entail, for instance, interpretivist research with those who take selfies, and critical examination of the socio-technical affordances of digital media for self-imaging.

Recent research on selfie practices reveals a complex array of social, cultural, economic, and political forces shaping their production. Abidin (2016) focuses on internet celebrity and those with large followings on social media, whom she calls Influencers. This term is used in both popular and academic literature to refer to social media users seen as credible, authentic, and able to engage a substantial audience in a particular industry, from beauty to fitness to travel and beyond. In her study of Singaporean Influencers, she finds that, despite the dismissal of selfies as frivolous or without any serious value or purpose, they are deeply entangled with commerce, providing the opportunity for these users to advertise products and services to audiences with whom they have cultivated intimacy through the sharing of their images. Selfies also serve to authenticate 'being there' at high-profile events and encounters with other Influencers and celebrities, becoming a mode of digital witnessing and verification. In these practices, Abidin argues, we can observe instances of subversive frivolity, which she defines as 'the under-visibilized and under-estimated generative power of an object or practice arising from its (populist) discursive framing as marginal, inconsequential, and unproductive' (2016: 2). The commodification activities she documents demonstrate that, far from being worthless, selfies are in fact profitable property, having a value that derives from their advertising potential but also from the tremendous labour invested in the production of a 'good selfie'. Abidin's study exemplifies how a careful analysis of the activities and objects associated with femininity in digital culture can reveal their power and value, despite the common view of such practices as requiring less expertise, skill, or effort, and as having no significant impact. Challenging normative constructions of the feminine as passive and the masculine as productive is an important part of feminist digital media studies, as demonstrated by work on women in games production (Harvey and Shepherd 2016) and in relation to geek culture (Reagle 2015).

Indeed, research on selfie practices demonstrates the skill and knowledge involved in self-reflexively assessing how to construct and represent oneself in the form of the selfie, as the person taking it acts as both an object and agent of representation (Frosh 2015), often taking into consideration a range of concerns related to privacy and purpose (Albury 2015). In her interviews with women who regularly create selfies, Warfield finds that they move between multiple subjectivities in their practices, 'trying to find a balance between an image that presents them as conventionally beautiful (the model), while also being an image that others would want to see (the self-conscious thespian) and finally an image that somehow represents a felt connection to the body and one's authentic sense of self', or the 'real me' (2015: 12). The reflexive engagement entailed in these negotiations belies the notion of selfie-taking as a simple form of expression, and can furthermore complicate any straightforward application of the theory of the male gaze to these representations, though as Warfield notes her avid selfie-takers do tend to follow the conventions of dominant Western visual culture, situating these digital media practices within a broader set of technologies for gender disciplining, including beauty apps that allow selfie-takers to filter, touch-up, and otherwise modify their posts (Elias and Gill 2017). Furthermore, as Naezer (2018) finds in her interviews with young Dutch girls, constructions of sexiness in selfies are informed by hegemonic values tied to body shape, skin colour, educational level, and class, reproducing dominant norms of feminine attractiveness and appropriate behaviour.

However, the hypervisibility of self-performance has been capitalized on by a plethora of users for varying purposes, including those who use the affordances of the selfie for identity play and body positive messaging. Proulx explores queer artistic responses to socio-technical norms related to the performance of gendered and sexualized bodies online, noting that the use of online affordances enables artists to create 'transitional imagery of bodies that are ambiguous, uncontrollable and often unrecognizable within the purview of digital culture' (2016: 117). A range of activists, artists, and everyday users deploy selfies to raise awareness of diverse bodies and selves, as demonstrated by the Black Muslim feminist Leah Vernon's fashion blogging, where imaging focuses on body positivity and self-love (Srouji 2018). It is important, however, to consider how the socio-technical norms, expected uses, and structures of a given digital media platform shape selfie production and reception, potentially amplifying or rendering invisible some kinds of non-normative performances (Duguay 2016).

Returning to the work involved in creating what is recognized as a 'good' selfie, it must be noted that the aesthetic frequently pursued, as exemplified in both Abidin's and Warfield's research, tends to resemble conventional beauty ideals related to the sexy body, reflecting the norms of postfeminist media culture. While this could be linked to critiques of narcissism and vanity in a moral judgement, it is useful to instead consider the question from a feminist perspective – 'how is beauty defined, deployed, defended, subordinated, marketed, or manipulated, and how do these tactics intersect with gender and value?' (Colebrook 2006: 132) – and also, as Figueroa (2013) adds, to examine the interaction of such beauty norms with race and nationality. Rather than dismissing selfies as being just another disciplinary mechanism under patriarchy, we can explore how, like other forms of beauty work, they may be pleasurable, social, and even a means by which marginalized people can gain recognition and generate feelings of belonging (Cho 2015). However, as Figueroa notes in her examination of the entanglement of racism and beauty, our experiences are shaped by visual racial logics that value certain skin colours, features, and bodily attributes over others. This insight is supported by research on the selfie production practices of queer and non-binary people undertaken by Vivienne (2017), who argues for a shift in discourses of empowerment circulating around non-normative gender representation to reflect instead the privilege of cisgender people posting selfies in a heteronormative and cissexist system of power. Vivienne's analysis also reveals the platform-specificity of meaning-making around selfies, highlighting how the affordances of Tumblr – such as reblogging, 'ask me anything' interactivity, and customization options – may present a distinctly different socio-technical apparatus for self-presentation than can be found on other social media sites. This work again challenges the simple binaries of empowerment or victimization, and indicates that while the theory of the gaze is not easily mapped onto selfie production, discussions of the politics of feminine beauty and gender disciplining are still relevant in the context of mass self-representation in participatory culture, where hierarchies of beauty and normative gender performance persist.

Despite the general emphasis on young women and vanity, internet scholars have noted that selfies, as visual communicative forms, express the intimate and personal in ways that can challenge dominant narratives in politics, creating new acts of citizenship (Kunstman 2017). They have been deployed in this way in activism to complicate the simplistic media framing of political events, emphasizing instead the lived experience and feeling of what it is to be a citizen. For example, selfies have been used as a mode of commenting on the ways in which people are dichotomously framed as victims or survivors of sexual assault in rape culture (Ferreday 2017). In Project Unbreakable, a crowdsourced online photography project, participants use selfies to make their experiences visible in ways that complicate the commonplace stories told about trauma and recovery. Because they involve visuals and text created by everyday users, selfies can contribute to a sense of the affective nuance of political questions – a personal approach to current affairs that harkens back to the earliest call of feminists that the personal is political.

That said, like other digitally mediated forms of expression, selfies are hinged implicitly on visibility politics – the valuation of being seen, being heard, being recognized. For those whose voices and experiences have been silenced and marginalized, digital media can provide a channel through which to challenge and resist epistemic violence, creating new representations and narratives that complicate stereotypes and highlight the multiplicity of lived experiences and cultures as well as critical perspectives. However, there are questions to be asked about who wants to be seen, how visibility is associated with power, and who gets to be seen and recognized in digital culture. In her discussion of selfies, Raji (2017) notes that there are bodies for whom visibility and recognition is a danger, for instance those who are oppressed based on their immigration status or racialized criminalization. As she argues, while selfie production may seem like a harmless everyday practice, the capturing and circulation of images is also a form of surveillance enabled by digital media, one that is a particular concern for those facing institutionalized and state violence. As much as visibility enabled by digital media can seem to rectify historical regimes of symbolic annihilation, it also prompts new questions, both theoretical and methodological.

The affordances of visibility, interactivity and spreadability enabled by digital media have played a role in supporting harassment and discrimination through misogynistic movements such as #GamerGate and The Fappening. Massanari (2017) argues that these two instances of 'toxic technoculture' are supported by Reddit's technical affordances, policy mechanisms, corporate oversight, and community culture. #GamerGate, which involved the online and offline harassment of well-known women in the video game industry, was characterized by ferocious attacks on women, people of colour, and queer and transgender people making an intervention into a masculinist games culture, enabled by the ease with which participants gathering around the hashtag could share personal information about their targets ('doxxing'), defamatory memes, and hateful, threatening, and violent comments across multiple platforms. Other highly visible female figures were the target of The Fappening, which involved the circulation of nude photos of celebrities – obtained by hacking Apple's cloud services – across image-based sites such as 4chan, Imgur, and Reddit. In both cases, visibility made a person a target and became intensified as mobs of online harassers focused on this identified target. Each of these sites, as Massanari demonstrates, have platform-specific technical, governance, and cultural features supporting this toxicity, including anonymity and forms of upvoting that allow some content to be foregrounded while critiques become hidden. In addition, the interconnectedness between sites (facilitated by the embedding of buttons to easily share content on other platforms) allows for materials and activity to be rapidly developed, shared, and modified – a feature of the commercialization of the social web (Gerlitz and Helmond 2013) that enables the intensification and spread of online harassment campaigns. Visibility can therefore become a liability on digital media, particularly for marginalized groups.

In addition to these conceptual considerations related to visibility, feminist media studies scholars also need to consider the methodological challenges that arise based on a feminist ethics of care as discussed in Chapter 2. Figueroa (2008) reflects on the decision of whether or not to include photographs from her research on race and beauty in the dissemination and presentation of her project. As she notes, gazing at images is a pleasure, but for those who share them these photographs may actually express or symbolize trauma, grief, humiliation, or other difficult emotions. For this reason, sometimes sharing photographs (or other visual content) is not the best approach, as the meaning given to them is indeterminate depending on their audiences. This is an important observation for feminist media studies broadly, as mediatized images often form part of our presentations as evidence. The poignancy of these insights is even more pronounced when our research images are 'found' on Instagram, Tumblr, Google Image Search, or other visual digital media. While we may have obtained these images in a manner that conforms to institutional ethical guidelines, we should also consider what the inclusion of such images can do and the multiple meanings they may carry. Such cautions are especially important in the pursuit of decolonizing feminist media studies, not least because, 'since the invention of photography and its "coincidence" with imperial expansion, scientific racism and changing forms of knowledge linked to logics of comparability and equivalency, images have symbolized a fascinating point of access to the "other"' (Figueroa 2008: 74). How we produce and consume images is shaped by this history, requiring attention and care in how we reproduce images, including selfies, as part of our research. Figueroa encourages us to consider this by 'looking emotionally', which means engaging critically with the social histories of those whom the photos make visible, and simultaneously considering what audiences they will be seen and understood by. This enables us 'to attend to webs of shared social understandings, individual perceptions of the past translated from the moment of the telling, and emotional reactions to the experience of reliving while narrating' (2008: 82).

The problem of visibility most obviously arises in relation to visually identifiable subjects, as in selfie research, but it is a broader methodological consideration in feminist media studies of digital communication and culture. Many of the affordances of digital media discussed in this chapter are underpinned by processes that are not visible to users, and these features enable widespread corporate and state surveillance of digital activities. Visibility, as Massanari (2018) points out, is actually difficult to escape in contemporary digital culture, with few socio-technical affordances enabling privacy online. As researchers, we need to address this for ourselves and for those with whom we conduct research. When conducting research on topics such as social justice, inclusion, and feminism, as well as hate, misogyny, and far-right politics, we can find ourselves at risk of surveillance and harassment, as was the case with video games academics and #GamerGate (Rambukkana 2019).

Furthermore, in contemporary work on digital media we see the rise in popularity of digitally driven methods including big data research, work that is itself enabled by normalized practices of collecting and collating massive amounts of information about digital media users, without the practices of informed consent underpinning ethical research. Indeed, the visibility of user actions to particular powerful interests through data 'scraping', 'mining', 'mapping', and 'visualization', can be seen as part of the 'ideology of direct, devouring, generative, and unrestricted vision' critiqued by Haraway (1988: 582). Leurs (2017) argues that data-driven research would benefit from the insights of feminist and postcolonial research, including a return to a focus on how data is not neutral but always represents a partial truth, context-specific, marked by power relations, and deeply subjective. The rise of big data analytics, applications, and research represents an opportunity for feminist media studies researchers to develop modes of analysis that highlight, as Leurs does, the importance of accounting for situated knowledges, lived experiences, and reflexive approaches in data-driven research. While as researchers we do not always have access to the invisible processes shaping participation on digital media (nor the mechanisms by which to modify them), we can engage in a feminist ethics of care when conducting our research by considering the questions posed by Luka and Millette in relation to rights, privileges, vulnerabilities, decision-making, and consent. They conclude their reflexive account of doing this kind of work by asking us to consider 'in what ways will our research contribute to a more equitable world?' (2018: 8). In the next section we will look at some initiatives explicitly pursuing this aim in digital media-based projects.

Towards feminist digital media action

In 2018, the American singer and songwriter Janelle Monáe released her album *Dirty Computer* with an accompanying 'emotion picture', a film constructed around the album's songs which features a transgressive queer android Black woman having her memories 'cleaned' by two men at a computer workstation. Monáe, who plays the android in the film, is a self-proclaimed 'dirty computer' in a totalitarian, surveillant, homophobic regime. In the process of her rebellious individuality being erased we are granted access to her memories of falling in love with a character played by the actress Tessa Thompson. The album and film have been widely discussed for their role in Monáe's public 'coming out', but they and the musician's previous work (Cárdenas 2015) are also worthy of attention for how they make the **Afrofuturist** genre more visible. Dating back to the 1950s, Afrofuturism is an aesthetic and philosophy focused on the intersection of technologies with African peoples and those of the African diaspora, often expressed through art, science fiction, and fantasy media texts. Indeed, with the 2018 film *Black Panther* and the setting of Numbani in the popular digital game *Overwatch*, as well as the successes of books such as *The Children of Blood and Bone* by Tomi Adeyemi, there appears to be a growing cultural shift away from the narratives associating technology and societal progress exclusively with Whiteness, the West, and masculinity, while marginalizing and erasing Black female subjects, as discussed by Hobson (2008). In the epilogue to *The Children of Blood and Bone*, Adeyemi clearly articulates the book's connection to the Black Lives Matter movement, highlighting the power and potency of even young adult fantasy fiction for making political arguments about ongoing oppression. It is significant too that in many cases the creators of these media representations of racialized people and their relationships to power and technology are themselves from marginalized groups, demonstrating again the importance of who has access to producing media.

Such images and narratives, alongside critical feminist research on digital media, are challenging 'the "ownership" of technoculture and showcasing computer technology, not as the HAL-like "master" of the information age, but as just another tool in the service of cultural agitation and social justice' (Hobson 2008: 123). Media representations of technology, however, are but one facet of the relations of power around digital media, and what should be evident from the themes and topics discussed throughout this chapter is the significant shaping role played by design. From the affordances and policies of social media sites, to the chat features of digital gaming worlds, to the largely invisible processes of artificial intelligence, machine learning, and algorithms, the socio-technical structures underpinning digital media enable activism *and* harassment. The architecture of, and discourses about, digital life facilitate some kinds of activity based on certain values while foreclosing or marginalizing others, all in ways that seem natural and inherent to the technology. Despite visibly widening participation, our digital spaces are not necessarily safe for women, people of colour, transgender users, and others from marginalized communities. In fact, there is increasing evidence that digital environments are active in the production and circulation of misogynistic discourse, articulated by both men and women (Dale 2016), as well as racist, homophobic, sexist, and otherwise discriminatory language. Less visibly, technical processes such as those embedded in algorithms are automated to make decisions that serve to discipline and regulate behaviours in ways that contribute to rather than dismantle inequalities, as demonstrated by Eubanks (2018) in her book *Automating Inequality*. Work in this vein demonstrates how the utopian, altruistic Golden Rule is practically impossible to apply given the socio-technical norms of the internet. We need instead to begin thinking in terms of social justice and adopting feminist approaches to design that recognize and address the systemic asymmetries in power in our digital media.

A range of organizations, networks, and projects engage in action for precisely these ends, including initiatives focused on data justice (Dencik et al. 2016), design justice (Costanza-Chock 2018), and the imagining and development of a feminist internet (Kee 2017). This work is broadly aimed at shifting the commonplace individualized discussions of privacy, choice, and empowerment towards structural and systemic issues as well as questions of social justice, thereby enabling the inclusion of other actors in civil society in these conversations. Within this growing field there is a recognition of differential experiences and inequality in our digital lives, but there remains a tremendous opportunity for feminist media studies to consider how these experiences are stratified according to gender and its intersections with other axes of oppression and points of privilege. *How, as Costanza-Chock (2018) asks, can we envision and design systems that are more equitable for those who are least powerful in our society?*

One important element of this work is **co-design**, which involves engaging communities and users in the design process so that priorities and challenges can be identified from the bottom-up, rather than by engineers, programmers, and other tech-focused stakeholders. Exemplary work in this area includes the Our Data Bodies project, whose website features a fact sheet and community report detailing how contextually sensitive participatory research has informed their insights on data collection and sharing in everyday life. Deriving conclusions on what justice in digital media looks like from the grassroots enables us to imagine alternatives informed by design traditions beyond those that have dominated computing culture, thereby decolonizing technology – as argued for by the research group Data Active in their call for Big Data from the South. Furthermore, working with communities can shift the largely tech-focused nature of 'design thinking' so that it better addresses human needs — such as the desire to have greater control over our data lives — by designing what Lee and Tolliver call 'consentful technologies'. This refers to 'applications and spaces in which consent underlies all aspects, from the way they are developed, to how data is stored and accessed, to the way interactions happen between users' (2017: n.p.) — in contrast to the normalized practices of location tracking and sharing of biometric data across agencies, as well as the revenge porn and doxxing that form part of the harassment campaigns discussed above. As this chapter has demonstrated, feminist media scholars have a great deal to contribute in conversations about how these visions can be further conceptualized and enacted in situated contexts and on a global level, joining the renewed movement for a cyberfeminism 2.0 (Gajjala and Ju Oh 2012) that understands digital media as a site of contestation which is neither exclusively progressive nor strictly regressive.

6   Gendered Media Work

Chapter 3 of this book opened by discussing the Bechdel Test and its variants as a means by which to assess the presence or, more frequently, the absence of diverse representation in the media. A dominant hypothesis about the reason for delimited portrayals of women, people of colour, and LGBTQ+ individuals, among others, is that these groups are equally under-represented within the ranks of creative media producers – those with the ability to tell and share stories. For instance, in an article entitled 'Hollywood's Gender Divide and Its Effect on Films', Friedman et al. argue that 'filmmakers, unintentionally, make movies about themselves (i.e., write what you know). Since the most powerful producers, writers, and directors are men, male-themes permeate into Hollywood's output' (2016: n.p.). They test this theory by analysing the gender breakdown of producers, directors, and writers credited on films released between 2005 and 2015, and find that films with one woman or more in a creative role are more likely to pass the Bechdel Test than those with all-male teams. Using their interactive visualization of the data, anyone can test out various configurations of gender and media-making roles across different Hollywood studios. Doing this, one thing becomes clear – the more you limit the criteria by selecting for women in writing, directing, and producing roles, the fewer the number of films in the sample become eligible for analysis. This reflects how, as the authors note, women are dramatically outnumbered in Hollywood productions, and tend to be linked to lower-budget independent film-making rather than to blockbuster titles. This imbalance in behind-the-screen work may also have an impact on the number of women on screen, with fewer roles available to female actors, who are in any case frequently paid substantially less than their male counterparts (Setoodeh 2015).

Homogeny in film work is not only an issue in Hollywood. Research on the UK film industry between 2003 and 2015 reveals a similarly imbalanced picture, with women of colour making up only 1 per cent of all directors and 0.3 per cent of all cinematographers, indicating intersectional inequalities in film-making (Cobb et al. 2018). Moreover, these imbalances in production roles are not changing, with the number of women in both UK and Hollywood-based film-making remaining below 20 per cent. Research on top-grossing films between 2007 and 2012 shows that across four of the years surveyed, women constituted less than 5 per cent of directors, and that when the number of female directors increased, this led to a subsequent decrease in their representation in the following year (Smith et al. 2013). This analysis also indicates a relationship between women in writing and directing roles and their representation on screen, though quantitative research cannot tell us whether this is because women creators are more interested in female-driven narratives, or because they are more likely to be assigned to make films intended for female audiences by production executives.

This last point is an important one for challenging what might be an overly simplistic argument about greater diversity in media production leading to wider representation or increased inclusion in media cultures. Such a perspective on individual creators – be they writers or directors in Hollywood or lyricists in the music industry, video game developers or editors in the magazine world – overlooks the broader cultural and economic system structuring media work. Despite the attention paid to high-profile auteurs in specific industries – the Quentin Tarantinos of film-making, the David E. Kelleys of television production, the Shigeru Miyamotos of digital games – media-making is a complex, increasingly global set of practices shaped by local relations of power, including economic, political, cultural, and social norms. The process of making media is also collaborative, involving teams of sometimes thousands of people to make blockbuster video games, television series, and films. Linking greater creative innovation in media to diverse teams of makers is a seductive correlation. As this chapter will demonstrate, the relationship between gender and media work is much more complex. Understanding the gendered dynamics in this domain necessitates qualitative analysis of the types and characteristics of media work, how it is defined, valued, and framed, and the structure of the media industries that shape it. While there are certainly indicators that women in creative positions are linked to more female-focused texts, such as the widely cited example of Shonda Rhimes' writing and producing of powerful roles for Black women in television, there are also examples of women's successes and stories being fuelled by the power (and for the profit) of male executives. For instance, the success of 'female-led' comedy projects including the films *Bridesmaids* and *Trainwreck* and the television series *Girls* was driven by Hollywood heavyweight Judd Apatow, a producer who does not identify as a feminist and is not motivated by more equal representation but simply by novelty in comedic storytelling (Fallon 2017).

Another, more recent example of this dynamic is the successful adaptation of Margaret Atwood's dystopian novel *The Handmaid's Tale* for television.

Widely celebrated as a feminist triumph after its critically acclaimed first season, which won awards for many female members of its production team, the second season was more contentiously received. Lisa Miller expressed concern that the narrative had devolved into gratuitous torture porn, noting that the executive team behind the programme was 70 per cent male: 'the irony, that the corporate beneficiaries of this show about the institutionalized oppression of women are white men, is, well, rich' (2018: n.p.). Furthermore, Smith et al.'s (2013) study demonstrates that while women in creative production roles are linked to films with less sexualization of female characters, their participation does not completely eradicate stereotypical framings of women and girls in film. The 'grammar of gender' discussed in Chapter 3, including the male gaze and the politics of feminine beauty, is normalized by a range of forces in media culture beyond the creator whose name is associated with a given production. In other words, representational tropes remain hegemonic, sometimes despite the diverse backgrounds of those in creative production roles. This indicates the importance of a structural analysis of power when examining gendered participation in media work. This chapter contributes to that analysis by exploring and developing key theories about the political economy of the media, communication, and cultural industries, providing a framework for those interested in examining long-standing and emerging trends in gendered media work.

Throughout this book, we have examined how gender shapes access to, representation within, and participation across media cultures. Here, the focus is on what is arguably the underlying dynamic for inequalities in media industries – how control over the modes of production shapes images, narratives, and expected audiences and uses in the media landscape. Specifically, this chapter puts forth key concepts for understanding media work from a feminist perspective, discussing the complex forces shaping gendered participation in production and highlighting how women's relative under-participation in some roles is but one topic relevant to a feminist media study of labour. We will see that when we take a broader view of the production cycle of media and communications, involving a wide range of forms of participation of varying degrees of formality, the extent of feminized labour across the media landscape is significant. How highly valued this work is (or is not) impacts on its visibility and recognition within media industries.

This chapter argues that material and historical analysis provides important insights into the character of women's media work, demonstrating how the kinds of stories we tell about industry pioneers and genius auteurs are shaped by gendered norms that can obfuscate women's roles in ways similar to those discussed in relation to computing in Chapter 5. Like programmes aiming to get more girls into coding, a range of organizations, groups, and projects specifically focus on the question of the under-representation of women in other forms of media work. In the final section of this chapter, we consider how these varying initiatives frame the mission of increasing the number of women in a given media field, highlighting the key differences that arise across seemingly similar forms of media action depending on whether the focus is on structural change or on individual efforts. As will become clear, despite the increased attention given to fostering diversity and democratization in media-making, inequalities may actually be deepening in the contemporary media landscape, a reality requiring an integrated quantitative and qualitative approach to change.

Feminist political economy of the media

Research in feminist media studies focused on the structural forces shaping women's work is informed by key concepts from the field of political economy, particularly **exploitation, ideology, labour,** and **commodification**. In *Das Kapital* (*Capital*), originally published in 1867, Marx (2004) argues that the core dynamic underpinning capitalism as an economic system is how, in production, a portion of work is unpaid and is therefore the source of profit for the owner. In other words, it is normalized in capitalism that our wages are a fraction of the profit made by our employer, and that the wealth of the owner of the organization for which we work is based on our pay being lower than our work is actually worth. This relationship between workers and owners, in which the derivation of surplus value from the non-payment of work is normalized, is what is called the **exploitation of labour**. In the process of selling their labour to an employer – the familiar practice of applying for jobs and accepting a wage or salary when hired – workers become commodified, which, as noted in Chapter 2, refers to the exchange value assigned to something previously not understood in economic terms.

Rather than working relations being understood as moral interactions between people, within the ideology of capitalism they are framed as solely rational economic transactions. This leads to the normalization, for instance, of the outsourcing of work to the Global South to reduce costs through lower pay, and to the trumpeting of enormous corporate profits despite downsizing, mergers, and mass layoffs, all of which amount to a greater exploitation of labour as well as lost jobs and wages for workers. As we saw in Chapter 4, at the global level, labour relations associated with capitalist ideology disproportionately impact on women's economic and social well-being, particularly those who have been historically exploited under colonialism (Lee 2011). These contours of inequality indicate that understanding the broader political and economic context is necessary for feminist critique, and the role of the media in reifying the dominant ideology highlights its importance in the analysis of such injustices.

A political economy approach in the study of media and communication enables an understanding of a range of dynamics, including the ownership of media channels and platforms, the control and regulation of channels of communication, and the role of media forms in perpetuating the normalization of exploitation within capitalist ideology. Because the majority of the media content to which we are exposed is produced and distributed by large-scale private corporations, such as Tencent, Fuji, Alphabet (the owner of Google), Disney, and Facebook, the starting point for all decisions related to the media these organizations produce will be based on the **profit motive**. Production decisions that may seem progressive – such as featuring Black female leads on television programmes, rebooting franchises by casting actors from previously under-represented groups, and developing new media platforms that allow non-professionals to create and share media content – are all premised on the notion that these choices will increase market share for the corporation that owns the media property and therefore result in larger profit margins for its shareholders. Feminist political economy research on communication considers these dynamics from the perspective that they are gendered and inequitable across production and consumption, and that capitalist ideology 'is used to stabilise the unequal social relations' (Lee 2011: 83).

Marxist political economy, with its critical approach to the organization of production, labour relations, wealth distribution, and resulting inequalities, has a clear parallel with intersectional feminist critique in its concern with not only examining the dynamics of power and oppression but also pursuing transformations in society, in this case through the redistribution of income and wealth. However, there has not always been a symmetrical interest in the intersectional nature of class-based oppression (Acker 2006), shaped as it is by gender, race, location, and sexuality. Indeed, it has been commonplace for Marxist theory to prioritize questions of economics and finance over questions of gender and race (Meehan and Riordan 2002). Feminist political economy has filled this gap, theorizing the relationship between capitalism and systems of domination including patriarchy and White supremacy, noting a commonality across these structures in terms of how power operates to maintain itself and the privileges of a relatively small group benefitting most from wealth inequalities. Riordan (2002) suggests that an important approach within feminist political economy is the consideration of the interaction of macro-institutions such as governments and industries with the day-to-day experiences of the individual. This would include an analysis of practices of consumption, which sustain capitalism and its class, race, and gender inequalities, as well as both paid and unpaid labour related to the media, which we discuss in greater detail below. An important point to keep in mind, however, is that class is not an essential internal category, nor is it determined by education or occupation, as is at times imagined when discussing 'social class'. In a feminist political economy, class must be understood as a function of our relations within capitalist economic structures, where the worker's labour is exploited by the owner (McLaughlin 2002).

Understanding the deep entanglement of class with race, gender, and sexuality is a key element of interest within Black feminist theory and its conceptualization of intersectional oppressions, and this emphasis pre-dates the emergence of the field of feminist political economy. Indeed, in the 1977 Combahee River Collective Statement, class-based oppression, socialist organizing, and Marxist theory are all explicitly referenced in relation to an interlocking axis of domination faced by women of colour. As Black feminist work has shown, the commodification of working bodies originates in the enslavement of people of colour by colonizing forces, indicating how the exploitation of labour is rooted in racial and colonial oppressions, and sustained by consumerist practices of 'eating the other' that perpetuate the commodification of racialized bodies (hooks 1992).

Within feminist theory and activism, however, the importance of class and the broader political-economic structures shaping women's unique lived experiences has not always been addressed. As Smith (2013–14) notes, Friedan's celebrated analysis in the *Feminine Mystique* (1963) of women's work in the home focused largely on White, college-educated, middle-class, suburban women, and did not address the lived experiences of Black women who were already working outside the domestic sphere. Indeed, at the time, Black women wage earners were framed as deviant and the cause of social ills and poverty because of how they inverted normative dynamics related to men as breadwinners. By ignoring the diversity of women's experiences, Friedan also overlooked the labour that would be needed to support the housewives she wrote about when they began working outside the home – female domestic workers, often women of colour, themselves hired to engage in housework and child care for others in addition to their own. This highlights a key distinction to be made between exploitation in economic relations and oppression based on gender, race, and sexuality. As Smith argues, 'both exploitation and oppression are rooted in capitalism.

Exploitation is the method by which the ruling class robs workers of surplus value; the various forms of oppression play a primary role in maintaining the rule of a tiny minority over the vast majority. In each case, the enemy is one and the same' (2013–14: n.p.). Smith further argues that the unification of oppressed people as part of a common struggle not only aligns with Marxist objectives but strengthens the liberatory project of rectifying economic injustice by providing a means to address all forms of tyranny, across class stratifications.

The shaping role of capitalist ideology will thus be central to an intersectional feminist media analysis, including how its norms structure media production and therefore representation. Consider for instance the various ways the media contribute to the vilification not only of alternative economic systems such as communism, but also of organizations such as unions and guilds that seek to protect and strengthen the rights of workers. Overall, across both fiction and non-fiction media, we can see a range of discourses and images that reify the dynamics of capitalism while vilifying the alternatives. This can be linked to the concentration of ownership within media industries, limiting diversity in voices and perspectives as well as opportunities for grassroots and independent producers to flourish. We can also observe how the media circulate negative stereotypes of those who are most disadvantaged by disparities in wealth distribution. For example, in her examination of television, newspaper, and online texts, Tyler finds that White British working-class people, and in particular mothers, are framed as 'chavs', a figure marked overwhelmingly by the affective response of disgust. She argues that 'the cumulative effect of disgust at chavs is the screening of the disenfranchised white poor from view; they are rendered invisible' (2008: 32), thereby reaffirming class hierarchies.

Smythe's (1981) theory of the **audience commodity** is useful for understanding the relationship between production and the content circulating within media culture. This concept highlights the importance of activities that might not be understood traditionally as work, in this case the attention of media audiences. As most media are delivered to audiences at a fraction of what they cost to produce – or indeed, as is the case with social media, for free – revenues are generated by the sale of advertising space or time to vendors. In this transaction, the eyeballs (or ears or clicks or interactions) of media audiences become a commodity, sold by media producers to marketers. Because the attention of audiences has an exchange value, there is an economic rationale for creating media that speaks to groups framed as lucrative based on their disposable income or spending power, as for instance in the case of tween girls discussed by Coulter (2014) or the development of the Black Entertainment Television cable network analysed by Smith-Shomade (2007). Analyses like these, considering the industrial context underlying the development of media, support Meehan's argument from her research on 1970s broadcast television, where, she states, 'taking a feminist perspective reveals that societal divisions of labor based on gender, plus prejudicial assumptions about gender, played a significant role in defining and differentiating the commodity audience' (2002: 216), leading to the valuation of the White male audience and the framing of all others as niche.

Taking an intersectional approach to the audience commodity allows us to address the relationship between the segmentation of markets based on demographics such as age, gender, race, and social class and the construction of audiences for media texts premised on distinctions such as 'chick flicks' and 'girl games'. How the context of production contributes to this is revealed in Saha's (2016) analysis of the publishing industry. He notes that risk-averse marketing strategies such as the recycling of images on book covers are part of a process of rationalization that structures the work of cultural workers such as editors as well as markets of readers. He finds that British Asian authors are categorized and positioned according to their ethnicity within 'multicultural' fiction, rather than according to genre or type of writing. In these normalized practices for minimizing uncertainty in the publishing industry, he argues, we can observe a 'rationalizing/racializing logic of capital' (2016: 2) that constructs niche cultural objects and audiences – a logic shaping many objects of intersectional feminist media analysis, such as those produced by and targeted at gendered subjects.

Another clear example of how industrial production practices marginalize and constrain seemingly 'diverse' media products can be found in the identification of lesbian, gay, and bisexual communities as viable consumer markets and the rise of texts, media properties, and sites aimed at gay audiences. Sender (2001) reviews how a US-based magazine for this audience, *The Advocate*, developed from a grassroots, activist publication into a glossy lifestyle magazine, delimiting its imagined 'gay' audience to affluent, socially mobile, frequently urban, White male professionals. As her example shows, marketing to previously marginalized groups is less an indicator of greater social acceptance of these communities than a method of seizing on opportunities presented by 'niche' markets, which entails the construction of particular tastes, knowledge, and aesthetics for an imagined consumer audience. Sender concludes, 'the profile of gay consumers the *Advocate's* publishers and others sold to interested corporate marketers has been distorted with considerable cost to lesbian and gay civil rights' (2001: 93), resulting in class, race, and gender-based differentiation and stratification within this subculture, as well as an emphasis on assimilation within the dominant culture rather than resistance or subversion. Shohat refers to this as the '**commodification of difference**' (1998: 5), a practice of explicitly committing to diversity in content without engaging in work to dismantle the systems of domination that marginalize those framed as 'different' to begin with. Overall, what these critiques should demonstrate is that the interests of commercially produced media, for instance in cultivating new consumer markets, do not equate to the progressive aims of feminism. The creation of products for marginalized groups to consume, and even the mobilization of liberatory, socially conscious discourse within those groups, should not be simplistically understood as representing a structural change leading to greater equity.

Despite the very real consequences of the profit motive driving concentrated global media ownership, political economists of communication do not advocate an understanding of the media as solely driven by finance, noting the importance of social relations and culture in shaping and potentially transforming the media landscape (Mosco 2009). Similarly, we must keep in mind that the creation of delimited markets such as the gay consumer group discussed by Sender does not determine media uses or indeed the possibility of resistance. Commodification presents challenges to political aims but does not foreclose them. As discussed in Chapter 5, the visibility of groups that were previously absent from mediated content is a complex question, risking depoliticization and co-optation by dominant culture but also presenting an opportunity to challenge marginalization and contest hegemonic ideas and framings circulating in the media. Sender (2005) highlights in her analysis that this is a key tension in the interplay of economics and politics. A feminist media critique should always keep these contradictions between resistance and commodification in mind when considering the industrial context underpinning media production and work.

As this brief overview indicates, while political economy and feminist theory have not always engaged with each other, there are clear parallels, symmetries, and points of complementarity valuable for feminist media studies. In the following sections, we draw on this critical approach to understand the relationship between economics and social forces in gendered media work by considering what women do in the media and the shape of this work. I divide the latter somewhat arbitrarily by degree of formality. First, we consider women's formal work in the media, which refers in the broadest sense to labour compensated by wages paid to the worker by the employer as part of the basic process of commodification at the heart of the capitalist system. We then turn to informal work, referring to a broad spectrum of activity not defined as traditional work, but which dynamically interacts with, supports, and shapes paid labour. We conclude by considering the concept of the **feminization of work** in the sphere of contemporary media production, before turning to action for change in this sphere.

The formal labour of women in the media

As with the statistics from film-making cited earlier in this chapter, more general surveys of the demographic breakdown of media industries and workplaces reveal severe imbalances in occupational presence, with women underemployed not only as film directors and writers but also as video game programmers, television editors, radio producers, and cinematographers, to name only a few high-profile roles. However, not all forms of work are equally visible or valued. For this reason, some forms of participation in the media are generally hidden from view because of how they are framed, measured, rewarded, and recognized within popular culture, their industries, and even in research. Consider for instance the less prestigious and significantly less well-paid media roles of costuming, production assistance, and make-up artistry, to name a few. These roles have been referred to as **below-the-line** work, which refers to how they are budgeted for in the production of movies, television, and commercials (Banks 2009). Fixed costs for high-profile roles – those of actors, directors, writers, producers, etc. – appear 'above-the-line', or at the top of the budget, whereas the tasks of others on a creative production team are considered variable and are metaphorically as well as literally positioned below the more prestigious roles in production planning. These include jobs that are typically contract-based as well as lower status, ranging from boom operators to directors of photography to light technicians. While within film these categories mark a distinction between creative production on the one hand and craft/technical work on the other, the implications for recognition and reward of media work can be extended beyond film to consider how different positions are hierarchized, and the implications of this for pay, job stability, and appreciation as well as the gendering of media work.

For instance, work may fall below-the-line because of its lack of visibility in relation to how medium-specific work is documented. In their discussion of film and television production, Ball and Bell explore how statistics reflecting the low numbers of women in the industry are exacerbated by how little of their work is recorded in documents such as memos and production files. Women in the screen industries have historically undertaken work that leaves 'little or no archival trace' (2013: 551), such as casting, continuity, editing, mixing, costume design, wardrobe, make-up, negative cutting and assembly, publicity, and secretarial, research, and library roles. Because these forms of participation in media work are not tracked or documented, they become instances of what is called **invisible labour** – contributions that are essential to the functioning of production but, being less traceable, are not attributed as much significance as more high-profile roles. The invisibility of this kind of labour means that workforce statistics must be read critically, and researchers may need to go beyond quantitative metrics such as workforce surveys to reveal what was always present. As discussed by Ball and Bell, this entails forms of research such as oral histories to bring women's contributions into view, or feminist media archaeologies that surface and re-presence the kinds of manual work that existing cultural narratives of invention and innovation obscure (Shorey and Rosner 2019).

Such approaches are central to feminist work in what is called **production studies**, a primarily qualitative approach to examining the conditions of media work and the processes, practices, and institutionalized forces shaping the media we engage with (see, for example, Mayer et al. 2009). For instance, Banks (2009) considers the constitution of professional identities to understand how media work is gendered through perceptions of skills and knowledges as well as how these are hierarchized. Her work with costume designers illuminates below-the-line workers' perspectives on their labour and the industry, challenging the norm of focusing on the viewpoints of singular creative auteurs (who are usually men). She defines the area of feminist production studies as research 'grounding a reading of production within a distinct sociohistorical and economic context to examine a text, a profession, a character – even an individual – as a cultural and anthropological artifact' (2009: 96). As this suggests, such an approach shares with feminist political economy an interest in examining the lived experiences of workers as well as the broader institutions shaping media production, considering how these together contribute to the gendering of media work and impact on the visibility of women's contributions.

In addition to how invisible some kinds of work are, women's contributions may be hierarchized as below-the-line because of how they are valued. Many forms of invisible labour undertaken by women in the media, and the skills they entail, are devalued as less creative, less technical, and therefore less meaningful in media-making. This echoes the differentiation of women's work across labour markets (Adkins 2005). Consider again Banks' research on the profession of costume design. She demonstrates how this work entails a great deal of expertise, and is essential to creating a believable scene, be it in a historical period film set in the Han Dynasty in China or a contemporary high school television series exploring interpersonal dynamics in a Scottish village. Despite its significance, costume design is devalued as 'women's work' due to the tools of the trade being cloth, thread, and needles, all of which are associated with traditional notions of domestic labour – a gendering of the profession that goes along with its underappreciation and undervaluation in terms of material compensation. In addition to this association, the work of a costume designer involves being physically close with actors' bodies, requiring the practitioner to develop a trusting rapport with them. As evidence, Banks quotes a television writer who refers to the emotional needs of the actor that the costume designer must attend to in their work. Therefore, part of the gamut of talents required in this below-the-line work is what we might understand informally as 'soft' or 'people' skills.

Within feminist theory, this kind of work has been conceptualized as **emotional labour**, which refers to 'the management of feeling to create a publicly observable facial and bodily display' (Hochschild 1983: 7), as required by one's profession. Hochschild coined this term when examining how feelings must be expressed or quashed 'in order to sustain the outward countenance that produces the proper state of mind in others' (1983: 7). Her theorization is based on research into the enforced friendliness of airline crew members as well as the performed irritability of debt collectors. In this ground-breaking study, she demonstrates how in service work the requirements placed by the employer on the worker to exercise this control over their feelings and those of their customers lead to emotions becoming commodified, alienating people from their feelings in the workplace. Expectations about who is good at what kinds of emotional labour are distinctly gendered (consider for instance the affect of police officers compared to that of social workers), and because of how care has been framed as a feminized practice in both domestic and working environments, women's emotional labour has been a topic of great research interest, including how undervalued this work is. We will return to this topic in more detail below.

Considering the histories of a given field can provide insight into how and why certain roles and contributions become less well-regarded and rewarded, obscuring in particular the participation of women in media work. Reynolds (1998) writes about women employed as editors in the French film industry in the 1930s, and details how as production became more formalized, sophisticated, and cost-intensive, ushering in formal hierarchies of work, women's participation become less common, aside from in acting roles. Where they did appear, primarily as editors, their work was framed according to feminized metaphors, including sewing, marriage, and child-birth, mirroring Banks' finding that costume design is discursively linked to shopping and an interest in fashion rather than skilful artistry. The archival work of Gaines et al. (2013), documenting the large number of women involved in silent film production across an array of roles, demonstrates how common histories of male pioneers belie the role of women in the early film industry. Hill's (2016) research on the wide-ranging contributions of women – including the wives of employees, and immigrants to the US – in Hollywood film-making details how their work was discursively framed as menial or mechanical despite its significance to the industry, linking 'women's work' to low pay and status. Ball and Bell (2013) explore the disappearance of women within television workplaces, noting how employment came to be structured according to categories determined by the unions, meaning that women working as production secretaries were categorized at the 'supplementary grade', a devalued status that framed their work as 'secretarial' rather than 'technical', making a career transition into editing, camera, or sound roles nearly impossible. We can observe these distinctions between technical/creative work and administrative/secretarial work at play in the video games industry, where statistics on the numbers of women in programming (5 per cent), audio (10 per cent), and design (10 per cent) belie the broader picture of where women do work – including in marketing, public relations and sales (25 per cent), and operations, IT, and human resources (47 per cent) (Prescott and Bogg 2011) – enabling discourse about the absence of women in the industry without recognition of their existing contributions. This intensifies the gendered dynamics of digital gaming, where, as we saw in Chapter 2 in relation to game designer Roberta Williams, women became invisible in game history with the prioritization of programming over narrative. Across these histories of different media industries, women's work is actively devalued and minimized as the sector becomes larger and more profitable, leading to the invisibility and denigration of their contributions, as well as lower pay, all of which amounts to a foreclosure on their participation with long-lasting repercussions.

Indeed, a focus on what we deem to be legitimately 'creative' media production work overlooks the extent and diversity of the labour entailed in the media. Nakamura asserts that 'cheap female labour is the engine that powers the internet' (2015: 106), and Mayer (2011) demonstrates how this is also the case with the electronic assembly entailed in the production of television sets. If we broaden our analysis to include the range of labour and locations involved in manufacturing the devices we rely on to access and engage with music, film, social media, and apps, then we can see how women are central to media production globally, and better understand the character of this work. Mayer argues that assembly line workers and others essential to the functioning of media production must be understood as 'producers betwixt and between the restrictive and expansive notions of production' (2011: 1), challenging simplistic ideas about the relationship between labour, identity, and the political economy of media. This is the case too with the broader range of labour underpinning the media, including those in Africa who mine the minerals essential to the construction of mobile phones, the workers who put together electronic devices in fabrication laboratories in East Asia, the hands that scan texts for Google Books, those who filter out the pornographic, abusive, and illegal content we do not see on social media, the people working in e-waste disposal and recycling centres in Pakistan, Vietnam, and Ghana, and many other workers engaged in the often physically and psychologically deleterious below-the-line labour that sustains media production (see Nakamura 2011 for an example related to the production of the iPhone). These forms of media labour are frequently undertaken by poor, racialized, and otherwise marginalized people in the Global South, and are then disavowed by the media industries they contribute to as not being part of the sector of production. Gendered stereotypes about nimble fingers (McLaughlin and Johnson 2008) and attention to detail (Nakamura 2014) are frequently deployed to naturalize and essentialize this work. The invisibility of these forms of dirty media work is partly the result of its effectiveness – as Roberts points out in relation to the work of behind-the-scenes online content moderation, 'who misses what is not there?' (2016: n.p.). In feminist approaches to media work, then, it is essential to shift the focus from the limited number of roles classified as 'creative media production' or 'above-the-line' work in order to recognize and analyse the breadth of formal media labour.

As this section has shown, women's paid work in the media, when it is not invisible, is framed according to gendered terms, metaphors, and labels, shaping who is hired for certain roles as well as how skills will be valued and rewarded. This is often based on common cultural stereotypes about who is best suited or more 'naturally' inclined to certain kinds of activities, but, as we have seen, these ideas are frequently challenged by historical analysis demonstrating how this work is structured and organized according to gender-based assumptions rather than actual performance. This gendering of the pathways and practices of women in media work is an important consideration for understanding the nature of their participation in formal creative media production as well as other kinds of media work. In the next section, we consider how new media have supported the rise of amateur production and examine how this kind of 'informal' work can be seen to extend and deepen inequalities when viewed through the lens of feminist theory and political economy critique.

The informal labour of women in the media

Many assumptions about the shape and nature of media work have been challenged by the rise of software, platforms, and technologies enabling amateur production, which forms part of what we might understand as informal labour in the landscape of media culture. As we saw in Chapter 5, 'new media' have been celebrated for their provision of accessible, do-it-yourself tools which allow users to create and distribute creative media productions, with possible benefits for young women in particular. Examples of informal media-making are prevalent online, with amateurs uploading videos showcasing their singing and dancing on YouTube, publishing their poetry and cultural critique on blogs, sharing their illustrations on Tumblr, and demonstrating their programming abilities by developing and modifying video games. As the argument goes, anyone with access to a networked computer, tablet or smartphone can garner an audience for their productions, democratizing a media system that is hierarchical, narrow, and homogeneous. Given the exclusion of women from creative roles in formal media production, new media's accessibility would seem to hold especial promise for them and for other marginalized communities. In this section, we take a brief overview of the affordances of new media enabling participation, and then look at what feminist theory has to offer for reconceptualizing these practices.

New media and in particular social media enable and indeed depend on a range of contributions and forms of participation enacted by users. The 'social' in social media refers to the way these platforms are fuelled by the activity and content generated by those engaging on these sites. Take for example YouTube. In addition to the DIY videos made by amateur musicians, YouTube personalities, make-up and hair artists, and comedians, the platform also depends on the activity of those who view, rate, subscribe to, and comment on their videos. The functioning of other social media sites such as Weibo, Twitter, and Instagram rely on the posts users make, from the most banal birthday greetings on Facebook to the carefully researched comment on a blog post. These activities are largely unpaid and are often neither strictly creative nor technical, and yet they are as essential to the basic functioning of these platforms as the invisible labourers engaged in hardware manufacturing and content moderation discussed above. As we will see, this work is also distinctly gendered.

Within the context of these ubiquitous informal contributions to the new media landscape, an array of forms of participation emerge that problematize the very distinction between informal and formal labour, making it at times difficult to discern the status of the media content producer. Consider for instance the video game streaming platform Twitch, acquired by Amazon for nearly 1 billion dollars in 2014, with a reported 2.2 million monthly streamers and 15 million daily users in 2018. Here, audiences gather to watch specific players or streams of games being played live, interacting using free or premium emojis on chat channels. There are, however, different tiers of streamers on this site, as those broadcasting their play can earn a profit via Twitch's Affiliate Program. Making money on the site is dependent on the individual streamer being able to **monetize** their channel by building an adequate following and so gaining the attention of advertisers and sponsors. Twitch is but one example of a key trend in participatory media culture, whereby everyday users can shift from being amateur producers to the status of compensated media-makers; first, however, they must do the work to be discovered, not in this case through an agent, casting director, or other formal talent-spotter, but by way of a multitude of other internet users. Building a sufficient audience on social media enables a user to participate in monetization strategies that will convert others on the platform into their very own audience commodities. In other words, at some point in this process, and perhaps unbeknownst to (or perhaps assumed by) the average viewer, unpaid work is being undertaken by a streamer, YouTube commentator, or fashion Instagrammer, in order to develop their own personal brand. The goal of this entrepreneurial informal labour, directed by the individual and supported by the affordances of the platform, is to shift into compensated media work, replicating some of the patterns of earlier media's political economy, such as the sale of eyeballs to advertisers, but on a more micro-level. As recent research indicating gender pay gaps for Twitch streamers indicates (Fogel 2018), these supposedly accessible routes to new media work remain riven by inequalities.

As this brief review of new media's capacity for shifting traditional patterns of content development demonstrates, 'media production is no longer the domain of the media industries proper' (Cavalcante et al. 2017: 5). It is easy to be seduced by the promises of democratization associated with new media production, particularly for marginalized communities who can use these platforms to make and share media as well as connect with like-minded others despite geographical distances. In Chapter 5 we reviewed how these opportunities have been seized by girls engaging in feminist media-making (Kearney 2006), particularly on blogging sites (Keller 2015). Research also demonstrates that these platforms enable the dissemination of critical commentary about Black womanhood (Brock et al. 2010), the storytelling and identity exploration of trans YouTube users (Raun 2014), and the development of **user-generated content** featuring portrayals of Native Americans that challenge stereotypes (Kopacz and Lawton 2011), to name a few positive findings.

Critical responses to the democratization of new media indicate that our assessment of its potential for creative expression does, however, need to be tempered. Turner argues that while new media have increasingly come to depend on the participation and content generation of everyday users – what he refers to a 'demotic turn' – nevertheless 'one can't jump to the conclusion that a widening of access necessarily carries with it a democratic politics' (2010: 1) – a point supported by the range of vitriolic misogynistic, racist, and otherwise hateful discourse circulating on digital media discussed in the previous chapter. Amateur media production online, users' aspirations to become social media celebrities, as well as participation in reality TV programmes and talk shows, are all examples of how media, new and old alike, have shifted to include content about, or generated by, 'ordinary people', making possible an audience interactivity that is unprecedented but of uncertain value when it comes to democracy, progress, and justice.

Furthermore, notions of empowerment based on new media become slightly less convincing when we consider the corporate infrastructure underpinning informal online media production activity. In 1999, only eight years after the internet was commercialized in the West, Dan Schiller authored *Digital Capitalism*, detailing networked communication's pervasive market-based logic premised on private ownership, deregulation, and the deepening of social inequalities. Subsequent research has found that the above-described shifts in the global media production process, from abundant audience activity to widespread content creation to accessible technologies of distribution, raise questions precisely because of how the internet has come to extend and even deepen the dynamics of exploitation and commodification by relying on the **free labour** of its users (Terranova 2000). We saw in Chapter 5 the structural and structuring power of the platform, and this shapes user activity in clearly defined ways, challenging triumphant notions of user agency in participatory culture (van Dijck 2009). The commercial nature of the internet and its dependence on unpaid user activity have necessitated conceptual development of the political economy of media, including approaches that capture how the goods and services circulating therein are often informational rather than tangible in nature. One important theory in this context is that of **immaterial labour**, which refers to the work entailed in creating and circulating information, wherein profit is generated through the commodification of cognitive and affective efforts (Lazzarato 1996). Media production is based on formal labour that may be material or immaterial, as we saw in the previous section. The business models of sites based on informal production depend on the extraction of value from precisely these kinds of efforts, without paying a wage to those who generate capital for the platform owners. However, immaterial labour is not unique to these platforms nor to technologies, and the longer history of thinking about the value of this kind of activity and how it is conceptualized and compensated reveals a clear connection between critiques of digital labour and feminist theory.

Some of the earliest debates about the nature of informal and immaterial work emerge from feminist action related to the domestic sphere, a site where emotional, affective work is undertaken on an everyday basis by women for no pay. In the period we identify as the second wave of feminism, the question of how to define work and labour arose in relationship to the largely invisible forms of domestic care work, from housework to sex to child-rearing, undertaken in the private realm of the home by women who were excluded from formal workplaces. Wages for Housework, a campaign spearheaded in Italy in 1972 by Marxist feminists including Selma James and Silvia Federici, aimed to initiate a global movement raising awareness of the essential role played by gendered care workers in sustaining the production process. The movement also sought to challenge the exclusion of housework from discussions of workers' struggles, as well as its devaluation in critical thought. Activists argue that the work performed by women outside formal production contexts – from biological reproduction and child care to food preparation and maintenance of the domestic environment – is labour essential to the well-being of paid workers and therefore to the functioning of capitalism. The Wages for Housework movement sought to gain international recognition for this work of **social reproduction**, not necessarily by literally securing wages for housework, but by opening a conversation about how this labour, its gendering as feminine, and its unwaged status create an oppressive dynamic between male and female working-class individuals and contribute to male domination (Fortunati 1988). As the idea spread, it was adapted to reflect the diverse concerns of women, including Black and lesbian women, who are required to engage in additional immaterial labour under a system of White supremacy and heteronormativity. Critiquing the status of this immaterial labour as unpaid and its framing as naturally and uniquely feminine – as though women are born loving to vacuum for free – reveals a lengthy historical trajectory linking certain kinds of work to certain kinds of bodies. Furthermore, insights on how forms of domestic care work are framed as 'labours of love' (Federici 1975: 2) indicates how free labour sustains capitalism through appeals to affective relations, a pattern replicated in discussions of informal digital labour.

This brief overview of feminist activism related to unwaged work in the home demonstrates the commonalities between housework and the formal and informal labour of women in the media, including its under- and unpaid status as well as its invisibility, denigration, and devaluation (Luxton 1997). There are clear parallels with how the freely given and uncompensated immaterial labour of internet users becomes a key source of value while being framed as 'not work'. Despite this denial of its status as labour, the activity and data of internet users is retained as the property of platform owners through legal mechanisms such as end-user licence agreements and terms of service. The Wages for Facebook art project (wagesforfacebook.com) draws on exactly these parallels in its manifesto, which notes that online platforms render invisible how user activities are generative of capital, naturalizing this work as based on social and affective relations of sharing, caring, and friendship. Both Jarrett (2016) and Gajjala (2018) draw explicit parallels between the labour undertaken in the digital and domestic spheres, referring respectively to 'the digital housewife' and 'digital domesticity' to shine a light on how commonplace framings of online activity render its affective and gendered work invisible. As Jarrett argues in relation to the digital housewife, while there is a history of such work being linked to women, this figure is not necessarily gendered. In contemporary economic relations we are witnessing what Haraway (1991) refers to as the feminization of work. Workers are feminized in new relations of production and reproduction as their work becomes increasingly vulnerable and exploited – lower paid, based on contracts, mobile by necessity – but also related to affective interactions entailing relationship-building, care, and emotion. In other words, the feminization of work occurs when it becomes like that associated with the attributes of women's work historically – immaterial, affective, largely invisible, and **precarious**.

Consider an example from informal media participation that has become increasingly formalized – social media engagement. In a report entitled 'Benchmarking Women's Leadership in the US', Lennon finds that 'in newer sectors, such as technology and social media, where gatekeepers have not yet emerged, women are better represented in positional leadership roles' (2013: 8). However, despite its centrality to the functioning of news agencies in particular, this work on social media is not necessarily highly valued. Levinson (2015) characterizes it as 'the pink ghetto of social media', referring to its marginalization in the news room despite the fact that social media editors are under immense pressure, responsible for filling any holes in the news cycle and at risk of the chopping block if any of their rapid-fire content is deemed objectionable. At the same time, however, this work is framed as easy compared to 'hard news', and is consequently paid less, often uncredited, infrequently rewarded by pay rises or promotions, and in many cases rendered invisible. It is also work that entails immediate contact between news producers and their reading public, requiring the emotional labour that has been associated with women's work in the media historically. Despite the promise of greater opportunities for women, shifts related to digital labour reify many of the gendered inequalities linked to recognition and reward observed in relation to formal media work. Furthermore, the invisibility and marginality of feminized social media labour extends far beyond news media, as demonstrated by recent research on job advertisements for this role (Duffy and Schwartz 2018).

And yet, as Duffy and Wissinger (2017) reveal in their examination of articles on social media celebrity published between 2006 and 2016, myths about this kind of work predominate, celebrating it as the height of 'doing what you love and getting paid' as well as an inherently meritocratic and democratic activity through which anyone can find fame as long as they are sufficiently talented and hard-working – what is called **aspirational labour**. The reality underpinning such myths includes the high barriers to entry in most industries related to social media celebrity (typically creative industries such as fashion, advertising, and games), as well as structural inequalities, persistent instability, the blurring of boundaries between the personal and the professional, and the need for constant self-improvement and technological upgrade. In sum, this work is precarious rather than stable, and depends on performances of positive affect such as passion and gratitude as well as high-risk entrepreneurial self-branding efforts that are often unpaid. The need to cultivate and maintain a normatively attractive appearance as part of this self-branding (Duffy and Hund 2015) – what has been referred to as glamour labour (Wissinger 2015) and aesthetic labour (Elias et al. 2017) – highlights how for women, on a transnational level, informal media work can demand stringent bodily disciplining according to status quo ideals of the body beautiful.

Many of these trends are an extension of patterns that have been identified in other forms of media work. Gill (2002) finds that gender inequalities in new media work are based on some of the values most celebrated in these 'cool, creative' jobs – autonomy, flexibility, and informality. A range of research on trends in creative and cultural work demonstrates how precarity – long hours, low pay, temporary contracts, the need for ongoing development, overall insecurity, judgement based on your last success, as well as self-branding activities – is intensified by the dynamics of free, immaterial, and affective labour in digital capitalism. While the do-it-yourself entrepreneurial approach is celebrated in a range of fields and types of work – perhaps most visibly in the rise of the sharing or gig economy supported by platforms and apps – this kind of **venture labour** is primarily characterized by high risks and not necessarily commensurately high rewards (Neff 2012). Unlike the kind of entrepreneurship where an individual sets up their own business, in this economy the precarious worker is still an employee and does not own the means of production, which means they are taking on the risks associated with innovation and development as part of the exploitation of their labour. While these trends impact on the workforce broadly, as the idea of the feminization of labour indicates, there remain additionally gendered implications that disproportionately impact on women and people of colour (van Doorn 2017), including lower pay despite longer working hours (Barzilay and Ben-David 2017) and the burden of unwaged labour required to combat normalized misogyny, racism, and abusive discourse on social media platforms through tactics such as public education, technical fixes, and social intervention (Nakamura 2015). As van Doorn concludes, 'in the world of platform labor, inequality is a feature rather than a bug' (2017: 907), an observation that presents a stark challenge to discourses of empowerment, democratization, and meritocracy.

When conducting a feminist media analysis of contemporary developments in gendered media work, then, it is vitally important to be attuned to continuities as much as to changes. Immaterial labour online generates commodities that may not have existed in the 1970s, but it remains no less linked to the physical world through bodies than was the labour of housewives agitating for wages. Women's entry into paid workforces was a major feminist victory but it did not resolve many issues, including how women are still largely responsible for a 'second shift' of unwaged domestic labour after their paid work ends (Hochschild and Machung 1989), a dynamic that may actually be further exacerbated by ICTs enabling work at all times of day (Gregg 2011) and by the reliance of women in the formal workforce on the care work provided by women from the Global South (Fraser 2016). The more things change, it seems, the more they stay the same when it comes to the gendering of work within and beyond the media.

Feminist media action in production and work

The unequal opportunities faced by women in media work have gained mainstream attention and motivated the formation of a wide range of groups and projects focused on 'getting more women into' creative media production, as well as on supporting women already working in media industries. For example, Women in Film and TV International (WIFTI) is a global network with the mission of 'uniting women working in the film, television and other screen-based industries including executive, creative, and technical fields' (WIFTI 'About Us' page). This objective is pursued through activities including mentorship, networking, research, lobbying, and the recognition and celebration of women's work through awards ceremonies. Similar language is used to describe the activities of Women in Animation, Women in Games International, and Women in Radio, to name but a few organizations, all of which refer to the 'advancement of women' in their mission statements. The processes through which this support is given, however, are not necessarily clear, particularly for those who have not paid (or may be unable to pay) membership dues, or who have not yet broken into the industry. *What does it mean to 'advance' women in fields they have been excluded from? What kinds of change are envisioned as possible by these organizations, and through what kinds of action? How might inclusion challenge or support trends towards precarity and the feminization of work?*

One area that has received sustained research and critique in this context is women in games initiatives. Research on digital games culture demonstrates how this media form has been gendered as masculine, leading to games, communities, sites, and experiences that can be exclusionary of women and girls (Jenson and de Castell 2013), people of colour (Gray 2012), and people in the LGBTQ+ community (Shaw 2014). Fron et al. (2007), theorizing what they call 'the hegemony of play', explore how the near-universal human activity of play became a delimited field when digitized, noting how a global system of industrial decision-making about design, marketing, and technologies contributed to a culture of exclusion. They delineate how the gendering of game culture is related to the homogeneous workforce in the games industry – by and large, its creative and technical roles are occupied by highly educated, heterosexual White and East Asian men. Within this narrow context of production, pervasive beliefs about the interests and desires of an imagined majority game-playing market circulate, mirroring the preferences of those who make the games. This echoes the argument about the relationship between those who create media and the texts they produce, and has been the motivation behind the formation of initiatives to encourage more women to make games.

As discussed in Chapter 2, to explore how the mission of getting more women into games has been envisioned and enacted, Fisher and I engaged in feminist participatory action research on several of these initiatives, participating in a short-term project (Fisher and Harvey 2013) as well as the community group it inspired in Toronto (Harvey and Fisher 2016). Along with Shepherd, I also researched a Montreal-based group formed to support women in games (Harvey and Shepherd 2016). Participating in these community initiatives allowed us to examine the complexities involved in such projects, including the tension between a quantitative approach to supporting individuals and a qualitative perspective focused on the structural exclusions that contribute to the need for such groups in the first place. The research revealed differences of opinion between stakeholders about how to effect change, including how to foster intersectionality, the importance and shape of 'safe spaces', the practicalities of engaging with corporate and other institutional partners, and even what kinds of games the participants should be making.

These differences cannot easily be linked to feminist waves, or the all-too-familiar intergenerational conflict narrative reviewed in Chapter 1 that frames disagreement as cat-fighting (Harvey and Fisher 2016). As Donegan discusses in her article on the internal debates characterizing the #MeToo campaign, disagreements about the action required to address sexism and gender-based inequalities have a long history in feminism. She frames these rifts in terms of the distinction between an individualistic feminism 'grounded in ideals of pragmatism, realism and self-sufficiency' and a social feminism that is 'expansive, communal, idealistic and premised on the ideals of mutual interest and solidarity' (2018: n.p.). Donegan notes that the focus of these debates is largely on how women's autonomy in relation to sexual harassment is envisioned, but the case of the #MeToo campaign is also relevant when considering how to address gaps in women's participation in media work.

The Me Too movement was originally conceived in 2006 by the activist Tarana Burke, as a tool for raising awareness of the ubiquity of sexual assault and abuse in society. In its recent resurrection by the American actress Alyssa Milano, to publicize normalized sexual harassment in Hollywood, it has been connected to the #TimesUp campaign focused on the intersection of sexualized abuse and labour in the media industries. The latter's website asserts that 'the clock has run out on sexual assault, harassment and inequality in the workplace. It's time to do something about it', though aside from instructions on how to contribute to the campaign's Legal Defense Fund, the means by which to participate in enacting this change are unclear. What this controversy has highlighted is how women's participation is not only less valued, recognized, and rewarded, but is also characterized by exploitative and abusive working conditions. While sometimes this is explicit, such as unwanted sexual advances towards actresses from men with the power to hire and fire them, in many industries it is more implicit, insidious, and based on dominant gender stereotypes and standardized professional norms. In the industries discussed above, such as film and television, assumptions about women's abilities shape whether or not they are hired (Ball and Bell 2013). Reliance on informal networks and apprenticeships also hinders the ability of women to gain experience, training, and access to opportunities in fields ranging from editing (Reynolds 1998) to ICT work (Eikhof 2012). Women furthermore face a lack of recognition and the delegitimization of their contributions within a field once they enter it, from documentary film-making (O'Brien 2018) to game development (Harvey and Shepherd 2016) and web design (Gill 2006).

While a handful of high-profile figures such as Bill Cosby, Woody Allen, and Harvey Weinstein have been linked to sexual harassment as part of #MeToo, these acts cannot be traced to just a few individuals. Feminist study and action needs to consider the cultural and structural features enabling this differential treatment, including the role women themselves play in perpetuating exclusionary and exploitative norms in the workplace. Consider for example O'Brien's (2017) research with women in senior management positions in the Irish media, across radio, television, and journalism. Despite what might seem to be a sign of positive change, with women appearing in leadership roles, O'Brien finds that the women she interviewed did not attempt to change masculinist norms or engage in structural transformation. Having women in leadership positions does not necessarily shift the overall representation of women in the media industries, nor the culture of their workplaces. For this reason, O'Brien argues that women in such roles might be understood as offering 'feminine leadership' rather than 'feminist leadership'. Feminist leadership is 'motivated by fairness, justice, and equality at micro and macro levels and is characterized by a transformative agenda that exposes and challenges patriarchy' (2017: 3). 'Feminine leadership' is exemplified by Sheryl Sandberg, COO of Facebook and author of the popular book *Lean In: Women, Work, and the Will to Lead* (2013), which explains how women can combat exclusions in the workplace on an individual level, focusing on tactics related to CV writing and interviewing as well as negotiating salary and pay rises. Sandberg embodies how women can shift gender norms by entering and succeeding in male-dominated fields, but do so without engaging in feminist action for structural change. 'Leaning in' instead normalizes inequalities by focusing on what individual women can do to help themselves in sexist cultures.

Farris and Rottenberg (2017) demonstrate that the feminist-inspired public discourse exemplified by 'Lean In' feminism tends to emphasize child-rearing and work-life balance as well as happiness and personal responsibility. In this way, such discourse turns away from previously core aims like liberation, justice, and equal rights, a shift that Farris and Rottenberg link to the embrace of an individualistic approach to gender parity. The focus on personal attributes and behaviours therefore aligns with the emphasis of capitalism on the power of the individual rather than transformations of systems premised on oppression, exploitation, and exclusion. Placing the onus on individual women to resist, not be too bothered, or get on with their work does not represent a sustainable, transformative solution to inequalities and abuse in media work. Furthermore, as Gill (2014) shows in her analysis of work in the creative and cultural industries, an emphasis on individualism and meritocracy can actually intensify gender inequalities by shutting down the ability to speak about and engage in action to change these norms. Finally, such individualized discourses about women's work in the media ignore the intersectional nature of exclusion, assuming a high degree of class-based privilege while ignoring the racialized elements of social reproduction historically and in contemporary arrangements (Glenn 1992). This has led to an alternative call for women who have been subject to abuse and exploitation to 'lean out' and refuse the toxicity of oppressive work environments (Shevinsky 2015).

Feminist media action focused on engaging with inequalities related to work and production must then consider alternatives to hegemonic, business-as-usual practices, including solidarity-building rather than individual efforts, an acceptance of difference and critical debate rather than oversimplified or universalizing approaches to women's experiences and perspectives, and transformative rather than status quo ways of thinking about media industries. As Donegan notes in her discussion of #MeToo, 'social feminism does not aspire to enable a few women to gain positions of power in patriarchal systems. It's not about giving women "a seat at the table". It's about taking the table apart, so that we can build a new one together' (2018: n.p.) This echoes Lorde and her famous assertion that 'the master's tools will never dismantle the master's house' (1984: n.p.). However, an important element of this oft-quoted insight that is not often highlighted is the fact that Lorde was speaking to White women about their exclusion of lesbians and women of colour in their organizing. To be effective, sustainable, and inclusive, feminist media action in the sphere of media production needs to address the intersections of exploitation and oppression within capitalism rather than celebrating individual success in exclusionary systems.

Part of this work entails re-envisioning how we think and talk about inequalities. Rather than taking an economic approach focused on how greater diversity in work may lead to better products, we might adopt a moral perspective on access and participation by considering Banks' proposal for thinking along the lines of **creative justice**. He argues that 'a job in culture is not only a significant material opportunity, it also provides the chance to secure status and recognition, as well as to participate in a practice, or more widely in the shared making of social and political life' (2017: 89). This perspective frames the equitable distribution of work as a question of social justice. In terms of tactics, Banks notes that quotas and other quantified metrics for inclusion have been criticized as setting diversity in opposition to merit. However, with the #MeToo and #TimesUp campaigns this idea has been given new life in mainstream culture, particularly with the notion of the 'inclusion rider'. Frances McDormand referred to this strategy in her acceptance speech at the 2018 Oscars (Dwyer 2018), drawing attention to Smith's (2014) suggestion that high-profile actors add a clause to their contracts stipulating that the gender balance of scripted characters match that of the film's setting, a tactic that could also be extended to representing people of colour. Powerful figures insisting on inclusion in this way is one key direction for justice in media work, particularly given the enduring nature of the challenges for intersectional gender equity discussed in the next chapter.

7 The Future of Feminist Media Studies and Action

As we have seen throughout the diverse approaches discussed in this book, feminism is a set of ideas and debates as well as a commitment to creating more equitable and just practices and institutions, including in media representations, cultures, industries, and research. Each chapter has showcased various actors and groups engaging with this objective of transformative change, highlighting the challenges as well as the opportunities presented by media cultures, platforms, and work, both contemporary and historical. In this final chapter, we look towards the future of feminist media studies and action based on the insights, challenges, debates, and examples examined throughout the book. While the way history is written tends to focus on breaks and conflicts, and contemporary research can fall into the trap of overemphasizing what appears to be new and different, this chapter aims to take stock of where we are in its continuities with where we have been. It does so in order to highlight the importance of drawing on the legacies and lessons of prior work for undertaking more rigorous, inclusive, and powerful analysis and action in the future. In this way, it provides a generative provocation for feminist media scholars moving forward.

As noted in Chapter 1, this book is inspired by and complements the original *Feminist Media Studies* written by Liesbet van Zoonen in 1994. She opens her book with an anecdote, recalling being asked by a journalist to comment on the release of American pop star Madonna's highly controversial album *Erotica*. It was assumed that as a feminist she would condemn in particular the explicitly sexual content of Madonna's work. In 2018, when the biggest news about Madonna was the celebration of her sixtieth birthday and her musical and cultural legacy, it seems almost quaint to reflect that her lingerie-inspired costuming and nude photos were once seen as taboo. The sexualization of culture has only intensified in the last twenty-five years, particularly within postfeminist media promising empowerment via the cultivation, maintenance, and display of a sexy body. However, just as quickly as the example appears dated, van Zoonen underlines the significance of the Madonna story, and its relevance today. When the journalist was disappointed by van Zoonen's enthusiastic and positive response, it became apparent that the request had been premised on the belief that 'a feminist viewpoint on the media implies a univocal, confident and unswerving denunciation of popular culture' (1994: 1). This framing of feminist commentators as killjoys is, it seems, timeless. But what this book has demonstrated throughout is that, despite such limiting frames, the field of feminist media studies is lively, growing, and productively engaging with pressing questions on an increasingly global level. Good thing too, as we have also explored a range of examples and developments in media culture indicating that intersectional and interdisciplinary research and action is even more necessary with the rise of digital media technologies and platforms.

As such developments highlight, our analysis needs to be timely, and it is therefore essential that we reflect on current affairs and emergent questions in the media. Recent research on the topic (Banet-Weiser 2018; Keller and Ryan 2018) has noted a key trend – the proliferation of 'feminisms' in media culture, particularly visible beginning in 2012. It seems that feminism is everywhere – in magazines, in the news, on T-shirts and notebooks, in every interview conducted with a prominent woman in the West. Neoliberal, liberal, popular, celebrity, consumer, and commodity feminism, as well as postfeminism – as we saw in Chapter 1 – are hotly contested but also highly visible, mediated expressions of feminist identifications and disavowals, constructing socially acceptable definitions of what it means to assert a feminist position. While they are diverse and at times contradictory, these articulations of what it means to be a feminist tend to share an emphasis on individual solutions to gender-based exclusions based on the privilege of purchasing power and self-disciplining practices in personal and professional domains. Through this, they serve to communicate that feminism is mainstream, common sense, and widely accepted, while actually supporting opposition to any critique of, or collective action against, the structural inequalities normalized by the connecting systems of domination composed of White supremacy, heteronormativity, patriarchy, and capitalism. As Renninger argues, such individualistic understandings of feminism promote 'a floating signifier label' (2018: 47) that comes unfixed from feminist dialogue, histories, and broader communities.

These expressions therefore contribute to the persistence of the killjoy figure by constructing feminism as little more than a brand to be traded and worn as an accessory, and by vilifying affects such as anger in the valuation of personal empowerment. Furthermore, as Gill (2016) notes in her discussion of the sale of feminism as part of 'cool capitalism' in brand culture, feminism as an identity is not accessible to all but celebrated when it is compatible with heterosexuality, fashion, beauty, and consumerism.

Finally, these articulations tend to reference and reinforce familiar discourses of intergenerational conflict, neutralizing the possibility of drawing power from the legacies, gains, and lessons afforded by engaging with feminist history. As such, contemporary articulations of feminism as a brand, identity, or label run directly in opposition to the aims of intersectional, collectivist action against oppression and marginalization. The prominence of these contemporary discourses is central to the field, as they contribute both to the complexity of our objects of analysis and to our broader understanding of its approach to scholarship and action.

As this would indicate, we should not be too quick to dismiss these discourses. Keller and Ryan (2018) note that something *feels different* about contemporary articulations of feminism in popular culture; and indeed, the idea of A-list celebrities such as Beyoncé and Emma Watson self-identifying as feminists would have been unthinkable even a few years ago. In their discussion of celebrity feminism, Hamad and Taylor argue that 'discursive struggles over the meanings of feminism are now, perhaps more than ever, largely staged in and through media culture' (2015: 126), which means that we ignore these struggles at our own peril. Furthermore, as Dejmanee (2016) demonstrates, wholly negative assessments of contemporary popular feminism, including celebrity feminism, bring us back to the intergenerational conflicts attributed to the shifts between feminist waves, particularly the second and third, about the ideal or perfect form of feminist action. For this reason, Keller and Ryan (2018) urge us to consider the complexities of these emergent feminisms in their convergences and divergences in relation to other and older forms of feminism, as these trends, while not wholly new, occur within a distinct media culture requiring careful scrutiny. This is why it is so vital to recall the broader history of feminism explored in Chapter 1 – without an eye to history we run the risk of contributing to depoliticizing narratives that reduce feminist debate to petty 'in-fighting'.

Of interest is how, alongside the sale of feminism as an identity, emergent feminisms include more critical, intersectional, action-oriented, and globally focused discourses and activities. This encompasses many of the examples of action we have considered throughout this book, including feminist media interventions such as the archiving projects considered in Chapter 2, the critical discourses about sexism and discrimination in media representations and work analysed in Chapters 3 and 6, the decolonizing knowledge work explored in Chapter 4, and the digital feminist activism discussed in Chapter 5. One well-known and oft-cited example of recent visible feminist action is the Everyday Sexism project initiated by British activist Laura Bates, seeking to raise awareness of the ongoing sexism faced in the daily lives of girls and women, on the streets, at school, and in the workplace. As noted in her book by the same name (2014), Bates takes her inspiration from statistics demonstrating major inequalities in the number of women in politics, the law, the sciences, the arts, and the media, despite the claims of mainstream discourse that 'we are all equal now'. The website she created in response has become a dynamic compendium of pervasive and banal experiences such as cat-calling, offensive advertising, and the dismissal of women's ideas in staff meetings, as well as sex- and gender-based violence including sexual assault and rape, on a global level. Crowdsourced from the experiences of thousands of women, this digital catalogue has garnered media attention, raised awareness, and generated conversation about a slew of structural and systemic forms of sexism in contemporary society. This example and the others explored throughout this book provide evidence of Gill's argument that, compared with just a few years ago when feminist issues had little traction in the media, now 'everything is a feminist issue. Feminism has a new luminosity in popular culture' (2016: 614). Gill wonders whether this might suggest that we are now in a **post-postfeminist** cultural moment, where the discourses of postfeminism no longer hold sway as feminism is so widely and exuberantly embraced. But taking a critical look at contemporary events as well as a long view of history demonstrates that we are in fact not 'post-' (in the sense of after or over) anything.

As the issues examined in Chapter 4 attest, we are not living in a post-racial world, but one in which race, migration status, colonial legacies, and location deeply shape one's possibilities. This is evidenced in the unevenness of the visibility of actors, topics, and actions in the landscape of proliferating feminisms manifesting in media culture. Campaigns aligning with familiar White feminist projects, including neo-colonial discourses of rescue such as #BringBackOurGirls and the celebration of Malala Yousafzai, obtain greater media prominence than local working-class or Black feminist campaigns, demonstrating the intersections of racism and classism within the new luminosity of feminism. Gill notes that across this landscape, 'visibility is also related to the ideological complexion of the politics and the campaign's degree of challenge to the status quo' (2016: 616), highlighting the significance of examining the forms of resistance to be found in the practices and sites we analyse. As Chapter 6 made clear, these constraints on visibility structure the relationship between the diversity within production teams and the representational regimes they can create. I have referred to the exemplary case of Shonda Rhimes several times to illustrate this tension between visibility and progress. Joseph's (2016) analysis of Rhimes' self-expression before and after the rise of the #BlackLivesMatter movement demonstrates that even the most powerful woman of colour in television feels obliged to conform to the 'politics of respectability' (Higginbotham 1994), placing limits on her public discourse about race, as indicated by her emphasis on 'colour-blind' casting for *Grey's Anatomy*.

Despite the promises of emergent feminisms, we are not yet living in an era that can be called post-sexist or post-misogynist. We have discussed how women and girls face ongoing inequalities in mediated representations and opportunities to participate in media cultures and production, even with the democratization promised by digital media. Indeed, as we saw in Chapter 5, the very same technologies enabling feminist discourses and communities to proliferate also support the establishment, growth, and reach of misogynistic and antifeminist discourses in response, what Banet-Weiser (2015) calls 'popular misogyny'. Examples of this kind of harassment are as plentiful as instances of networked feminist activism. Alongside the prominence of feminist hashtags related to sexual violence, it has become an everyday occurrence to hear about yet another case of digitally mediated harassment, via the tactics of broadcasting women's personal information (doxxing), circulating intimate photos without consent (revenge porn), and tarnishing reputations through the creation of defamatory memes, Wikipedia vandalism, and websites dedicated to negative reviews. Racist, misogynistic, and homophobic attacks have been launched against women in all walks of life, all for the crime of being a woman visible in public life. British journalist Caroline Criado-Perez was harassed for campaigning for a female historical figure to appear on the currency. Canadian pop culture critic Anita Sarkeesian was the subject of a coordinated online campaign of harassment because she organized a Kickstarter campaign to raise funds for her video series on sexist representations in video games. Diane Abbott, a seasoned Black politician in the UK, received ten times more abusive tweets during the 2017 election campaign than any other MP. The American actress Kelly Marie Tran was driven off Instagram after racist harassment from those objecting to her being cast in a film in the *Star Wars* franchise. As these and myriad other instances reveal, the affordances of digital media can support and amplify both feminist and antifeminist voices, demonstrating the continuities between 'new media' and older discourses, debates, and problems. In the introduction to their book on the mediation of misogyny, Vickery and Everbach (2018) evidence these enduring norms by drawing a potent parallel between the US elections of 1913 and those of 2016 in relation to the feminist activism that was sparked by both. Digital media does not naturally create the grounds for emergent feminisms or popular misogyny. Critically assessing these discourses and activities enables an understanding of the ways the media make visible some articulations and voices rather than others, and highlights how the goals of feminist action remain timely and significant across online and offline spaces.

In recognition of the uneven visibilities of the current luminosity of feminism, Gill (2016) concludes that the issues arising within the contemporary media environment underline the value of examining the circulation of postfeminist logic. 'Post-' does not in this case mean 'after' feminism. Rather, as we saw in Chapter 1, taking postfeminism as an object of analysis is particularly valuable for revealing the contradictions in intersectional gendered relations across the media, popular culture, and a range of institutions. Tracing the origins of the idea of postfeminism back to its theorization in Stacey's (1987) ethnographic research in Silicon Valley, the value of analysing it in contemporary society becomes even clearer. Stacey explored the relationship between experiences of feminism, working conditions, and family life in 'post-industrial' society, when work in the Global North began to shift from industrial manufacturing to the kinds of knowledge and service work that Silicon Valley has become famous for. While her respondents could attribute the increasing opportunities for women beyond the domestic sphere to feminism, it was not something they felt they could turn to for support with difficult family situations, including the challenges arising from non-unionized work and decreasing wages in post-industrial America. Returning to Stacey's research and analysis, published over thirty years ago, underscores how feminist ideas and actions are not experienced in a vacuum but in response to intergenerational contact, family relations, and economic conditions, highlighting the ways in which the personal and the political remain deeply entangled. Examinations of postfeminist media cultures should remain grounded in this understanding of the underlying web of factors shaping intergenerational and individual experiences, and remind us of the worth of tracing the heritage of the research and activism we undertake. Looking to history also ensures that we do not participate in rendering the work of those who preceded us invisible, thereby contributing to the epistemic violence discussed in Chapter 4.

The point is an urgent one. While the diverse and dynamic landscape of anti-, post-, and feminist discourse demonstrates the value of intersectional feminist media studies, the very foundations of this area of scholarship and engagement are under attack in the contemporary political environment. The far-right government in Hungary recently implemented a ban on gender studies, with government officials challenging its validity as a field of study and claiming that the existence of such programmes represents an assault on traditional, socially conservative family values. As Zsubori points out, this state intervention into academia is an assault on intellectual freedom as well as democracy, and by 'defining strict social expectations regarding roles of women (and men)', its 'rhetoric is an attack on the very idea of gender equality' (2018: n.p.). Gender studies is not the only area under attack; the Hungarian government has also begun to levy a 25 per cent tax on universities with programmes supporting migrants, resulting in the suspension of teaching and research activities related to migration (Wilson 2018). In a time of resurgent nationalistic ideology across the world, these attacks on critical, social justice-oriented forms of knowledge production and inquiry are of concern within feminist media studies and beyond.

Understanding the political and economic context referenced in this chapter is essential to our analysis moving forward, as we cannot make sense of the present without considering the past, including how previous generations of feminists made the gains that contemporary forces are attempting to undo and that postfeminism has to thank for its existence. Still, the example of Hungary indicates that the questions addressed by feminist media studies are seen as threatening by some, and this should in turn highlight the power and potency of this work, past, present, and future. Harnessing this power entails rejecting invidious individualism to be sure, but as this book has argued it also requires us to be critical when we think about visibility. As Keller and Ryan (2018) note, the mediation of feminism does not shine its light equally on all kinds of articulations, subjects, bodies, spaces, and questions, and therefore many continue to be marginalized, including people of colour and others. For example, Duguay (2016) highlights how the visibility of LGBTQ+ people in the media tends to focus on sameness rather than presenting a challenge to the status quo, nullifying the potential for these mediated visibilities to create queer publics. This depoliticization of queer politics, alongside battles against feminist and anti-racist thought and action, provides the background for the contemporary attacks on transgender people in the US. This already marginalized group faces becoming no longer recognized and protected by law, with the proposed introduction of a definition of gender as determined at birth and immutable (Green et al. 2018). While visibility does not necessarily entail a transformation of dominant norms, silencing the voices of people – whether in media representations or in policy-making and law – severely diminishes their ability to survive and thrive. For this reason, feminist media analysts must heed Cárdenas when she argues that a failure to acknowledge and address the violence faced by transgender women of colour 'reproduces that violence through exclusion' (2015: n.p.). To paraphrase the activist

Emi Kane, feminism as a movement will only be truly transformational if it includes and acknowledges the voices of the most marginalized in society (Bhattacharjya et al. 2013: 287), and that holds equally true for feminist media studies.

The intersectional approach delineated throughout this book aims to ensure that the future of feminist media studies is one that does not reproduce violence, but fiercely combats multifaceted exclusions, by addressing the differential privilege experienced by women around the world. As a way of thinking, it reminds us that feminism is not an identity, a word simply affixed to something, such as media studies. The theorization, development, and exploration of intersectionality represents a key moment in feminist history, and it should therefore ground us in a contextually sensitive approach to our objects of study. Throughout this book we have considered how intersectionality in our theorizing, research methods, and action enhances the critical and political power of the field. While I have attempted throughout these discussions to integrate insights about where gender intersects with race, nationality, migration and citizenship status, ability, age, sexuality, and religion, it has not been possible to provide a full sense of what critical thought in these areas affords feminist media work. Nevertheless, the future of feminist media studies depends on its further engagement with existing and developing scholarship in critical race studies, queer theory, critical disability studies, postcolonial theory, and a range of complementary fields related to social justice. Only by engaging with the insights afforded by this interdisciplinary and international work can we address the myriad, multifaceted, and global intersectional challenges facing women today.

In recognition of the importance of reflecting on history, I conclude the book by quoting in full Mary Celeste Kearney's (2012) manifesta for feminist media criticism. Although written on the cusp of the flourishing of feminist discourses discussed in this chapter, Kearney's manifesta strikingly reveals how little has changed in the media in the intervening years of visible discourse and activity. I have reproduced her list of reasons for the existence of this field in the hope that feminist media scholars reading this book can take inspiration from the challenges she articulates. I finish here with the aspiration that by the time an update to this book is needed, we will be able to look back at this end point and use it to draw up a list of gains and wins across media representation, production, and research. If we draw on the tremendous contributions of the feminist killjoys who have come before us, and embrace an interdisciplinary, intersectional, and international approach to the field, I truly believe this is possible.

A manifesta for feminist media criticism by Mary Celeste Kearney

Because we are committed to critically analysing systems of power in all their forms – but especially with regard to gender and media culture – and we want others to be as well.

Because we believe our culture and society can be better, and we can play an active role in transforming them.

Because we share in the fight to end oppression so all individuals everywhere can be who they want to be and reach their potential happily and without suffering.

Because we believe that biology is not destiny, that gender and other identity norms are socially constructed, and that they can and should be deconstructed.

Because we are angry at a society that continues to tell us that a woman's first priority is to be sexy, that to be smart is to be unattractive, and that feminism is no longer necessary and/or that feminist = anti-male, feminist = humorless, and feminist = nazi.

Because too many of our female students, colleagues, and friends say, 'I'm not a feminist', despite acknowledging they want equality with men and don't experience it in many aspects of their lives.

Because there are not more men who are willing to join our fight.

Because we refuse to assimilate to someone else's standards of what makes a good scholar, teacher, artist, writer, activist, citizen, consumer, or person.

Because we understand the media industries as comprising the most powerful and influential social institution today, and they traffic in normative values harmful to many.

Because we want to destroy the domination of global media culture by those who want us to keep consuming whatever they churn out, buying whatever their sponsors are shilling, ignoring politics, hating ourselves, and competing with each other rather than producing our own media, working to end oppression, fighting for social justice, loving ourselves, and supporting each other.

Because we want more movies, TV shows, songs, games, websites, comics, radio programs, and news stories that don't infantilize, hyper-sexualize, demonize, exoticize, marginalize, exclude, or demean us – or anyone else.

Because we value our media tastes and pleasures and want them affirmed rather than ignored for those of a more lucrative market.

Because we are troubled that popular culture has become more focused on sex and violence than when feminist media criticism emerged four decades ago.

Because women in the news are consistently discussed in relation to their appearance, and men hardly ever are.

Because we are frustrated that women are always seen as women first, and whatever other role we have is secondary.

Because Kathryn Bigelow is the only woman to have earned the Academy Award for Best Director, and because most people don't even know who Kathryn Bigelow is.

Because so many female characters on television are victims of assault and murder, and because so many girl characters are motherless and sisterless.

Because women-made and women-themed movies are considered 'niche'.

Because the privileged role for girl musicians is still the sexy vocalist, and playing instruments continues to be seen as a 'guy thing'.

Because many journalists see 'women's issues' as not serious and apolitical and thus ghettoize them in the Life and Style section of newspapers.

Because we know reading/watching/hearing/writing/doing things that validate and challenge us can help us to build the knowledge, strength, and community we need to overcome the sexism, racism, classism, ageism, heterocentrism, able-bodieism, thinism, and xenophobia writ large, which structure our lives, our communities, and our culture.

Because we understand the power of media as tools for documenting lives, expressing creativity, exploring identity, and building community, and we want all people to have equal access to those tools and those powers.

Because we are committed to supporting feminist, queer, and anti-racist media producers and know that doing so is integral to changing our society for the better.

Because many media studies programs do not have classes specifically devoted to exploring gender in media culture.

Because so many media history and production classes continue to focus on the Great White Men of Celluloid, of Video, of the Air, of the Tubes, of the Internet, of Gaming, and of Comics … and privilege the work of only the male scholars who write about them.

Because so many girls, parents, and teachers the world over don't see media production as a worthwhile profession for women, and males continue to dominate both production programs and the media industries at all levels.

Because female media critics and producers tend to earn less and are promoted less than their male peers, and women are more affected by contingent labor practices than are men.

Because we know being multiply oppressed as a result of sexuality, race, or ability makes all this much, much, much more difficult.

Because we are encouraged to remain quiet or tone down our activist rhetoric and activities to get better teaching evaluations, promotion reviews, and salary increases.

Because we know the heart of academic life is about participating in critical debates started many years before us, about having our beliefs and expectations challenged, about facilitating learning in community with others, and about mentoring others so they can develop as participatory citizens, discerning consumers, and genuinely nice people.

Because we are interested in creating ways of learning, teaching, mentoring, administrating, and sharing research that privilege collaboration and communication over competition and celebrity.

Because we want to make it easier for feminist media scholars to read and hear each other's work so we can share strategies and resources, critique each other, and support one another.

Because we honor, draw strength from, and want to continue the work of older feminist media critics, and because we desire to teach, mentor, and collaborate with younger scholars who will do the same, until such a time when that work is no longer necessary.

And, last but not least:

Because we believe, with all our hearts/minds/bodies, that progressive change is necessary, that progressive change is possible, and that feminist media critics constitute a revolutionary force that transforms academia and popular culture – for real.

(Reproduced with the permission of Mary Celeste Kearney and the Antenna blog where it was originally published: http://blog.commarts.wisc.edu/2012/12/11/feminist-media-criticism-is-part-2.)

References

Abbate, Janet (2012) *Recoding Gender: Women's Changing Participation in Computing*. MIT Press.

Abetz, Jenna and Moore, Julia (2018) '"Welcome to the Mommy Wars, Ladies": Making Sense of the Ideology of Combative Mothering in Mommy Blogs', *Communication, Culture & Critique*, 11, pp. 265–81.

Abidin, Crystal (2016) '"Aren't These Just Young, Rich Women Doing Vain Things Online?": Influencer Selfies as Subversive Frivolity', *Social Media + Society*, 2(2).

Acker, Joan (2006) *Class Questions: Feminist Answers*. Rowman & Littlefield International.

Adkins, Lisa (2005) *Gendered Work: Sexuality, Family and the Labour Market*. Open University Press.

Ahmed, Sara (2004) 'Affective Economies', *Social Text*, 22(2), pp. 117–39.

Ahmed, Sara (2010) 'Feminist Killjoys (and Other Willful Subjects)', *The Scholar and Feminist Online*, http://sfonline.barnard.edu/polyphonic/ahmed_01.htm#text1.

Ahmed, Sara (2013) 'Making Feminist Points', *Feministkilljoys*, 11 September, https://feministkilljoys.com/2013/09/11/making-feminist-points.

Ahmed, Sara (2016) 'Interview with Judith Butler', *Sexualities*, 19(4), pp. 482–92.

Albury, Kath (2015) 'Selfies, Sexts, and Sneaky Hats: Young People's Understandings of Gendered Practices of Self-Representation', *International Journal of Communication*, 9, pp. 1734–45.

Alhayek, Katty (2014) 'Double Marginalization: The Invisibility of Syrian Refugee Women's Perspectives in Mainstream Online Activism and Global Media', *Feminist Media Studies*, 14(4), pp. 696–700.

Alper, Meryl (2018) 'Inclusive Sensory Ethnography: Studying New Media and Neurodiversity in Everyday Life', *New Media & Society*, 20(10), pp. 3560–79.

Amos, Valerie and Parmar, Pratibha (1984) 'Challenging Imperial Feminism', *Feminist Review*, 17, pp. 3–19.

Anderson, Monica, Perrin, Andrew, and Jiang, Jingjing (2018) '11% of Americans Don't Use the Internet. Who Are They?', *Pew Research Centre*, 5 March, www.pewresearch.org/fact-tank/2018/03/05/some-americans-dont-use-the-internet-who-are-they.

Andrejevic, Mark (2007) 'Surveillance in the Digital Enclosure', *The Communication Review*, 10(4), pp. 295–317.

Ang, Ien (1985) *Watching Dallas: Soap Opera and the Melodramatic Imagination*. Methuen.

References

Anzaldúa, Gloria E. (2015) 'Speaking in Tongues: A Letter to Third World Women Writers', in *This Bridge Called My Back: Writings by Radical Women of Color*, 4th edition, ed. Cherríe Moraga and Gloria Anzaldúa. SUNY Press, pp. 163–72.

Appadurai, Arjun (1990) 'Disjuncture and Difference in the Global Cultural Economy', *Theory, Culture and Society*, 7(2/3), pp. 295–310.

Arvin, Maile, Tuck, Eve, and Morrill, Angie (2013) 'Decolonizing Feminism: Challenging Connections between Settler Colonialism and Heteropatriarchy', *Feminist Formations*, 25(1), pp. 8–34.

Ashley, Laura and Olsen, Beth (1998) 'Constructing Reality: Print Media's Framing of the Women's Movement 1966–1986', *Journalism and Mass Communication Quarterly*, 75, pp. 263–77.

Attwood, Feona (2006) 'Sexed Up: Theorizing the Sexualization of Culture', *Sexualities*, 9(1), pp. 77–94.

Bachmann, Chaka L. and Gooch, Becca (2017) 'LGBT in Britain – Hate Crime and Discrimination', *Stonewall*, www.stonewall.org.uk/sites/default/files/lgbt_in_britain_hate_crime.pdf.

Bailey, Moya (2010) 'They Aren't Talking about Me…', *The Crunk Feminist Collective*, www.crunkfeministcollective.com/2010/03/14/they-arent-talking-about-me.

Bailey, Moya (2016) 'Redefining Representation: Black Trans and Queer Women's Digital Media Production', *Screen Bodies*, 1(1), pp. 71–86.

Ball, Vicky and Bell, Melanie (2013) 'Introduction: Working Women: Women's Work: Production, History, Gender', *The Journal of British Cinema and Television*, 10(3), pp. 547–62.

Banet-Weiser, Sarah (2007) 'What's Your Flava? Race and Postfeminism in Media Culture', in *Interrogating Postfeminism: Gender and the Politics of Popular Culture*, ed. Yvonne Tasker and Diane Negra. Duke University Press, pp. 201–26.

Banet-Weiser, Sarah (2011) 'Branding the Post-Feminist Self: Girls' Video Production and YouTube', in *Mediated Girlhoods: New Explorations of Girls' Media Culture*, ed. Mary Celeste Kearney. Peter Lang, pp. 277–94.

Banet-Weiser, Sarah (2015) '"Confidence You Can Carry!" Girls in Crisis and the Market for Girls' Empowerment Organizations', *Continuum: Journal of Media & Cultural Studies*, 29(2), pp. 182–93.

Banet-Weiser, Sarah (2018) *Empowered: Popular Feminism and Popular Misogyny*. Duke University Press.

Banks, Mark (2017) *Creative Justice: Cultural Industries, Work and Inequality*. Rowman & Littlefield.

Banks, Miranda J. (2009) 'Gender Below-the-Line: Defining Feminist Production Studies', in *Production Studies: Cultural Studies of Media*, ed. Vicki Mayer, Miranda J. Banks and John Thornton Caldwell. Routledge, pp. 87–98.

Barlow, John P. (1996) 'A Declaration of the Independence of Cyberspace', Electronic Frontier Foundation, www.eff.org/cyberspace-independence.

Barzilay, Arianne and Ben-David, Anat (2017) 'Platform Inequality: Gender in the Gig-Economy', *Seton Hall Law Review*, 47(393), pp. 393–431.

Bates, Laura (2014) *Everyday Sexism*. Simon & Schuster.

Bathla, Sonia (2004) 'Gender Construction in the Media: A Study of Two Indian Women Politicians', *Asian Journal of Women's Studies*, 10(3), pp. 7–34.

Baym, Nancy (2010) *Personal Connections in the Digital Age*. Polity.

Berger, John (1972) *Ways of Seeing*. Penguin Modern Classics.

Berlant, Lauren (2011) *Cruel Optimism*. Duke University Press.

Berlant, Lauren and Warner, Michael (1998) 'Sex in Public', *Critical Inquiry*, 24(2), pp. 547–66.

Bhabha, Homi K. (2004) *The Location of Culture*. Routledge Classics.

Bhattacharjya, Manjima, Birchall, Jenny, Caro, Pamela, Kelleher, David, and Sahasranaman, Vinita (2013) 'Why Gender Matters in Activism: Feminism and Social Justice Movements', *Gender & Development*, 21(2), pp. 277–93.

Bivens, R. (2015) 'The Gender Binary Will Not Be Deprogrammed: Ten Years of Coding Gender on Facebook', *New Media & Society*, 19(6), pp. 880–98.

Boom, Kesiena (2015) '4 Tired Tropes That Perfectly Explain What Misogynoir Is – And How You Can Stop It', *Everyday Feminism*, 3 August, https://everydayfeminism.com/2015/08/4-tired-tropes-misogynoir.

Boyle, Karen (2010) 'Introduction: Everyday Pornography', in *Everyday Pornography*, ed. Karen Boyle. Routledge, pp. 1–13.

Brock, André, Kvasny, Lynette, and Hales, Kayla (2010) 'Cultural Appropriations of Technical Capital: Black Women, Weblogs, and the Digital Divide', *Information, Communication & Society*, 13(7), pp. 1040–59.

Burgess, Melinda C. R., Dill, Karen E., Stermer, S. Paul, Burgess, Stephen R., and Brown, Brian P. (2011) 'Playing with Prejudice: The Prevalence and Consequences of Racial Stereotypes in Video Games', *Media Psychology*, 14, pp. 289–311.

Burns, Anne (2015) 'Self(ie)-Discipline: Social Regulation as Enacted Through the Discussion of Photographic Practice', *International Journal of Communication*, 9, pp. 716–33.

Butler, Jess (2013) 'For White Girls Only? Postfeminism and the Politics of Inclusion', *Feminist Formations*, 25(1), pp. 35–58.

Butler, Judith (1990) *Gender Trouble*. Routledge.

Calhoun, Craig (2003) '"Belonging" in the Cosmopolitan Imaginary', *Ethnicities*, 3(4), pp. 531–53.

Cárdenas, Micha (2015) 'Shifting Futures: Digital Trans of Color Praxis', *Ada: A Journal of Gender, New Media, and Technology*, 6.

Cassell, Justine and Cramer, Meg (2008) 'High Tech or High Risk: Moral Panics About Girls Online', in *Digital Youth, Innovation, and the Unexpected*, ed. Tara McPherson. MIT Press, pp. 53–75.

Cavalcante, Andre (2017) 'Breaking into Transgender Life: Transgender Audiences' Experiences with "First of its Kind" Visibility in Popular Media', *Communication, Culture, & Critique*, 10, pp. 538–55.

Cavalcante, Andre, Press, Andrea, and Sender, Katherine (2017) 'Feminist Reception Studies in a Post-Audience Age: Returning to Audiences and Everyday Life', *Feminist Media Studies*, 17(1), pp. 1–13.

Chakravartty, Paula, Kuo, Rachel, Grubbs, Victoria, and McIlwain, Charlton (2018) '#CommunicationSoWhite', *Journal of Communication*, 68, pp. 254–66.
Charlton, James I. (2000) *Nothing About Us Without Us: Disability Oppression and Empowerment*. University of California Press.
Chen, Eva (2012) 'Shanghai(ed) Babies', *Feminist Media Studies*, 12(2), pp. 214–28.
Cho, Alexander (2015) 'Queer Reverb: Tumblr, Affect, Time', in *Networked Affect*, ed. Susanna Paasonen, Ken Hillis and Michael Petit. MIT Press.
Cho, Alexander (2017) 'Default Publicness: Queer Youth of Color, Social Media, and Being Outed by the Machine', *New Media & Society*, 20(9), pp. 3183–200.
Chua, Trudy Hui Hui and Chang, Leanne (2016) 'Follow Me and Like My Beautiful Selfies: Singapore Teenage Girls' Engagement in Self-Presentation and Peer Comparison on Social Media', *Computers in Human Behavior*, 55(A), pp. 190–7.
Chun, Wendy Hui Kyong (2016) *Updating to Remain the Same: Habitual New Media*. MIT Press.
Citron, Danielle Keats (2016) *Hate Crimes in Cyberspace*. Harvard University Press.
Cobb, Shelley, Williams, Linda Ruth, and Wreyford, Natalie (2018) 'Calling the Shots: Women Directors and Cinematographers on British Films since 2003', https://wftv.org.uk/wp-content/uploads/2018/02/Calling-the-Shots-Report-Feb-2018-Women-directors-and-cinematographers.pdf.
Cockburn, Cynthia (1988) *Machinery of Dominance: Women, Men, and Technical Know-How*. Northeastern University Press.
Cohen, Nicole S. (2008) 'The Valorization of Surveillance: Towards a Political Economy of Facebook', *Democratic Communiqué*, 22(1).
Colebrook, Claire (2006) 'Introduction: Special Issue on Beauty and Feminist Theory', *Feminist Theory*, 7(2), pp. 131–42.
Collins, Patricia Hill (2008) *Black Feminist Thought: Knowledge, Consciousness, and the Politics of Empowerment*, 2nd edition. Routledge.
Combahee River Collective (1977) 'The Combahee River Collective Statement', http://historyisaweapon.com/defcon1/combrivercoll.html.
Connell, R.W. (2005) *Masculinities*, 2nd edition. University of California Press.
Corbin, Juliet and Strauss, Anselm (2008) *Basics of Qualitative Research: Techniques and Procedures for Developing Grounded Theory*, 3rd edition. SAGE.
Costanza-Chock, Sasha (2018) 'Design Justice: Towards an Intersectional Feminist Framework for Design Theory and Practice', Proceedings of the Design Research Society, University of Limerick, Ireland, 25–28 June.
Coulter, Natalie (2014) *Tweening the Girl: The Crystallization of the Tween Market*. Peter Lang.
Cowan, Ruth Schwartz (1985) *More Work for Mother: The Ironies of Household Technology from the Open Hearth to the Microwave*. Basic Books.
Crenshaw, Kimberlé (1989) 'Demarginalizing the Intersection of Race and Sex: A Black Feminist Critique of Antidiscrimination Doctrine, Feminist Theory and

Antiracist Politics', *University of Chicago Legal Forum*, 1(8), http://chicagounbound.uchicago.edu/uclf/vol1989/iss1.

Daalmans, Serena, Kleemans, Mariska, and Sadza, Anne (2017) 'Gender Representation on Gender-Targeted Television Channels: A Comparison of Female- and Male-Targeted TV Channels in the Netherlands', *Sex Roles*, 77, pp. 366–78.

D'Acci, Julie (1994) *Defining Women: Television and the Case of Cagney and Lacey*. University of North Carolina Press.

Dale, Jack (2016) 'The Scale of Online Misogyny', *Demos*, 26 May, www.demos.co.uk/blog/misogyny-online.

Dargis, Manohla (2016) 'Sundance Fights Tide With Films Like "The Birth of a Nation"', *New York Times*, 29 January, https://nyti.ms/1PZshO5.

Davis, Angela Y. (1983) *Women, Race and Class*. Ballantine Books.

Debbagh, Mohammed (2012) 'Discourse Analysis of the Representations of Women in Moroccan Broadcast News', *Journal of North African Studies*, 17(4), pp. 653–70.

de Beauvoir, Simone (1949) *Le Deuxième Sexe*. Gallimard.

Dejmanee, Tisha (2016) 'Waves and Popular Feminist Entanglements: Diffraction as a Feminist Media Methodology', *Feminist Media Studies*, 16(4), pp. 741–5.

de Lauretis, Teresa (1987) *Technologies of Gender: Essays on Theory, Film, and Fiction*. Indiana University Press.

Dencik, Lina, Hintz, Arne, and Cable, Jonathan (2016) 'Towards Data Justice? The Ambiguity of Anti-Surveillance Resistance in Political Activism', *Big Data & Society*, 3(2), pp. 1–12.

de Saussure, Ferdinand (1983) *Course in General Linguistics*. Duckworth.

Dever, Maryanne (2017) 'Archives and New Modes of Feminist Research', *Australian Feminist Studies*, 32(91–2), pp. 1–4.

Dibbell, Julian (1993) 'A Rape in Cyberspace', *The Village Voice*, 21 December, www.juliandibbell.com/articles/a-rape-in-cyberspace.

Dobson, Amy Shields (2011) 'Hetero-Sexy Representation by Young Women on MySpace: The Politics of Performing an "Objectified" Self', *Outskirts*, 25, www.outskirts.arts.uwa.edu.au/volumes/volume-25/amy-shields-dobson.

Dobson, Amy Shields (2012) '"Individuality is Everything": "Autonomous" Femininity in MySpace Mottos and Self-Descriptions', *Continuum: Journal of Media & Cultural Studies*, 26 (3), pp. 371–83.

Dobson, Amy Shields (2015) *Postfeminist Digital Cultures: Social Media and the Politics of Self-Representation*. Palgrave.

Donegan, Moira (2018) 'How #MeToo Revealed the Central Rift within Feminism Today', *Guardian*, 11 May, www.theguardian.com/news/2018/may/11/how-metoo-revealed-the-central-rift-within-feminism-social-individualist.

Dosekun, Simidele (2015) 'For Western Girls Only? Post-feminism as Transnational Culture', *Feminist Media Studies*, 15(6), pp. 960–75.

Doty, Alexander (1993) *Making Things Perfectly Queer: Interpreting Mass Culture*. University of Minnesota Press.

Douglas, Susan J. (2010) *Enlightened Sexism: The Seductive Message That Feminism's Work Is Done*. Times Books.

Döveling, Katrin, Harju, Ana A., and Sommer, Denise (2018) 'From Mediatized Emotion to Digital Affect Cultures: New Technologies and Global Flows of Emotion', *Social Media + Society*, DOI: 10.1177/2056305117743141.

Duffy, Brooke Erin and Hund, Emily (2015) '"Having it All" on Social Media: Entrepreneurial Femininity and Self-Branding Among Fashion Bloggers', *Social Media + Society*, 1(2).

Duffy, Brooke Erin and Schwartz, Becca (2018) 'Digital "Women's Work?": Job Recruitment Ads and the Feminization of Social Media Employment', *New Media & Society*, 20(8), pp. 2972–89.

Duffy, Brooke Erin and Wissinger, Elizabeth (2017) 'Mythologies of Creative Work in the Social Media Age: Fun, Free and "Just Being Me"', *International Journal of Communication*, 11, pp. 4652–71.

Duguay, Stefanie (2016) 'Lesbian, Gay, Bisexual, Trans, and Queer Visibility Through Selfies: Comparing Platform Mediators Across Ruby Rose's Instagram and Vine Presence', *Social Media + Society*, 2(2).

Dwyer, Colin (2018) 'What's An Inclusion Rider? Here's The Story Behind Frances McDormand's Closing Words', *NPR*, 5 March, www.npr.org/sections/thetwo-way/2018/03/05/590867132/whats-an-inclusion-rider-here-s-the-story-behind-frances-mcdormand-s-closing-wor.

Dyer, Richard (1982) 'Don't Look Now', *Screen*, 23(3–4), pp. 61–73.

Dyer, Richard (1984) 'Stereotyping', in *Gays and Film*, ed. Richard Dyer. Zoetrope, pp. 27–39.

Edwards, Paul N. (2003) 'Industrial Genders: Soft/Hard', in *Gender and Technology: A Reader*, ed. Nina E. Lerman, Ruth Oldenziel and Arwen P. Mohun. Johns Hopkins University Press, pp. 177–203.

Eichorn, Kate (2013) *The Archival Turn in Feminism*. Temple University Press.

Eikhof, Doris Ruth (2012) 'A Double-Edged Sword: Twenty-First Century Workplace Trends and Gender Equality', *Gender in Management: An International Journal*, 27(1), pp. 7–22.

Electronic Freedom Foundation (2015) 'Appendix to October 5, 2015 Coalition Letter to Facebook', www.eff.org/files/2015/10/05/10052015_appendix.pdf.

Elias, Ana Sofia and Gill, Rosalind (2017) 'Beauty Surveillance: The Digital Self-Monitoring Cultures of Neoliberalism', *European Journal of Cultural Studies*, 21(1), pp. 59–77.

Elias, Ana Sofia, Gill, Rosalind, and Scharff, Christina (eds) (2017) *Aesthetic Labour: Rethinking Beauty Politics in Neoliberalism*. Palgrave Macmillan.

Ellcessor, Elizabeth (2016) *Restricted Access: Media, Disability, and the Politics of Participation*. New York University Press.

Ensmenger, Nathan L. (2010) *The Computer Boys Take Over: Computers, Programmers, and the Politics of Technical Expertise*. MIT Press.

Eubanks, Virginia (2018) *Automating Inequality: How High-Tech Tools Profile, Police, and Punish the Poor*. Macmillan.

Fairclough, Norman (2012) 'Critical Discourse Analysis', *International Advances in Engineering and Technology (IAET)*, 7, pp. 452–87.
Fallon, Claire (2017) 'Judd Apatow Isn't a Feminist, According to Judd Apatow', *HuffPost*, 7 August, www.huffingtonpost.co.uk/entry/judd-apatow-feminist-vulture_us_59887d1ce4b08b75dcc8679e?guccounter=1&guce_referrer_us=aHR0cHM6Ly93d3cuZ29vZ2xlLmNvLnVrLw&guce_referrer_cs=I6k_Zp-d-QOvlYafldI40w.
Faludi, Susan (1991) *Backlash: The Undeclared War Against American Women*. Crown.
Fanon, Frantz (1963) *The Wretched of the Earth*. Grove Press.
Farris, Sara and Rottenberg, Catherine (2017) 'Introduction: Righting Feminism', *New Formations*, 91, pp. 5–15.
Federici, Silvia (1975) 'Wages Against Housework', published jointly by the Power of Women Collective and the Falling Wall Press, https://monoskop.org/images/2/23/Federici_Silvia_Wages_Against_Housework_1975.pdf.
Fernández, María (1999) 'Postcolonial Media Theory', *Art Journal*, 58(3), pp. 58–73.
Ferreday, Debra (2017) 'Like a Stone in Your Stomach: Articulating the Unspeakable in Rape Victim-Survivors' Activist Selfies', in *Selfie Citizenship*, ed. Adi Kuntsman. Palgrave Macmillan, pp. 127–36.
Figueroa, Mónica G. Moreno (2008) 'Looking Emotionally: Racism, Photography and Intimacies in Research', *History of the Human Sciences*, 21(4), pp. 66–83.
Figueroa, Mónica G. Moreno (2013) 'Displaced Looks: The Lived Experience of Beauty and Racism', *Feminist Theory*, 14(2), pp. 137–51.
Firestone, Shulamith (1970) *The Dialectic of Sex: The Case for Feminist Revolution*. Farrar, Straus and Giroux.
Fisher, Stephanie and Harvey, A. (2013) 'Intervention for Inclusivity: Gender Politics and Indie Game Development', *Loading … Journal of the Canadian Game Studies Association*, 7(11), pp. 25–40.
Fogel, Stefanie (2018) 'Study: Almost Half of Women Streamers Don't Get Paid For Content', *Variety*, 30 May, https://variety.com/2018/gaming/news/paypal-superdata-streamer-study-1202825734.
Fortunati, Leopoldina (1988) *The Arcane of Reproduction: Housework, Prostitution, Labor and Capital*. Autonomedia.
Fotopoulou, Aristea (2016) *Feminist Activism and Digital Networks: Between Empowerment and Vulnerability*. Palgrave Macmillan.
Foucault, Michel (1990) *The History of Sexuality. Volume 1: An Introduction*, trans. Robert Hurley. Vintage Books.
Fraser, Nancy (2016) 'Contradictions of Capital and Care', *New Left Review*, 100, pp. 99–117.
Friedan, Betty (1963) *The Feminine Mystique*. W.W. Norton.
Friedman, Lyle, Daniels, Matt, and Blinderman, Ilia (2016) 'Hollywood's Gender Divide and Its Effect on Films', *Polygraph*, http://poly-graph.co/bechdel.
Frith, Katherine, Shaw, Ping and Cheng, Hong (2005) 'The Construction of

Beauty: A Cross-Cultural Analysis of Women's Magazine Advertising', *Journal of Communication*, 55(1), pp. 56–70.

Fron, Janine, Fullerton, Tracy, Ford Morie, Jacquelyn, and Pearce, Celia (2007) 'The Hegemony of Play', paper presented at the annual meeting for the Digital Games Research Association, Tokyo, Japan, 24–28 September.

Frosh, Paul (2015) 'The Gestural Image: The Selfie, Photography Theory, and Kinesthetic Sociability', *International Journal of Communication*, 9, pp. 1607–28.

Fusco, Coco (2001) *The Bodies That Were Not Ours and Other Writings*. Routledge.

Gaines, Jane, Vatsal, Radha, and Dall'Asta, Monica (eds) (2013) 'Women Film Pioneers Project', Center for Digital Research and Scholarship, Columbia University Libraries, https://wfpp.cdrs.columbia.edu/about.

Gajjala, Radhika (2002) 'An Interrupted Postcolonial/Feminist Cyberethnography: Complicity and Resistance in the "Cyberfield"', *Feminist Media Studies*, 2(2), pp. 177–93.

Gajjala, Radhika (2004) *Cyber Selves: Feminist Ethnographies of South Asian Women*. Rowman Altamira.

Gajjala, Radhika (2018) *Digital Diasporas: Labour, Affect and Technomediation of South Asia*. Rowman & Littlefield International.

Gajjala, Radhika and Ju Oh, Yeon (eds) (2012) *Cyberfeminism 2.0*. Peter Lang.

Gajjala, Radhika and Mamidipudi, Annapurna (1999) 'Cyberfeminism, Technology, and International "Development"', *Gender and Development*, 7(2), pp. 8–16.

Gajjala, Radhika, Zhang, Yahui, and Dako-Gyeke, Phyllis (2010) 'Lexicons of Women's Empowerment Online', *Feminist Media Studies*, 10(1), pp. 69–86.

Geena Davis Institute on Gender in Media (2016) 'The See Jane Top 50: Gender Bias in Family Films of 2016', https://seejane.org/wp-content/uploads/see-jane-top-50-gender-bias-in-family-films-of-2016.pdf.

Geena Davis Institute on Gender in Media and J. Walter Thompson (2017) 'Gender Bias in Advertising: Research, Trends, and New Visual Language', https://seejane.org/wp-content/uploads/gender-bias-in-advertising.pdf.

Gerlitz, Carolin and Helmond, Anne (2013) 'The Like Economy: Social Buttons and the Data-Intensive Web', *New Media & Society*, 15(8), pp. 1348–65.

Gill, Rosalind (2002) 'Cool, Creative and Egalitarian? Exploring Gender in Project-Based New Media Work in Europe', *Information, Communication & Society*, 5(1), pp. 70–89.

Gill, Rosalind (2006) 'Technobohemians or the New Cybertariat? New Media Work in Amsterdam a Decade after the Web', *Network Notebooks*, Institute of Network Cultures.

Gill, Rosalind (2007) 'Postfeminist Media Culture: Elements of a Sensibility', *European Journal of Cultural Studies*, 10(2), pp. 147–66.

Gill, Rosalind (2009) 'Beyond the "Sexualization of Culture" Thesis: An Intersectional Analysis of "Sixpacks", "Midriffs" and "Hot Lesbians" in Advertising', *Sexualities*, 12(2), pp. 137–60.

Gill, Rosalind (2014) 'Unspeakable Inequalities: Post-Feminism, Entrepreneurial

Subjectivity, and the Repudiation of Sexism among Cultural Workers', *Social Politics*, 21(4), pp. 509–28.

Gill, Rosalind (2016) 'Post-Postfeminism? New Feminist Visibilities in Postfeminist Times', *Feminist Media Studies*, 16(4), pp. 610–30.

Gillies, Val and Alldred, Pam (2012) 'The Ethics of Intention: Research as a Political Tool', in *Ethics in Qualitative Research*, 2nd edition, ed. Tina Miller, Maxine Birch, Melanie, Mauthner and Julie Jessop. SAGE, pp. 43–60.

GLAAD (nd) 'GLAAD Media Reference Guide – Transgender', www.glaad.org/reference/transgender.

Glenn, Evelyn Nakano (1992) 'From Servitude to Service Work: Historical Continuities in the Racial Division of Paid Reproductive Labor', *Signs*, 18(1), pp. 1–43.

Gomez, Stephanie L. and McFarlane, Megan D. (2017) '"It's (Not) Handled": Race, Gender, and Refraction in *Scandal*', *Feminist Media Studies*, 17(3), pp. 362–76.

Gonick, Marnina (2006) 'Between "Girl Power" and "Reviving Ophelia": Constituting the Neoliberal Girl Subject', *NWSA Journal*, 18(2), pp. 1–23.

Gray, Kishonna L. (2012) 'Intersecting Oppressions and Online Communities: Examining the Experiences of Women of Color in Xbox Live', *Information, Communication & Society*, 15(3), pp. 411–28.

Gray, Kishonna L. (2013) 'Collective Organizing, Individual Resistance, or Asshole Griefers? An Ethnographic Analysis of Women of Color in Xbox Live', *Ada: A Journal of Gender, New Media & Technology*, 2.

Gray, Kishonna L. (2018) 'Masculinity Studies', *Feminist Media Histories*, 4(2), pp. 107–12.

Gray, Mary (2009) *Out in the Country: Youth, Media, and Queer Visibility*. New York University Press.

Green, Erica L., Benner, Katie, and Pear, Robert (2018) '"Transgender" Could Be Defined Out of Existence Under Trump Administration', *New York Times*, 21 October, https://nyti.ms/2R9W1jB.

Gregg, Melissa (2011) 'Do Your Homework', *Feminist Media Studies*, 11(1), pp. 73–81.

Gregg, Melissa (2018) 'AI in the Home', paper presented at the Queensland University of Technology DMRC Summer School, Brisbane, Australia, 5–9 February.

Grewal, Inderpal (2005) *Transnational America: Feminisms, Diasporas, Neoliberalisms*. Duke University Press.

Grewal, Inderpal and Kaplan, Caren (1994) *Scattered Hegemonies: Postmodernity and Transnational Feminist Practices*. University of Minnesota Press.

Grewal, Inderpal and Kaplan, Caren (2001) 'Global Identities: Theorising Transnational Studies of Sexuality', *GLQ*, 7(4), pp. 663–79.

Griffin, F. Hollis (2017) *Feeling Normal: Sexuality and Media Criticism*. Indiana University Press.

Guha, Pallavi (2014) 'Hash Tagging But Not Trending: The Success and Failure of the News Media to Engage with Online Feminist Activism in India', *Feminist Media Studies*, 15(1), pp. 155–7.

Gumbs, Alexis Pauline (2011) 'Seek the Roots: An Immersive and Interactive Archive of Black Feminist Practice', *Feminist Collections*, 32(1), pp. 17–20.

Gunaratnam, Yasmin and Hamilton, Carrie (2017) 'The Wherewithal of Feminist Methods', *Feminist Review*, 115(1), pp. 1–12.

Gwynne, Joel (2013) 'Japan, Postfeminism, and the Consumption of Sexual(ised) Schoolgirls in Male-Authored Contemporary Manga', *Feminist Theory*, 14(3), pp. 325–43.

Haimson, Oliver L. and Hoffman, Anna Lauren (2016) 'Constructing and Enforcing "Authentic" Identity Online: Facebook, Real Names, and Non-normative Identities', *First Monday*, http://firstmonday.org/ojs/index.php/fm/article/view/6791/5521.

Halberstam, Judith (2011) *The Queer Art of Failure*. Duke University Press.

Halberstam, J. Jack (2012) *Gaga Feminism: Sex, Gender, and the End of Normal*. Beacon Press.

Hall, Stuart (1980) 'Encoding/Decoding', in *Culture, Media, Language: Working Papers in Cultural Studies*. Hutchinson, pp. 128–38.

Hall, Stuart (1995) 'The Whites of their Eyes: Racist Ideologies and the Media', in *Gender, Race, and Class in Media*, ed. Gail Hines and Jean M. Humez. SAGE, pp. 18–22.

Hall, Stuart (ed.) (1997) *Representation: Cultural Representations and Signifying Practices*. Sage.

Hamad, Hannah and Taylor Anthea (2015) 'Feminism and Contemporary Celebrity Culture', *Celebrity Studies Forum Special*, 6(1), pp. 126–7.

Haraway, Donna (1988) 'Situated Knowledges: The Science Question in Feminism and the Privilege of Partial Perspective', *Feminist Studies*, 14(3), pp. 575–99.

Haraway, Donna (1991) 'A Cyborg Manifesto: Science, Technology, and Socialist-Feminism in the Late Twentieth Century', in *Simians, Cyborgs and Women: The Reinvention of Nature*. Routledge.

Harp, Dustin, Harlow, Summer, and Loke, Jaime (2013) 'The Symbolic Annihilation of Women in Globalization Discourse: The Same Old Story in US Newsmagazines', *Atlantic Journal of Communication*, 21(5), pp. 263–77.

Harris, Anita (2004) *Future Girl: Young Women in the Twenty-First Century*. Routledge.

Harvey, Alison (2015) *Gender, Age, and Digital Games in the Domestic Context*. Routledge.

Harvey, Alison and Fisher, Stephanie (2016) 'Growing Pains: Intergenerational Feminisms in Digital Games', *Feminist Media Studies*, 16(4), pp. 648–62.

Harvey, Alison and Shepherd, Tamara (2016) 'When Passion Isn't Enough: Gender, Affect and Credibility in Digital Games Design', *International Journal of Cultural Studies*, 20(5), pp. 492–508.

Hasinoff, Amy Adele (2015) *Sexting Panic: Rethinking Criminalization, Privacy, and Consent*. University of Illinois Press.

Hegde, Radha (2011) *Circuits of Visibility: Gender and Transnational Media Cultures*. New York University Press.
Helsper, Ellen J. and Reisdorf, Bianca C. (2017) 'The Emergence of a "Digital Underclass" in Great Britain and Sweden: Changing Reasons for Digital Exclusion', *New Media & Society*, 19(8), pp. 1253–70.
Herzog, Herta (1941) 'On Borrowed Experience: An Analysis of Listening to Daytime Sketches', *Studies in Philosophy and Social Science*, 9(1), pp. 65–95.
Hicks, Marie (2017) *Programmed Inequality: How Britain Discarded Women Technologists and Lost Its Edge in Computing*. MIT Press.
Higginbotham, Evelyn Brooks (1994) *Righteous Discontent: The Women's Movement in the Black Baptist Church, 1880–1920*. Harvard University Press.
Hill, Erin (2016) *Never Done: A History of Women's Work in Media Production*. Rutgers University Press.
Hobson, Janell (2008) 'Digital Whiteness, Primitive Blackness: Racializing the "Digital Divide" in Film and New Media', *Feminist Media Studies*, 8(2), pp. 111–26.
Hobson, Janell (2016) 'Celebrity Feminism: More Than a Gateway', *Signs*, http://signsjournal.org/currents-celebrity-feminism/hobson.
Hochschild, Arlie Russell (1983) *The Managed Heart: Commercialization of Human Feeling*. University of California Press.
Hochschild, Arlie Russell and Machung, Anne (1989) *The Second Shift: Working Parents and the Revolution at Home*. Viking Penguin.
Hogan, Mél (2018) 'Data is Airborne; Data is Inborn: The Labor of the Body in Technoecologies', *First Monday*, http://firstmonday.org/ojs/index.php/fm/article/view/8285/6650.
Holland, Patricia (1983) 'The Page Three Girl Speaks to Women, Too', *Screen*, 24(3), pp. 84–102.
Hong Fincher, Leta (2018) *Betraying Big Brother: The Feminist Awakening in China*. Verso Books.
hooks, bell (1981) *Ain't I a Woman? Black Women and Feminism*. South End Press.
hooks, bell (1989) *Talking Back: Thinking Feminist, Thinking Back*. Between the Lines.
hooks, bell (1992) *Black Looks: Race and Representation*. Between the Lines.
Horak, Laura (2018) 'Trans Studies', *Feminist Media Histories*, 4(2), pp. 201–6.
Jackson, Sarah J., Bailey, Moya, and Foucault Welles, Brooke (2018) '#GirlsLikeUs: Trans Advocacy and Community Building Online', *New Media & Society*, 20(5), pp. 1868–88.
Jackson-Edwards, Phoebe (2015) 'Twitter Backlash over Photographer's REFUGEE Fashion Shoot', *Daily Mail*, 7 October, www.dailymail.co.uk/femail/article-3263017/This-utterly-sick-Twitter-backlash-photographer-s-REFUGEE-fashion-shoot-complete-models-wearing-designer-clothes-dragged-away-police.html.
Jane, Emma A. (2014) '"You're a Ugly, Whorish, Slut": Understanding E-Bile', *Feminist Media Studies*, 14(4), pp. 531–46.

Jarrett, Kylie (2016) *Feminism, Labour, and Digital Media: The Digital Housewife*. Routledge.

Jenson, Jennifer and de Castell, Suzanne (2013) 'Tipping Points: Marginality, Misogyny, and Videogames', *Journal of Curriculum Theorizing*, 29(2), pp. 72–81.

Jeppesen, Sandra, Hounslow, Toni, Khan, Sharmeen and Petrick, Kamilla (2017) 'Media Action Research Group: Toward an Antiauthoritarian Profeminist Media Research Methodology', *Feminist Media Studies*, 17(6), pp. 1056–72.

Jermyn, Deborah (2016) 'Pretty Past It? Interrogating the Post-Feminist Makeover of Ageing, Style, and Fashion', *Feminist Media Studies*, 16(4), pp. 573–89.

Jhally, Sut (2018) 'Image-based Culture: Advertising and Popular Culture', in *Gender, Race, and Class in Media*, ed. Gail Hines and Jean M. Humez. SAGE, pp. 226–33.

Joerges, Bernward (1999) 'Do Politics Have Artefacts?' *Social Studies of Science*, 29(3), pp. 411–31.

Johnson, Jim [Bruno Latour] (1988) 'Mixing Humans and Non-Humans Together: The Sociology of a Door-Closer', *Social Problems: Special Issue on the Sociology of Science and Technology*, 35(3), pp. 298–310.

Johnson, Maisha Z. (2015) 'What's Wrong with Cultural Appropriation? These 9 Answers Reveal Its Harm', *Everyday Feminism*, 14 June, https://everydayfeminism.com/2015/06/cultural-appropriation-wrong.

Joseph, Ralina L. (2009) '"Tyra Banks is Fat": Reading (Post-) racism and (Post-) feminism in the New Millennium', *Critical Studies in Media Communication*, 26(3), pp. 237–54.

Joseph, Ralina L. (2016) 'Strategically Ambiguous Shonda Rhimes: Respectability Politics of a Black Woman Showrunner', *Souls*, 18(2–4), pp. 302–20.

Kanai, Akane (2017) 'The Best Friend, the Boyfriend, Other Girls, Hot Guys, and Creeps: The Relational Production of Self on Tumblr', *Feminist Media Studies*, 17(6), pp. 911–25.

Katz, Cindi (2001) 'On the Grounds of Globalization: A Topography for Feminist Political Engagement', *Signs: Journal of Women in Culture and Society*, 26(4), pp. 1213–34.

Katz, Jackson (2011) 'Advertising and the Construction of Violent White Masculinity: From BMWs to Bud Light', in *Gender, Race and Class in Media*, ed. Gail Dines and Jean M. Humez. SAGE, pp. 261–9.

Kearney, Mary Celeste (1998) 'Producing Girls: Rethinking the Study of Female Youth Culture', in *Delinquents and Debutants: Twentieth Century American Girls' Culture*, ed. Sherrie Inniss. New York University Press, pp. 285–310.

Kearney, Mary Celeste (2006) *Girls Make Media*. Routledge.

Kearney, Mary Celeste (2012) 'A Manifesta for Feminist Media Criticism', at http://blog.commarts.wisc.edu/2012/12/11/feminist-media-criticism-is-part-2.

Kee, Jac sm (2017) 'Imagine a Feminist Internet', *Development*, 60(1), pp. 83–89.

Keller, Jessalynn (2011) 'Virtual Feminisms: Girls' Blogging Communities, Feminist Activism, and Participatory Politics', *Information, Communication & Society*, 15(3), pp. 429–47.

Keller, Jessalynn (2015) *Girls' Feminist Blogging in a Postfeminist Age*. Routledge.
Keller, Jessalynn and Ryan, Maureen E. (2018) 'Introduction: Mapping Emergent Feminisms', in *Emergent Feminisms: Complicating a Postfeminist Media Culture*, ed. Jessalynn Keller and Maureen E. Ryan. Routledge, pp. 1–21.
Keller, Jessalynn, Mendes, Kaitlynn, and Ringrose, Jessica (2016) 'Speaking "Unspeakable Things": Documenting Digital Feminist Responses to Rape Culture', *Journal of Gender Studies*, 27(1), pp. 22–36.
Kendall, Lori (2011) '"White and Nerdy": Computers, Race, and the Nerd Stereotype', *The Journal of Popular Culture*, 44(3), pp. 505–24.
Khoja-Moolji, Shenila (2015a) 'Reading Malala: (De)(Re)Territorialization of Muslim Collectivities', *Comparative Studies of South Asia, Africa and the Middle East*, 35(3), pp. 539–56.
Khoja-Moolji, Shenila (2015b) 'Becoming an "Intimate Public": Exploring the Affective Intensities of Hashtag Feminism', *Feminist Media Studies*, 15(2), pp. 347–50.
Kilbourne, Jean (2010) *Killing Us Softly 4: Advertising's Image of Women*. Media Education Foundation.
Kinane, Ruth (2017) 'Why Shonda Rhimes Hates Being Asked How She Writes Strong Female Characters', *Entertainment Weekly*, 7 September, https://ew.com/tv/2017/09/07/shonda-rhimes-time-firsts-strong-female-characters.
Kinser, Amber E. (2004) 'Negotiating Spaces For/Through Third-Wave Feminism', *NWSA Journal*, 16(3), pp. 124–53.
Kopacz, Maria and Lawton, Bessie Lee (2011) 'The YouTube Indian: Portrayals of Native Americans on a Viral Video Site', *New Media & Society*, 13(2), pp. 330–49.
Kunstman, Adi (ed.) (2017) *Selfie Citizenship*. Palgrave Macmillan.
Latif, Nadia and Latif, Leila (2016) 'How to Fix Hollywood's Race Problem', *Guardian*, 18 January, www.theguardian.com/film/2016/jan/18/hollywoods-race-problem-film-industry-actors-of-colour.
Lauzen, Martha M. (2017) 'Boxed In 2016–17: Women on Screen and Behind the Scenes in Television', *Center for the Study of Women in Television and Film*, https://womenintvfilm.sdsu.edu/wp-content/uploads/2017/09/2016-17_Boxed_In_Report.pdf.
Lawson, Caitlin E. (2018) 'Platform Vulnerabilities: Harassment and Misogynoir in the Digital Attack on Leslie Jones', *Information, Communication & Society*, 21(6), pp. 818–33.
Lazar, Michelle M. (2006) '"Discover the Power of Femininity!" Analyzing Global Power Femininity in Local Advertising', *Feminist Media Studies*, 6(4), pp. 505–17.
Lazar, Michelle M. (2011) 'The Right to Be Beautiful: Postfeminist Identity and Consumer Beauty Advertising', in *New Femininities: Postfeminism, Neoliberalism and Subjectivity*, ed. Rosalind Gill and Christina Scharff. Palgrave Macmillan, pp. 37–51.
Lazzarato, Maurizio (1996) 'Immaterial Labor', in *Radical Thought in Italy: A*

Potential Politics, ed. Paolo Virno and Michael Hardt. University of Minnesota Press, pp. 133–48.

Lebesco, Kathleen A. (2003) *Revolting Bodies? The Struggle to Redefine Fat Identity*. University of Massachusetts Press.

Lee, Micky (2011) 'A Feminist Political Economy of Communication', *Feminist Media Studies*, 11(1), pp. 83–7.

Lee, Una and Tolliver, Dan (2017) 'Building Consentful Tech', http://ripplemap.io/zine.pdf.

Lennon, Tiffani (2013) 'Benchmarking Women's Leadership in the US', University of Denver, Colorado Women's College, www.womenscollege.du.edu/media/documents/BenchmarkingWomensLeadershipintheUS.pdf.

Leurs, Koen H. A. (2015) *Digital Passages: Migrant Youth 2.0: Diaspora, Gender and Youth Cultural Intersections*. Amsterdam University Press.

Leurs, Koen (2017) 'Feminist Data Studies: Using Digital Methods for Ethical, Reflexive, and Situated Socio-Cultural Research', *Feminist Review*, 115, pp. 130–54.

Levinson, Alana Hope (2015) 'The Pink Ghetto of Social Media', *Medium*, 16 July, https://medium.com/matter/the-pink-ghetto-of-social-media-39bf7f2fdbe1.

Levy, Ariel (2005) *Female Chauvinist Pigs: Women and the Rise of Raunch Culture*. Free Press.

Lim, Sun Sun and Soon, Carol (2010) 'The Influence of Social and Cultural Factors on Mothers' Domestication of Household ICTs: Experiences of Chinese and Korean Women', *Telematics and Informatics*, 27(3), pp. 205–16.

Lincoln, Yvonna S. and Guba, Egon G. (1985) *Naturalistic Inquiry*. SAGE.

Livingstone, Sonia (1998) 'Relationships between Media and Audiences: Prospects for Future Audience Reception Studies', in *Media, Ritual and Identity*, ed. Tamar Liebes and James Curran. Routledge, pp. 237–55.

Loken, Meredith (2014) '#BringBackOurGirls and the Invisibility of Imperialism', *Feminist Media Studies*, 14(6), pp. 1100–1.

Lorde, Audre (1984) *Sister Outsider: Essays and Speeches*. The Crossing Press.

Loza, Susana (2014) 'Hashtag Feminism, #SolidarityisForWhiteWomen, and the Other #FemFuture', *Ada: A Journal of Gender, New Media, and Technology*, 5.

Lugones, María (2010) 'Toward a Decolonial Feminism', *Hypatia*, 25(4), pp. 742–59.

Luka, Mary Elizabeth and Millette, Mélanie (2018) '(Re)framing Big Data: Activating Situated Knowledges and a Feminist Ethics of Care in Social Media Research', *Social Media + Society*. DOI: 10.1177/2056305118768297.

Lupton, Deborah (2000) 'The Embodied Computer/User', in *The Cybercultures Reader*, ed. David Bell and Barbara M. Kennedy. Routledge, pp. 477–87.

Luxton, Meg (1997) 'The UN, Women, and Household Labour: Measuring and Valuing Unpaid Work', *Women's Studies International Forum*, 20(3), pp. 431–9.

Lynch, Teresa, Tompkins, Jessica E., van Driel, Irene I., and Fritz, Niki (2016) 'Sexy, Strong, and Secondary: A Content Analysis of Female Characters in Video Games across 31 Years', *Journal of Communication*, 66(4), pp. 564–84.

McDougall, Sophia (2013) 'I Hate Strong Female Characters', *New Statesman*, 15 August, www.newstatesman.com/culture/2013/08/i-hate-strong-female-characters.

McIntosh, Peggy (1988) 'White Privilege and Male Privilege: A Personal Account of Coming to See Correspondences Through Work in Women's Studies', Wellesley: Center for Research on Women, Working Paper 189.

McLaughlin, Lisa (2002) 'Something Old, Something New: Lingering Moments in the Unhappy Marriage of Marxism and Feminism', in *Sex & Money: Feminism and Political Economy in the Media*, ed. Eileen R. Meehan and Ellen Riordan. University of Minnesota Press, pp. 30–46.

McLaughlin, Lisa and Johnson, Helen (2008) 'Women and Knowledge Work in the Asia Pacific: Complicating Technological Empowerment', in *Knowledge Workers in the Information Society*, ed. Catherine McKercher and Vincent Mosco. Lexington Books, pp. 249–66.

McRobbie, Angela (1978) 'Jackie: An Ideology of Adolescent Femininity', Centre for Contemporary Cultural Studies, http://epapers.bham.ac.uk/1808/1/SOP53.pdf.

McRobbie, Angela (2004) 'Post-feminism and Popular Culture', *Feminist Media Studies*, 4(3), pp. 255–64.

McRobbie, Angela (2007a) 'Postfeminism and Popular Culture: Bridget Jones and the New Girl Regime', in *Interrogating Postfeminism: Gender and the Politics of Popular Culture*, ed. Yvonne Tasker and Diane Negra. Duke University Press, pp. 27–39.

McRobbie, Angela (2007b) 'Top Girls? Young Women and the Post-Feminist Sexual Contract', *Cultural Studies*, 21(4–5), pp. 718–37.

McRobbie, Angela (2009) *The Aftermath of Feminism: Gender, Culture, and Social Change*. SAGE.

Mahmood, Saba (2011) *Politics of Piety: The Islamic Revival and the Feminist Subject*. Princeton University Press.

Marston, Kendra (2016) 'The World Is Her Oyster: Negotiating Contemporary White Womanhood in Hollywood's Tourist Spaces', *Cinema Journal*, 55(4), pp. 3–27.

Martínez, Elizabeth (1993) 'Beyond Black/White: The Racisms of our Times', *Social Justice*, 20 (1/2), pp. 22–34.

Marwick, Alice E. (2015) 'Instafame: Luxury Selfies in the Attention Economy', *Public Culture*, 27(1(75)), pp. 137–60.

Marwick, Alice E. and boyd, danah (2010) 'I Tweet Honestly, I Tweet Passionately: Twitter Users, Context Collapse, and the Imagined Audience', *New Media & Society*, 13(1), pp. 114–33.

Marx, Karl (2004) *Capital: A Critique of Political Economy*, trans. Ben Fowkes. Penguin Books.

Massanari, Adrienne (2017) '#Gamergate and The Fappening: How Reddit's Algorithm, Governance, and Culture Support Toxic Technocultures', *New Media & Society*, 19(3), pp. 329–46.

References

Massanari, Adrienne L. (2018) 'Rethinking Research Ethics, Power, and the Risk of Visibility in the Era of the "Alt-Right" Gaze', *Social Media + Society*, pp. 1–9.

Mayer, Vicki (2011) *Below the Line: Producers and Production Studies in the New Television Economy*. Duke University Press.

Mayer, Vicki, Banks, Miranda J., and Caldwell, John T. (eds) (2009) *Production Studies: Cultural Studies of Media Industries*. Routledge.

Meehan, Eileen R. (2002) 'Gendering the Commodity Audience: Critical Media Research, Feminism, and Political Economy', in *Sex & Money: Feminism and Political Economy in the Media*, ed. Eileen R. Meehan and Ellen Riordan. University of Minnesota Press, pp. 209–22.

Meehan, Eileen R. and Riordan, Ellen (2002) 'Introduction', in *Sex & Money: Feminism and Political Economy in the Media*, ed. Eileen R. Meehan and Ellen Riordan. University of Minnesota Press, pp. ix–xiii.

Mignolo, Walter D. (2011) 'The Global South and World Dis/Order', *Journal of Anthropological Research*, 67(2), pp. 165–88.

Miller, Lisa (2018) 'The Relentless Torture of The Handmaid's Tale', *The Cut*, 2 May, www.thecut.com/2018/05/the-handmaids-tale-season-2-review.html.

Mishna, Faye, Schwan, Kaitlin J., Birze, Arija, Van Wert, Melissa, Lacombe-Duncan, Ashley, McInroy, Lauren, and Attar-Schwartz, Shalhevet (2018) 'Gendered and Sexualized Bullying and Cyber Bullying: Spotlighting Girls and Making Boys Invisible', *Youth & Society*. DOI: 10.1177/0044118X18757150.

Mohanty, Chandra Talpade (1984) 'Under Western Eyes: Feminist Scholarship and Colonial Discourses', *boundary* 2, 12(3), pp. 333–58.

Molina-Guzmán, Isabel and Cacho, Lisa Marie (2013) 'Historically Mapping Contemporary Intersectional Feminist Media Studies', in *The Routledge Companion to Media and Gender*, ed. Cynthia Carter, Linda Steiner and Lisa McLaughlin. Routledge, pp. 71–80.

Mooney, Annabelle (2008) 'Boys Will Be Boys: Men's Magazines and the Normalisation of Pornography', *Feminist Media Studies*, 8(3), pp. 247–65.

Morley, David and Robins, Kevin (1995) *Spaces of Identity: Global Media, Electronic Landscapes and Cultural Boundaries*. Routledge.

Morton, Katherine (2018) 'Ugliness as Colonial Violence: Mediations of Murdered and Missing Indigenous Women', in *On the Politics of Ugliness*, ed. Sara Rodrigues and Ela Przybylo. Palgrave Macmillan, pp. 259–89.

Mosco, Vincent (2009) *The Political Economy of Communication*, 2nd edition. SAGE.

Mosco, Vincent and Foster, Derek (2001) 'Cyberspace and the End of Politics', *Journal of Communication Inquiry*, 25(3), pp. 218–36.

Mott, Carrie and Cockayne, Daniel (2017) 'Citation Matters: Mobilizing the Politics of Citation Toward a Practice of "Conscientious Engagement"', *Gender, Place & Culture*, 24(7), pp. 954–73.

Mukherjee, Sumita (2018) *Indian Suffragettes: Female Identities and Transnational Networks*. Oxford University Press.

Mulvey, Laura (1999) 'Visual Pleasure and Narrative Cinema', in *Film Theory and*

Criticism: Introductory Readings, ed. Leo Braudy and Marshall Cohen. Oxford University Press, pp. 833–44.

Muñoz, José Esteban (1999) *Disidentifications: Queers of Color and the Performance of Politics*. University of Minnesota Press.

Murray, Dara Persis (2012) 'Branding "Real" Social Change in Dove's Campaign for Real Beauty', *Feminist Media Studies*, 13(1), pp. 83–101.

Naezer, Marijke (2018) 'Sexy Selves: Girls, Selfies and the Performance of Intersectional Identities', *European Journal of Women's Studies*. DOI: 10.1177/1350506818804845.

Nagar, Richa, Lawson, Victoria, McDowell, Linda, and Hanson, Susan (2002) 'Locating Globalization: Feminist (Re)readings of the Subjects and Spaces of Globalization', *Economic Geography*, 78(3), pp. 257–84.

Nagy, Peter and Neff, Gina (2015) 'Imagined Affordance: Reconstructing a Keyword for Communication Theory', *Social Media + Society*, 1(2).

Nakamura, Lisa (2000) '"Where Do You Want to Go Today?" Cybernetic Tourism, the Internet, and Transnationality', in *Race in Cyberspace*, ed. Beth E. Kolko, Lisa Nakamura and Gilbert B. Rodman. Routledge, pp. 15–26.

Nakamura, Lisa (2002a) 'After/Images of Identity: Gender, Technology, and Identity Politics', in *Reload: Rethinking Women + Cyberculture*, ed. Mary Flanagan and Austin Booth. MIT Press, pp. 321–31.

Nakamura, Lisa (2002b) *Cybertypes: Race, Ethnicity, and Identity on the Internet*. Routledge.

Nakamura, Lisa (2008) *Digitizing Race: Visual Cultures of the Internet*. University of Minnesota Press.

Nakamura, Lisa (2011) 'Economies of Digital Production in East Asia: iPhone Girls and the Transnational Circuits of Cool', *Media Fields Journal*, 2.

Nakamura, Lisa (2014) 'Indigenous Circuits: Navajo Women and the Racialization of Early Electronic Manufacture', *American Quarterly*, 66(4), pp. 919–41.

Nakamura, Lisa (2015) 'The Unwanted Labour of Social Media: Women of Colour Call Out Culture as Venture Community Management', *New Formations*, 86, pp. 106–12.

Neff, Gina (2012) *Venture Labor: Work and the Burden of Risk in Innovative Industries*. MIT Press.

Negra, Diane (2001) 'Romance and/as Tourism: Heritage Whiteness and the Inter(national) Imaginary in the New Woman's Film', in *Keyframes: Popular Cinema and Cultural Studies*, ed. Matthew Tinkcom and Amy Villarejo. Routledge, pp. 82–97.

Negrón-Muntaner, Frances with Chelsea Abbas, Luis Figueroa, and Samuel Robson (2014) 'The Latino Media Gap: A Report on the State of Latinos in U.S. Media', National Association of Latino Independent Producers, https://media-alliance.org/wp-content/uploads/2016/05/Latino_Media_Gap_Report.pdf.

Nguyen, Viet Thanh (2018) 'Asian-Americans Need More Movies, Even Mediocre Ones', *New York Times*, 21 August, https://nyti.ms/2nVAZZ7.

Noble, Safiya Umoja (2018) *Algorithms of Oppression: How Search Engines Reinforce Racism*. New York University Press.

Noble, Safiya Umoja and Tynes, Brendesha M. (eds) (2015) *The Intersectional Internet: Race, Sex, Class, & Culture Online*. Peter Lang.

Nooney, Laine (2013) 'A Pedestal, A Table, A Love Letter: Archaeologies of Gender in Videogame History', *Game Studies*, 13(2), http://gamestudies.org/1302/articles/nooney.

Noriega, Chon (1999) 'Race Matters, Media Matters', in *Viewing Race: A Videoforum Publication. A Videography and Resource Guide*, ed. Chon Noriega. National Video Resources, pp. 5–7.

Nussbaum, Martha C. (1999) *Sex and Social Justice*. Oxford University Press.

Nussbaum, Martha C. (2000) *Women and Human Development*. Cambridge University Press.

O'Brien, Anne (2017) 'Feminine or Feminist? Women's Media Leadership', *Feminist Media Studies*, 17(5), pp. 835–50.

O'Brien, Anne (2018) '(Not) Getting the Credit: Women, Liminal Subjectivity, and Resisting Neoliberalism in Documentary Production', *Media, Culture & Society*, 40(5), pp. 673–88.

O'Riordan, Kate and Phillips, David J. (eds) (2007) *Queer Online: Media Technology and Sexuality*. Peter Lang.

Ozkazanc-Pan, Banu (2012) 'Postcolonial Feminist Research: Challenges and Complexities', *Equality, Diversity and Inclusion: An International Journal*, 31(5/6), pp. 573–91.

Parameswaran, Radhika (2004) 'Global Queens, National Celebrities: Tales of Feminine Triumph in Post-Liberalization India', *Critical Studies in Media Communication*, 21(4), pp. 346–70.

Parameswaran, Radhika (2013) 'Studying the Elusive Audience: Consumers, Readers, Users, and Viewers in a Changing World', in *The International Encyclopedia of Media Studies Volume IV: Audience and Interpretation*, ed. Radhika Parameswaran. Wiley-Blackwell, pp. 1–24.

Patel, Vibhuti (1985) 'Women's Liberation in India', *New Left Review*, I/153.

Patil, Vrushali and Purkayastha, Bandana (2015) 'Sexual Violence, Race and Media (In)Visibility: Intersectional Complexities in a Transnational Frame', *Societies*, 5, pp. 598–617.

Phipps, Alison (2016) 'Whose Personal is more Political? Experience in Contemporary Feminist Politics', *Feminist Theory*, 17(3), pp. 303–21.

Pink, Sarah (2015) *Doing Sensory Ethnography*, 2nd edition. SAGE.

Plant, Sadie (1998) *Zeroes and Ones: Digital Women and the New Technoculture*. Fourth Estate.

Prescott, Julie and Bogg, Jan (2011) 'Segregation in a Male-Dominated Industry: Women Working in the Computer Games Industry', *International Journal of Gender, Science and Technology*, 3, pp. 206–27.

Probyn, Elspeth (2001) 'Teaching in the Field: Gender and Feminist Media Studies', *Feminist Media Studies*, 1(1), pp. 35–9.

Projansky, Sarah (2014) *Spectacular Girls: Media Fascination and Celebrity Culture*. New York University Press.

Propp, Vladimir (1968) *Morphology of the Folktale*, 2nd edition, trans. Laurence Scott. University of Texas Press.

Proulx, Mikhel (2016) 'Protocol and Performativity: Queer Selfies and the Coding of Online Identity', *Performance Research*, 21(5), pp. 114–18.

Quail, Christine (2011) 'Nerds, Geeks, and the Hip/Square Dialectic in Contemporary Television', *Television & New Media*, 12(5), pp. 460–82.

Radway, Janice (1984) *Reading the Romance: Women, Patriarchy, and Popular Literature*. University of North Carolina Press.

Raji, Sanaz (2017) '"My Face is Not for Public Consumption": Selfies, Surveillance and the Politics of Being Unseen', in *Selfie Citizenship*, ed. Adi Kuntsman. Palgrave Macmillan, pp. 149–58.

Rambukkana, Nathan (ed.) (2015) *Hashtag Publics: The Power and Politics of Discursive Networks*. Peter Lang.

Rambukkana, Nathan (2019) 'The Politics of Gray Data: Digital Methods, Intimate Proximity, and Research Ethics for Work on the "Alt-Right"', *Qualitative Inquiry*, 25(3), pp. 312–23.

Raun, Tobias (2014) 'Video Blogging as a Vehicle of Transformation: Exploring the Intersection between Trans Identity and Information Technology', *International Journal of Cultural Studies*, 18(3), pp. 365–78.

Raval, Noopur (2014) 'The Encyclopedia Must Fail! – Notes on Queering Wikipedia', *Ada: A Journal of Gender, New Media, and Technology*, 5.

Rawson, K. J. (2014) 'Transgender Worldmaking in Cyberspace: Historical Activism on the Internet', *QED: A Journal in GLBTQ Worldmaking*, 1(2), pp. 38–60.

Reagle, Joseph (2015) 'Geek Policing: Fake Geek Girls and Contested Attention', *International Journal of Communication*, 9, pp. 2862–80.

Reddy, Vanita (2006) 'The Nationalization of the Global Indian Woman', *South Asian Popular Culture*, 4(1), pp. 61–85.

Reinke, Rachel and Todd, Anastasia (2016) '"Cute Girl in Wheelchair—Why?" Cripping YouTube', *Transformations: The Journal of Inclusive Scholarship and Pedagogy*, 25(2), pp. 168–74.

Renninger, Bryce (2018) '"Are You a Feminist?" Celebrity, Publicity, and the Making of a PR-Friendly Feminism', in *Emergent Feminisms: Complicating a Postfeminist Media Culture*, ed. Jessalynn Keller and Maureen E. Ryan. Routledge, pp. 42–56.

Rentschler, Carrie A. (2014) 'Rape Culture and the Feminist Politics of Social Media', *Girlhood Studies*, 7(1), pp. 65–82.

Rentschler, Carrie A. (2017) 'Bystander Intervention, Feminist Hashtag Activism, and the Anti-Carceral Politics of Care', *Feminist Media Studies*, 17(4), pp. 565–84.

Resmer, Cathy (2005) 'The Rule', *Dykes to Watch Out For*, http://dykestowatchoutfor.com/the-rule.

Reynolds, S. (1998) 'The Face on the Cutting-Room Floor: Women Editors in the French Cinema of the 1930s', *Labour History Review*, 63(1), pp. 66–82.

Rich, Adrienne (1980) 'Compulsory Heterosexuality and Lesbian Existence', *Signs*, 5(4), pp. 631–60.

Riordan, Ellen (2002) 'Intersections and New Directions: On Feminism and Political Economy', in *Sex & Money: Feminism and Political Economy in the Media*, ed. Eileen R. Meehan and Ellen Riordan. University of Minnesota Press, pp. 3–15.

Rivers, Nicola (2017) *Postfeminism(s) and the Arrival of the Fourth Wave: Turning Tides*. Palgrave Macmillan.

Roberts, Sarah T. (2016) 'Digital Refuse: Canadian Garbage, Commercial Content Moderation and the Global Circulation of Social Media's Waste', *Wi: Journal of Mobile Media*, 10(1), http://wi.mobilities.ca/digitalrefuse.

Rottenberg, Catherine (2013) 'The Rise of Neoliberal Feminism', *Cultural Studies*, 28(3), pp. 418–37.

Saha, Anamik (2016) 'The Rationalizing/Racializing Logic of Capital in Cultural Production', *Media Industries*, 3(1).

Said, Edward W. (1978) *Orientalism*. Pantheon Books.

Sandberg, Sheryl (2013) *Lean In: Women, Work, and the Will to Lead*. W. H. Allen.

Santos, Boaventura de Sousa (2014) *Epistemologies of the South: Justice Against Epistemicide*. Routledge.

Sassen, Saskia (1999) *Globalization and Its Discontents: Essays on the New Mobility of People and Money*. The New Press.

Schiller, Dan (1999) *Digital Capitalism: Networking the Global Market System*. MIT Press.

Sender, Katherine (2001) 'Gay Readers, Consumers, and a Dominant Gay Habitus: 25 Years of the Advocate Magazine', *Journal of Communication*, 51(1), pp. 73–99.

Sender, Katherine (2005) *Business, Not Politics: The Making of the Gay Market*. Columbia University Press.

Senft, Theresa M. and Baym, Nancy K. (2015) 'What Does the Selfie Say? Investigating a Global Phenomenon', *International Journal of Communication*, 9, pp. 1588–606.

Sensoy, Özlem and Marshall, Elizabeth (2010) 'Missionary Girl Power: Saving the "Third World" One Girl at a Time', *Gender and Education*, 22(3), pp. 295–311.

Setoodeh, Ramin (2015) 'Equal Pay Revolution: How Top Actresses Are Finally Fighting Back', *Variety*, 10 November, http://completesleeper.co.uk/2015/film/news/hollywood-gender-pay-gap-inequality-1201636553.

Shade, Leslie Regan (2002) *Gender and Community in the Social Construction of the Internet*. Peter Lang.

Shaw, Adrienne (2014) *Gaming at the Edge: Sexuality and Gender at the Margins of Gamer Culture*. University of Minnesota Press.

Shaw, Adrienne (2017) 'Encoding and Decoding Affordances: Stuart Hall and Interactive Media Technologies', *Media, Culture & Society*, 29(4), pp. 592–602.

Shepherd, Tamara (2017) 'Neocolonial Intimacies', *California Review of Images and Mark Zuckerberg*, 1, http://zuckerbergreview.com/shepherd.html.

Shepherd, Tamara, Harvey, Alison, Jordan, Tim, Srauy, Sam, and Miltner, Kate (2015) 'Histories of Hating', *Social Media + Society*, 1(2).
Shevinsky, Elissa (ed.) (2015) *Lean Out: The Struggle for Gender Equality in Tech and Start-Up Culture*. OR Books.
Shigematsu, Setsu (2012) *Scream from the Shadows: The Women's Liberation Movement in Japan*. University of Minnesota Press.
Shohat, Ella (1998) *Talking Visions: Multicultural Feminism in Transnational Age*. MIT Press.
Shome, Raka (2006) 'Transnational Feminism and Communication Studies', *The Communication Review*, 9(4), pp. 255–67.
Shorey, Samantha and Rosner, Daniela K. (2019) 'A Voice of Process: Re-Presencing the Gendered Labor of Apollo Innovation', *communication+1*, 7(2), https://scholarworks.umass.edu/cpo/vol7/iss2/4.
Shugart, Helene A. (2007) 'Crossing Over: Hybridity and Hegemony in the Popular Media', *Communication and Critical/Cultural Studies*, 4(2), pp. 115–41.
Shukla, Nikesh (2013) 'After the Bechdel Test, I Propose the Shukla Test for Race in Film', *New Statesman*, 18 October, www.newstatesman.com/2013/10/after-bechdel-test-i-propose-shukla-test-race-film.
Simmons, Aishah Shahidah (2002) 'Using Celluloid to Break the Silence About Sexual Violence in the Black Community', *Women & Therapy*, 25(3–4), pp. 179–85.
Smith, Sharon (2013–14) 'Black Feminism and Intersectionality', *International Socialist Review*, 91, https://isreview.org/issue/91/black-feminism-and-intersectionality.
Smith, Stacy L. (2014) 'Hey, Hollywood: It's Time to Adopt the NFL's Rooney Rule', *The Hollywood Reporter*, 15 December, www.hollywoodreporter.com/news/hey-hollywood-time-adopt-nfls-754659.
Smith, Stacy L., Choueiti, Marc, and Pieper, Katherine, with assistance from Yu-Ting Liu and Christine Song (2014) 'Gender Bias Without Borders: An Investigation of Female Characters in Popular Films Across 11 Countries', The Geena Davis Institute on Gender in Media, http://seejane.org/wp-content/uploads/gender-bias-without-borders-executive-summary.pdf.
Smith, Stacy L., Choueiti, Marc, and Pieper, Katherine (2017) 'Inequality in 900 Popular Films: Examining Portrayals of Gender, Race/Ethnicity, LGBT, and Disability from 2007–2016', Media, Diversity, and Social Change Initiative, https://annenberg.usc.edu/sites/default/files/Dr_Stacy_L_Smith-Inequality_in_900_Popular_Films.pdf.
Smith, Stacy L., Choueiti, Marc, Scofield, Elizabeth, and Pieper, Katherine (2013) 'Gender Inequality in 500 Popular Films: Examining On-Screen Portrayals and Behind-the-Scenes Employment Patterns in Motion Pictures Released between 2007–2012', Media, Diversity, and Social Change Initiative, https://annenberg.usc.edu/sites/default/files/MDSCI_Gender_Inequality_in_500_Popular_Films_-_Smith_2013.pdf.
Smith-Shomade, Beretta E. (2002) *Shaded Lives: African-American Women and Television*. Rutgers University Press.

References

Smith-Shomade, Beretta E. (2007) *Pimpin' Ain't Easy: Selling Black Entertainment Television*. Routledge.

Smythe, Dallas W. (1981) 'On the Audience Commodity and its Work', in *Dependency Road: Communications, Capitalism, and Canada*. Ablex Publishing Corporation, pp. 22–51.

Spivak, Gayatri Chakravorty (1988) 'Can the Subaltern Speak?', in *Marxism and the Interpretation of Culture*, ed. Cary Nelson and Lawrence Grossberg. University of Illinois Press, pp. 271–313.

Spivak, Gayatri Chakravorty (1999) *A Critique of Postcolonial Reason: Toward a History of the Vanishing Present*. Harvard University Press.

Springer, Kimberly (2007) 'Divas, Evil Black Bitches, and Bitter Black Women: African American Women in Postfeminist and Post-Civil Rights Popular Culture', in *Interrogating Postfeminism: Gender and the Politics of Popular Culture*, ed. Diane Negra and Yvonne Tasker. Duke University Press, pp. 249–76.

Srivastava, Prachi and Hopwood, Nick (2009) 'A Practical Iterative Framework for Qualitative Data Analysis', *Interactive Journal of Qualitative Methods*, 8(1), pp. 76–84.

Srouji, Mayada (2018) 'A Body-Positive Black Muslim Feminist: Leah Vernon Uses Fashion as a Statement', *Mvslim*, http://mvslim.com/a-body-positive-black-muslim-feminist-leah-vernon-uses-fashion-as-a-statement.

Stacey, Judith (1987) 'Sexism by a Subtler Name? Postindustrial Conditions and Postfeminist Consciousness in the Silicon Valley', *Socialist Review* 96, 17(6), pp. 7–28.

Stacey, Judith (1988) 'Can There Be a Feminist Ethnography?' *Women's Studies International Forum*, 11(1), pp. 21–7.

Stoler, Ann Laura (2009) *Along the Archival Grain: Epistemic Anxieties and Colonial Common Sense*. Princeton University Press.

Stone, Sandy (1994) 'Split Subjects, Not Atoms; or, How I Fell in Love with my Prosthesis', *Configurations*, 2(1), pp. 73–190.

Storr, Will (2018) *Selfie: How We Became So Self-Obsessed and What It's Doing to Us*. Overlook Press.

Sultana, Farhana (2007) 'Reflexivity, Positionality and Participatory Ethics: Negotiating Fieldwork Dilemmas in International Research', *ACME: An International Journal for Critical Geographies*, 6(3), pp. 374–85, www.acme-journal.org/index.php/acme/article/view/786.

Sundén, Jenny and Paasonen (2018) 'Shameless Hags and Tolerance Whores: Feminist Resistance and the Affective Circuits of Online Hate', *Feminist Media Studies*, 18(4), pp. 643–56.

Taft, Jessica K. (2004) 'Girl Power Politics: Pop-Culture Barriers and Organizational Resistance', in *All About the Girl: Culture, Power and Identity*, ed. Anita Harris. Routledge, pp. 69–78.

Tasker, Yvonne and Negra, Diane (2005) 'Postfeminism and Contemporary Media Studies', *Cinema Journal*, 44(2), pp. 107–10.

Terranova, Tiziana (2000) 'Free Labor: Producing Culture for the Digital Economy', *Social Text*, 63, 18(2), pp. 33–58.

Thomas, Amber (2017) 'Women Only Said 27% of the Words in 2016's Biggest Movies', *Medium*, 12 January, https://medium.freecodecamp.org/women-only-said-27-of-the-words-in-2016s-biggest-movies-955cb480c3c4.

Trott, Verity (2018) 'Black "Rantings": Indigenous Feminisms Online', in *Emergent Feminisms: Complicating a Postfeminist Media Culture*, ed. Jessalynn Keller and Maureen E. Ryan. Routledge, pp. 143–58.

Tuchman, Gaye (1978) 'Introduction: The Symbolic Annihilation of Women by the Mass Media', in *Hearth and Home: Images of Women in the Mass Media*, ed. Gaye Tuchman, Arlene Kaplan Daniels and James Benet. Oxford University Press, pp. 3–38.

Tuhiwai Smith, Linda (2012) *Decolonizing Methodologies: Research and Indigenous Peoples*. Otago University Press.

Turkle, Sherry (1984) *The Second Self: Computers and the Human Spirit*. Simon & Schuster.

Turner, Graeme (2010) *Ordinary People and the Media: The Demotic Turn*. SAGE.

Tyler, Imogen (2008) '"Chav Mum Chav Scum": Class Disgust in Contemporary Britain', *Feminist Media Studies*, 8(1), pp. 17–34.

UN Broadband Commission for Sustainable Development (2017) 'The State of Broadband 2017: Broadband Catalyzing Sustainable Development', *ITU Publications*, www.itu.int/dms_pub/itu-s/opb/pol/S-POL-BROADBAND.18-2017-PDF-E.pdf.

van Dijck, José (2009) 'Users Like You? Theorizing Agency in User-Generated Content', *Media, Culture & Society*, 31(1), pp. 41–58.

van Doorn, Niels (2011) 'Digital Spaces, Material Traces: How Matter Comes to Matter in Online Performances of Gender, Sexuality and Embodiment', *Media, Culture & Society*, 33(4), pp. 531–47.

van Doorn, Niels (2017) 'Platform Labor: On the Gendered and Racialized Exploitation of Low-Income Service Work in the "On-Demand" Economy', *Information, Communication & Society*, 20(6), pp. 898–914.

van Zoonen, Liesbet (1994) *Feminist Media Studies*. SAGE.

Vickery, Jacqueline Ryan and Everbach, Tracy (2018) 'The Persistence of Misogyny: From the Streets, to Our Screens, to the White House', in *Mediating Misogyny: Gender, Technology, and Harassment*, ed. Jacqueline Ryan Vickery and Tracy Everbach. Palgrave Macmillan, pp. 1–27.

Vivienne, Son (2017) '"I Will Not Hate Myself Because You Cannot Accept Me": Problematizing Empowerment and Gender-Diverse Selfies', *Popular Communication*, 15(2), pp. 126–40.

Wajcman, Judy (1991) *Feminism Confronts Technology*. Polity.

Wakeford, Nina (2000) 'Network Women and Grrrls with Information/Communication Technology', in *The Cybercultures Reader*, ed. David Bell and Barbara M. Kennedy. Routledge, pp. 350–9.

Warfield, Katie (2015) 'The Model, The #Realme, and the Self-Conscious

Thespian: Digital Subjectivities, Young Canadian Women, and Selfies', *The International Journal of the Image*, 6(2), pp. 1–16.

Warner, Michael (1991) 'Introduction: Fear of a Queer Planet', *Social Text*, 29, pp. 3–17.

Weiner Mahfuz, Lisa and Farrow, Kenyon (2012) 'Movement Building: Past and Present Strategies', in *Resisting the Rainbow: Right-Wing Responses to LGBT Gains*. A publication of Political Research Associates, compiled by Pam Chamberlain, www.politicalresearch.org/wp-content/uploads/downloads/2012/12/Resisting-the-Rainbow-Full-Report.pdf#page=108.

Wekker, Gloria (2006) *The Politics of Passion: Women's Sexual Culture in the Afro-Surinamese Diaspora*. Columbia University Press.

Wekker, Gloria (2016) *White Innocence: Paradoxes of Colonialism and Race*. Duke University Press.

Whitlock, Gillian (2007) *Soft Weapons: Autobiography in Transit*. University of Chicago Press.

Williams, Dmitri, Martins, Nicole, Consalvo, Mia, and Ivory, James D. (2009) 'The Virtual Census: Representations of Gender, Race and Age in Video Games', *New Media & Society*, 11(5), pp. 815–34.

Williams, Raymond (1974) *Television: Technology and Cultural Form*. Fontana.

Wilson, Leslie (2018) 'State Control over Academic Freedom in Hungary Threatens all Universities', *Guardian*, 6 September, www.theguardian.com/higher-education-network/2018/sep/06/state-control-over-academic-freedom-in-hungary-threatens-all-universities.

Winner, Langdon (1980) 'Do Artifacts Have Politics?' *Daedalus*, 109(1), pp. 121–36.

Wissinger, Elizabeth (2015) '#No Filter: Models, Glamour Labor, and the Age of the Blink', *Interface*, 1(1), pp. 1–20.

Wodak, Ruth (2001) 'What CDA is About: A Summary of its History, Important Concepts, and its Developments', in *Methods of Critical Discourse Analysis*, ed. Ruth Wodak and Michael Meyers. SAGE, pp. 1–13.

Wolf, Naomi (1990) *The Beauty Myth: How Images of Beauty Are Used Against Women*. Chatto & Windus.

Woolcock, Nicola (2017) 'Great Thinkers Too Male and Pale, Students Declare', *The Times*, 9 January, www.thetimes.co.uk/article/great-thinkers-too-male-and-pale-students-declare-scq98txld.

Wreyford, Natalie and Cobb, Shelley (2017) 'Data and Responsibility: Toward a Feminist Methodology for Producing Historical Data on Women in the Contemporary UK Film Industry', *Feminist Media Histories*, 3(3), pp. 107–32.

Zeng, Meg Jing (2018) 'From #MeToo to #RiceBunny: How Social Media Users are Campaigning in China', *The Conversation*, 6 February, https://theconversation.com/from-metoo-to-ricebunny-how-social-media-users-are-campaigning-in-china-90860.

Zhang, Tracy Y. (2007) '"Deaf-mutes, Illiterates, and Women": Ethnicity, Gender, and Labor Policy in a Tibetan Carpet Factory', *Feminist Media Studies*, 7(4), pp. 381–96.

Zsubori, Anna (2018) 'Gender Studies Banned at University – the Hungarian Government's Latest Attack on Equality', *The Conversation*, 9 October, https://theconversation.com/gender-studies-banned-at-university-the-hungarian-governments-latest-attack-on-equality-103150f.

Index

#BeenRapedNeverReported 128
#BlackLivesMatter (BLM) 21, 107, 139
#BringBackOurGirls 100–1, 130–1, 171
#bystanderintervention 128
#croptopday 128
#distractinglysexy 128
#FemFuture 131
#GamerGate 136, 138
#GirlsLikeUs 129
#handsoffaboriginalkids 127
#HeForShe 17
#MeToo 109, 128, 164–7
#RiceBunny 109
#SayHerName 107
#SolidarityisForWhiteWomen 129, 131
#TimesUp 164, 167
#WhatIReallyReallyWant 96, 100
#WorldPitch 85, 97, 100
#YesAllWomen 128
#YouOKSis 128
4chan 126, 136
10 Hours of Walking in New York 130

Abbott, Diane 172
ability 24, 42 *see also* disability
abolitionism 6–7, 16
access
  to communities 36–7
  to education 3, 11, 96
  to opportunities 11, 20–1, 49, 94, 165
  to physical spaces 23–4
  to technology 94–5, 113, 116, 122, 125, 131
  to work 3, 11
action for change 11, 14–15, 51–7, 105–11, 131–41, 163–7, 170–1 *see also* activism and intervention
activism 8, 11, 52, 55–6, 97–100, 107, 109, 135, 159
  hashtag 96, 100, 107, 109, 127–31
  social media 84
  see also action for change and intervention
activism-research 54–5

'Add More Women and Stir' 30
A Declaration of the Independence of Cyberspace 120 *see also* John Perry Barlow
Adichie, Chimamanda Ngozi 106
advertising 62, 69, 72–5, 102–4, 122, 133, 148, 157, 161
Advocate, The 149–50
affect 45, 48–9, 53, 89, 128–9, 131–2, 135, 148, 153, 159–62, 169
affordances 121, 124–6, 128–9, 132, 134–9, 157, 172
Afrofuturism 139
age 17, 22, 40, 49, 73, 85, 97–8, 100–1, 132
agency 11, 16, 26, 50–1, 84, 99, 127
algorithms 124
Alphabet 146
alterity industry, the 103
Amazon 157
anger 12, 31, 64, 169
Angry Black Woman stereotype 67
Annenberg Inclusion Initiative 61
anonymity 125–7, 136
antifeminism 27, 129, 172 *see also* backlash
Apatow, Judd 81, 143
Arab Spring, the 107
A Rape in Cyberspace 121
archetypes 64–6
archives 52–3, 151, 154
artificial intelligence 116, 139
audience 41, 45, 62–4, 133, 157–8
  Black 70
  commodity 148–9, 157 *see also* commodification
  gay 70, 149
  studies 44, 46–8, 51, 108
  transgender 47
Australia 127
authenticity 126, 132–4

Bachelor, The 78
backlash 12, 18, 72–3, 83 *see also* antifeminism

205

Banet-Weiser, Sarah 79
Banks, Miranda 151–4
Barlow, John Perry 120, 122 see also *A Declaration of the Independence of Cyberspace*
beauty 10–11, 16, 24, 72–5, 7, 89, 125, 134–5
Beauty Myth, The 72 see also Wolf, Naomi
Bechdel Test, the 58, 82, 142
below-the-line work 151–3, 155
Benchmarking Women's Leadership in the US 160
Beyoncé 17, 170
Bieber, Justin 101
big data 95, 138
Big Data from the South 140
bisexuality 22
Bitch Media 56
Blackface 102
Black Jezebel stereotype 70
Black Panther 76, 139
blogs 14, 45, 60, 72, 120, 122, 134–5, 156
Buffy the Vampire Slayer 13
Burke, Tarana 164
Butler, Judith 13

Cagney & Lacey 51
Canada 7, 91, 125, 163–4
capitalism 10, 15, 19, 119, 145–8, 159–60
care 45, 64, 67, 70, 88, 147, 153, 159–60, 162 *see also* self-care, feminist ethics of care
censorship 109
Center for the Study of Women in Television and Film 61
chavs 148
chick flicks 149
chick lit 27, 77, 107
child marriage 96, 98
Children of Blood and Bone, The 139
China 54, 107, 109, 125
choice 16, 26, 73, 89, 98–9
citational politics 91, 105–6
citizenship 21–2, 94, 135
civil rights 9, 103, 149
class 21, 26, 61, 75, 89–90, 106–7, 146–8, 159
co-design 140
colonialism 21, 90–2, 97–9, 110
Combahee River Collective 19, 147
commodification
of difference 101–3, 150
of emotions 153
of feminism 15, 21, 28, 77
of labour 145–8, 158–9
of selfies 133
of user-generated content 50
see also audience commodity
commodity image system 72
compulsory heterosexuality 22
connotation 40
consentful technologies 141
constraints 124
content analysis 35, 42–3, 79
content moderation 128, 155
context collapse 126–7
cosmopolitanism 94, 96, 103
costume design 151–4
countertypes 65, 81
creative justice 167
Crenshaw, Kimberlé 19
Criado-Perez, Caroline 172
cultural appropriation 66–7, 101–4, 121
cultural relativism 97
cyberethnography 49
cyberfeminism 117–18, 141
Cyberspace and the American Dream: A Magna Carta for the Knowledge Age 119

d'Acci, Julie 51
data justice 140
decolonization 85, 88, 105–11, 137, 140
deductive approaches 35
democratization of media, the 79, 156–8
denotation 40
design justice 140
desire 11–2, 48, 68–9, 74, 99
deterritorialization 89, 107
digital capitalism 158, 161–2
digital divides 94–5, 122
digital games 53, 56, 61, 136, 138, 163–4
digital housewife, the 160
disability 23–4, 36–7, 49 *see also* ability
discourse 4, 43
discourse analysis 43–6, 110, 129
disgust 148
Disney 146
Dobson, Amy Shields 79
do-it-yourself (DIY) media 14, 156
dominant readings 45–6, 124
Dosekun, Simidele 106
Doty, Alexander 41–2
doxxing 136, 172
DuVernay test, the 58, 82
Dyer, Richard 69

Index

eating the other 101–2, 147
e-bile 125
embodiment *see also* postfeminism and the body
    and the internet 122
    fatphobia and fat positivity 24
    pathologized bodies 22, 36, 49, 93
emic and etic accounting 48
empowerment 13–15, 77, 79, 94, 96, 99, 103–4, 135, 158 *see also* postfeminism and empowerment
encoding/decoding model of communication 45–6
epistemic violence 95, 105, 108, 130–1, 173
equality 8–10, 80, 85, 120
Equal Pay Act of 1963, The 8
ethics 34, 138
ethnography 48–50, 57, 173
Everyday Sexism 128, 170–1
exploitation 90–1, 145–8, 158, 162

Facebook 2, 45, 50, 89, 118, 126–7, 146, 156, 160, 165
Fappening, The 136
fashion 11, 40, 72–5, 89, 102, 134
feelings 45, 153
female genital mutilation (FGM) 97–8
female leads 63, 76, 103, 146
Femen 98–9
Femina 107
Feminine Mystique, The 8–9, 147 *see also* Friedan, Betty
feminism
    and media studies 3–4, 168–9
    and single-issue approaches 7, 9, 19, 106
    Black feminist theory 147–8
    celebrity 16–17, 169–70
    commodity 21, 169
    consumer 21, 169
    co-optation of 13, 77
    definitions of 4, 15, 17
    intergenerational conflict 17, 22, 170
    liberal 99, 169
    mediation of 10, 16–17, 169
    neoliberal 28, 169
    popular 16, 170
    popular criticism of 12
    structural critique versus individualist approaches 13–16, 80, 164–6, 169
    the killjoy figure 12, 17, 31, 64, 78, 169
    White 7–9, 130–1
    see also waves of feminism

feminist ethics of care 34–5, 57, 137–8 *see also* care, self-care
Feminist Five, The 109
Feminist Frequency 56
feminist internet, the 140
feminist participatory action research 55–6, 163–4
Feminist Voices 109
feminization of work 160
film 42, 47, 54, 58–63, 68–70, 74, 81–2, 103, 109, 138–9, 142–4, 151–4, 167
France 98
freedom 99, 117–22
Friedan, Betty 8, 17, 147 *see also Feminine Mystique, The*
Fuji 146

gaze
    male 26, 68–70, 75, 77, 79, 101, 134–5
    narcissistic 26
    oppositional 70–1
    White 67, 87
Geena Davis Institution on Gender in Media, The 61
gender
    as social construct 3, 8, 18, 32
    definition of 3
    disciplining 25–6, 72–3, 114, 125, 134, 161
    essentialism 3, 12, 18, 25–7, 118, 174
    identity 3, 18, 22–3, 174
    performance 4, 10, 13–14, 72
    poststructural approaches 3, 12, 18
    socialization 12, 65, 72
    subjectivity 4, 77–8, 114, 120,
gender pay gap 18, 88, 142, 154, 157, 161–2
Ghana 155
Ghostbusters (2016) 76, 82
Gill, Rosalind 25–7, 171
girl empowerment organizations 80, 95–6
girl games 149
girl power 13–15, 96, 100
girls 14, 25, 40, 73, 79, 80, 85, 97–8, 100–1, 125, 130, 134, 157 *see also* tween girls and youth
'giving voice' 34, 50, 107
GLAAD media reference guide, the 23
global cultural flows 89–90, 94
globalization 75, 86, 88–90, 107, 110
Global South, the 85–6, 89–90, 100–1, 106, 108, 110, 130–1, 155

Golden Rule, the 120, 140
Gomez, Selena 101
Google 1, 98, 115, 119, 124, 130, 137, 146, 155
grammar of gender 66, 144
grammar of race 66
Grey's Anatomy 76, 172
Growing Up Married 109

Handmaid's Tale, The 143–4
happiness 8, 65, 77, 165
Haraway, Donna 38
hashtag publics 128
hate crime 13
hegemony of play, the 163
heteronormativity 21–2, 58
histories of
   computing 91, 115–18
   digital games 53, 154
   film 153–4
   television 54, 151, 154
   the internet 114–16
Hochschild, Arlie Russell 153
Hollaback! 129–30
Hollywood 69, 142, 164
hooks, bell 70, 102–4
How to Get Away with Murder 76
humour 67
Hungary 173–4
hybridity 96–7
Hypersexual Jezebel stereotype 67

ICT4D 94–5
identity play 79, 121, 126, 134
identity tourism 121
ideology 4, 145
   hegemonic 43–4, 63–66
Imgur 136
imperialism 21, 85, 90–2, 97–8, 100, 103, 122
inclusion rider 167
India 7, 9, 42–3, 94, 96, 107, 110, 129
Indigenous people 7, 22, 90–2, 98, 118, 127
inductive approaches 35
informed consent 34, 138
Influencers 133
Instagram 137, 156–7, 172
interactivity 50, 82, 120, 123, 125, 135–6, 158
interdisciplinarity of feminist media studies 2, 11, 29, 32, 175
international development 94–6

interpretivism 33–4
intersectionality
   definition of 2–3, 19
   in action 19–20
intervention 13, 47, 55, 86, 100, 127, 136, 162, 170 *see also* action for action and activism
interviewing 8, 35, 37, 39, 43, 47–9, 53–5, 86, 133–4, 165
intimacy 133
Islamophobia 23–4
Italy 10, 159
iteration 35–6

Jackie magazine 40–1
Japan 10
Jones, Felicity 60
Jones, Leslie 82–3 *see also Ghostbusters* (2016)

Kloss, Karlie 101

labour
   aesthetic 161
   aspirational 161
   care 88
   emotional 131, 153, 161
   exploitation of 145–7
   formal 151–6
   free 158, 160
   glamour 161
   immaterial 158–60
   informal 156–61
   invisible 91, 152
   unpaid 50
   venture 162
LambdaMoo 121
language 21–2, 38, 43–5, 95
Latif and Latif test, the 59, 82
Latino Media Gap report 62
Laverne & Shirley 41
Lean In: Women, Work, and the Will to Lead 165 *see also* Sandberg, Sheryl
lean out 166
Lopez, Jennifer 96
Lovelace, Ada 117
'Love Your Body' 16
low culture texts 40, 46–7, 132
L Word, The 61

McDormand, Frances 167
McRobbie, Angela 40
Madonna 168

Index

magazines
  feminist 56–7
  gay 149–50
  lad 41, 78
  teen 14, 40–1
  news 88
  women's 16, 25, 41, 75, 107
  see also zines
magical negro stereotype 59, 67
Mahmood, Saba 99
makeover paradigm 26
Mammy stereotype 66, 70
manufacturing 154–5
marginalization 53–4, 105, 107, 124, 149–150, 174–5
Marx, Karl 145
masculinities 64, 81–2, 93, 114–6
mastery 114–15
Media Action Research Group 55
media archaeology 53, 152
media effects 11, 50, 71, 74
media industries 50–1, 62–3, 69, 142–4, 148–55, 163, 165–6
media ownership 50, 127, 146, 148, 158
meritocracy 80, 161
migration 22, 86, 103, 174
Milano, Alyssa 164
Minaj, Nicki 27
misogynoir 20–1, 67
misogyny 20, 172
missing and murdered Indigenous women 91
mixed methods 33, 41–2, 49, 51, 54
Monáe, Janelle 138–9
monetization 157
moral panics 125
Morocco 44
Mulvey, Laura 68–9
MySpace 79, 120

narcissism 26, 68, 132
narrative scarcity and narrative plenitude 82
National Organization for Women, The 8
negotiated readings 45–7, 70, 124
neoliberalism 14–15, 88, 119
nerd stereotype 64, 115
news media 42–4, 62, 66, 73, 88–9, 110, 160–1
Newsweek 88
New Yorker, The 121
New York Times, The 110
Nigeria 27, 89, 96, 100–1, 106, 130
normative research 51
'Nothing About Us Without Us' 36–7

objectification 10, 26, 68–9, 71, 74, 78, 103–4
objectivity 33–4, 37–8
One Laptop Per Child 95
online community 14, 121, 126
online harassment 82–3, 120, 132, 136–7, 162, 172
oppositional readings 45–7, 70–1
Oppression Olympics 20
oral history 53–4, 152
Orientalism 92–3
Othering 64, 66, 92, 101–4, 121–2
Our Data Bodies 140
Overwatch 139

Page Three girl 11, 71
Pakistan 155
participant observation 48–9, 55
participatory culture 123, 157–8
paternalism 98–100, 108
patriarchy 10, 19–20, 99–100, 105
Perry, Katy 66–7
place 1, 89, 92, 110, 120
platforms 50, 83, 120, 126–8, 135–7, 156–7, 160, 162
pleasure 11–12, 41, 47–8, 68–71, 74, 102–4, 137
political economy 50, 145–7, 152, 158
politics of respectability 172
polysemy 46
popular misogyny 172
pornography 11, 41, 71, 74, 78–9, 112, 124, 144, 155
positionality 36–9, 87
positivism 33
postcolonial theory 21, 85, 93, 96
postfeminism 25–8, 77, 173
  and empowerment 79, 168 *see also* empowerment
  and individualism 80
  and irony 78
  and Non-Western subjects 86–7, 89, 104, 106
  and race 87, 101–4, 107
  and the body 71, 73, 168 *see also* embodiment
post- 171
poststructuralism 3–4
post-racial society 100–3
power
  in knowledge production 34, 55, 57, 86–7, 91, 107–8, 175
  of the media 4, 50, 74, 127
  redistribution of 117, 119

precarity 160–2
privacy 49–50, 126–7, 138
privatization 119
privilege 9, 19–24, 36, 102, 105
production studies 152
profit motive 146, 150
progress narratives 75–7, 80–1, 91–2, 94, 97–100, 110, 122, 139, 146
Project Unbreakable 135
Propp, Vladimir 65
publishing 149

queer theory 22, 41
quotas 167

race 7–8, 19–21, 27, 49, 59, 63, 66, 76–7, 101, 103–4, 115, 121–2, 137, 147, 172
racism 66, 75, 78, 82–3, 91–2, 102, 135, 137
  overt and inferential 66
  reverse 129
radio 46, 165
rape culture 71, 110, 128, 131, 135
raunch culture 78–9
reality television 78
reappropriation 45, 70
Reddit 126, 136
reflexivity 34, 36–7, 49, 53, 86–7, 138
Refugees Not Captives (RNC) 84, 89, 93–4
religion 23–4, 98–9
representation 24, 42–3, 58–63, 67–9, 76–9, 81, 106–7
  of age 22
  of class 21, 73
  of disability 23, 36
  of indigenous people 91
  of non-Western people 21–3, 87, 92–4, 107
  of race 20–1, 64–6, 70, 87, 121, 139
  of sexuality 21–2
  of transgender people 22–3, 47–8, 76
  of women 41, 44, 51
  see also self-representation
reproductive rights 10–11
resistance 4, 45–6, 70–1, 150
revenge porn 141, 172
Rhimes, Shonda 76, 143, 171–2
rigor 34
Riot Grrls 14
Run Lola Run 82

Saha, Anamik 149
Sandberg, Sheryl 165 *see also Lean In: Women, Work, and the Will to Lead.*

Sapphire stereotype 70
Sarkeesian, Anita 56, 172
Sassy Black Woman stereotype 67
Scandal 76–8
science and technology studies (STS) 123
scopophilia 68
self-branding 79, 157, 161
self-care 28 *see also* care, feminist ethics of care
selfies 132–6
self-representation 79, 133–5 *see also* representation
semiotics 40
Seneca Falls Declaration 6
sensory ethnography 49
sexism 78, 170–1
sexuality 11, 21–2, 25, 41, 78–9, 93, 97
sexualization 11, 25, 61, 77–9, 102, 127, 144
  of culture 25, 71, 168
sex wars 11–12
shame 22, 26, 45
Shape of Water, The 36
Shukla Test, the 59, 82
signification 4, 40
Silicon Valley 115, 173
Sina Weibo 109, 156
Singapore 73, 75, 104, 133
situated knowledges 30, 34, 38, 106, 138
social determinism 123, 127
social reproduction 159, 166
socio-technical approaches 123–4, 126, 131, 134–5, 138–9
social web 136–7
Sojourner Truth 7
South Africa 7, 96
South Korea 125
Spice Girls 13, 17, 96
spreadability 125, 136
Stacey, Judith 173
Stanton, Elizabeth Cady 6, 8
Steinem, Gloria 17
stereotyping 61–2, 65, 101, 106
Steubenville rape case 110
Stonewall 13
Storify 52
street harassment 52, 128–30
Strong Black Woman stereotype 67
Strong Female Characters 65, 76–8, 81
subaltern 92
subjectivity 4
  and technology 114
subject positions 20, 32, 44, 80, 115

Index

subversive frivolity 133
suffrage 6–8
surveillance 26, 44, 50, 112, 119, 136, 138
Swift, Taylor 17, 103
symbolic annihilation of women 65, 88–9, 136
Syria 84, 94

Taiwan 75
taste 104, 149
technological determinism 112–13, 115, 120, 125, 127
techno-utopianism 95, 117–18, 120, 122–3, 126, 140
television 44, 51, 61–2, 76–8, 143, 148–9, 151, 153–4, 165, 172
Tencent 146
textual analysis 39–42, 49
theoretical saturation 35–6
thick description 48, 54
Tibet 54
Times of India, The 110
Time Magazine 13, 88
'The Personal is Political' 10, 135
tokenism 60, 121
toxic technoculture 136
Tran, Kelly Marie 172
trans-exclusionary radical feminism 18
transnational thought 86–7, 110–11
Transparent 23
travel narratives 103
tropes 64, 66–7, 76–7, 101, 103, 114–16, 144
Tumblr 60, 126 135, 137
Turing, Alan 117
tween girls 14, 148 *see also* girls and youth
Twitch 157
Twitter 127–8, 156

ubiquity of media 1–2
United Kingdom 6-7, 41, 54, 95–6, 106, 142–3, 172
United Nations 17, 94–6, 98
United States 6, 8–10, 23, 49, 70, 75–6, 78, 92, 106, 109–10, 122, 130, 154, 172–3, 154
user-generated content 50, 156–8
uses and gratifications 46–7

van Zoonen, Liesbet 168–9
victimization 14, 23, 98, 100, 106, 125
Vietnam 82, 155
visibility 9–10, 42, 82–3, 107, 110, 136–8, 171, 174

Wages for Facebook 160
Wages for Housework 159
Watson, Emma 17, 170
waves of feminism 5 *see also* feminism
   criticisms of 5, 12
   first wave 6–8
   fourth wave 16–18, 26, 128
   second wave 8–12, 17, 19, 72, 159, 170
   third wave 11–19, 26, 72, 170
WeChat 109
Wekker, Gloria 38
White Man's Burden 92, 99
White Supremacy 19, 67, 70, 102
White-washing 6, 59
Wikipedia 123, 172
Williams, Roberta 53, 154
Wolf, Naomi 72, *see also Beauty Myth, The*
women
   in film 142–3, 151, 163
   in games 53, 56, 133, 154, 163–4
   in leadership roles 160, 165
   in politics 42–3, 78, 172
   in television 76, 143, 151, 154, 163, 165, 172
Women Deliver Young Leaders Program 85
Women in Animation 163
Women in Film and Television International 163
Women in Games International 163
Women in Radio 163
Women of Freedom 109

YouPorn 120
Yousafzai, Malala 100–1, 171
youth 13, 49, 73 *see also* girls and tween girls
YouTube 23, 79, 89, 156–8

Zeisler, Andi 56
zines 14 *see also* magazines